BLACK   SEA

THE KINGDOM OF
MITHRIDATES

BITHYNIA

GREECE

ASIA

LESBOS
Mytilene

ATHENS

CILICIA

RHODES

NDISIUM

THE YOUNG CAESAR

IN THIS autobiographical novel Rex Warner makes the great Caesar tell the story of his life up to the close of his first consulate.

It is a story which deals with the least known, but in many ways the most perilous, years of Caesar's life; the years when the old Roman constitution was palpably breaking down, when revolution was succeeded by revolution, proscription by massacre. It was in such a society that the young Caesar grew up and learned those lessons in politics which he put into practice in his later years.

These were for him years of adventure, enquiry, experience—and survival, and Mr. Warner gives the reader the opportunity to see the world of that day, its wonders as well as its horrors, through his eyes. He has as his hero one of the world's most remarkable men; a man of letters and a man of action, a convivial friend, a promiscuous lover, and an epileptic who was one of the world's greatest generals.

BY THE SAME AUTHOR

Novels
THE WILD GOOSE CHASE
THE PROFESSOR
WHY WAS I KILLED?
THE AERODROME
MEN OF STONES

Mythology
MEN AND GODS
GREEKS AND TROJANS
THE VENGEANCE OF THE GODS

Poetry
POEMS AND CONTRADICTIONS

Essays
THE CULT OF POWER

Travel
VIEWS OF ATTICA

REX WARNER

THE YOUNG CAESAR

COLLINS

ST JAMES'S PLACE, LONDON

1958

© REX WARNER, 1958

PRINTED IN GREAT BRITAIN

COLLINS CLEAR-TYPE PRESS : LONDON AND GLASGOW

To Barbara

CONTENTS

7

CONTENTS

BOOK THREE

BOOK FOUR

PROLOGUE

On the evening of 14th March, 44 B.C., Caesar was dining in
Rome at the house of Lepidus. After dinner he withdrew to a
side table and began to write. He was now fifty-eight years of
age and for some time had been bald. His baldness, however,
was concealed by the triumphal wreath which, by a decree of
the senate, he was entitled to wear on all occasions. He had
recently been made Dictator for life and about a month before
the date of this dinner party had refused, some said with reluctance, the offer of a crown made to him by Antony. It was believed
that this offer was to be made again, though in a different form,
on the next day, which was the Ides of March. Caesar's old
uncle, Lucius Cotta, was to propose formally in the senate that
the Dictator should be given the title of " King." He would
justify the proposal by producing a statement from the Oracular
Books to the effect that only a King was fated to conquer the
great eastern Kingdom of Parthia. As Caesar himself, directly
after the meeting of the senate on the Ides of March, was to set
out against Parthia on a final military campaign, the proposal of
Cotta could be represented as a patriotic one.

We do not know what was occupying Caesar's attention as he
sat writing, listening from time to time to the conversation of
his fellow guests. He may have been busy with orders for his
divisional commanders or with instructions for the conduct of
his troops ; he may have been drafting regulations designed to
curb the luxury and extravagance of Roman women or business
men ; he may have been recording one of his own campaigns,
or composing a poem or literary treatise ; he may have been
writing a love letter to Cleopatra, the Queen of Egypt, who was

then in Rome, or to any one of a number of other women. Bridges, aqueducts, roads, finance, religion, municipal charters, traffic control, alterations in the calendar, an anthology of witty sayings, which he was at this time compiling, the Jewish problem, details of uniform, statues, the difficulties of his friends—on all or any or many more of these subjects may his mind have been either ranging or concentrated, so numerous were his cares, interests and responsibilities, so active and energetic still were his body and his mind.

It was true that in recent years he had suffered increasingly from a form of epilepsy, and there were some who would maintain that because of his fear of these attacks (since he hated anything indecorous) or because of the mental disturbance of which the attacks themselves were a symptom, his conduct and manner had somehow changed. His well-known affability and courteousness could no longer, it was said, be entirely depended upon. There had been, for instance, an occasion when he had offended the senate by receiving them sitting down. Was this a mark of tyranny or of physical exhaustion? And in the last great battle of the civil war, he was held by some experts to have shown an astonishing recklessness and impatience which might well have cost him both life and honour. His friends, however, could justly reply that he had always been reckless and that this was by no means the first battle which he had won at the last moment and as the result of exposing his own person to the utmost danger. As for his manners they declared them to be as friendly and affable as ever. For friendship indeed he had a gift which seemed unique. No other great man in history, it was claimed, had so many friends in so many different circles of society ; and if Caesar had often made friends, as with Pompey or with Crassus, partly in order to promote his own interests, far more numerous were the cases when his friendship was freely offered and freely accepted as something sincere, enjoyable and disinterested. So far as the senate was concerned, it was no new thing for Caesar to react somewhat violently to pomposity and obstructionism. It was perhaps a mistake to have received the senators without bothering to rise from his chair, but it was the kind of apparent

mistake which Caesar often made and which finally turned out
to have been a gesture which did good to his party and to himself. In all probability the incident would be remembered in
future as just another example of Caesar's unconventionality, of
the supreme self-confidence which sprang from his utter fearlessness. Not that at this stage of his life he had any superior power
to fear. Yet he must have known that, although the whole
proud state of Rome was at his feet or in his hand, there were
still many individuals who from ambition, envy, rancour or
even patriotism hated him, and even that he may have been
most hated by some of those to whom he had been most
merciful. He was not ignorant of human nature and his
whole life had been spent in revolutionary politics. The only
danger to which he was exposed was that of assassination.
Characteristically he took no precautions against this danger
at all.

It would have been unlike him, however, not to have given
the matter some thought. Certainly at this dinner party of
Lepidus on the evening before the Ides of March he looked up
for some moments from his work and listened attentively to his
fellow guests who were discussing in general terms what sort of
death was most to be desired. The others were not aware that he
was listening and were surprised when he broke rapidly into the
conversation with the words, " A sudden one." He then turned
once more to whatever business it was that had been occupying
him.

One of his fellow guests must have been disturbed by his
words. This was Decimus Brutus, who, though he did not
know it, had been named second heir in Caesar's will. He was
a man of great military ability who had served Caesar well in
many campaigns and who owed everything to Caesar's friendship.
Yet he was among the conspirators who, headed by another
Brutus, the son of Caesar's old mistress Servilia, a young man of
whom the Dictator was particularly fond, had planned the
assassination for the following day. Decimus Brutus must have
wondered, as we wonder to-day, what feeling, what knowledge,
what intuition or apprehension lay behind those calmly spoken

words commending a death that was sudden and a death that had been already planned.

That Caesar had no knowledge of the precise nature and extent of the conspiracy is certain. The stories, however, which have come down to us concerning the disturbed night which he passed after the dinner party, the omens and dreams and hesitations, provide evidence that his mind may have been affected by some dreadful apprehension. Could he have surmised that for the first and only time luck, violence and his own character had combined against him? Could he have imagined that his hours were numbered? And, had he done so, might he not have seen, as certain people are supposed to see before death, the whole process of his life pass before him rapidly and in a flash? What he would have seen and how he would have judged we do not know but may venture partially to imagine. Our imagination must be selective, since even the events themselves which we assume to have passed before his eyes either in a moment at the house of Lepidus or in wakeful intervals of the night which followed are too numerous to be recorded; and it is proper also that we should be circumscribed by a respect for truth, although in such a venture as this objectivity is not possible. Caesar often took the trouble to explain himself, but he was not used to self-criticism. His greatness is indisputable. Whether such greatness is an admirable or disastrous thing is a different question altogether.

Caesar knew that he was great, though the knowledge seems to have come to him gradually. Before his death we may imagine him reflecting in some such terms as these upon the life that was so nearly over :

BOOK ONE

CHAPTER I

MY FAMILY

MY FAMILY is descended from the ancient Kings of Rome and, if the story is true that Venus was our ancestress, from the immortal gods. Whether the gods exist or not, that power in nature and in personality to which we give the name of "Venus" has proved most kindly to me except, strangely enough, in her procreative aspect. Now that my daughter Julia is dead, I have no child of my own body, and though Cleopatra claims that I am the father of her child Caesarion, her word is not to be believed. But our ancient family, raised again by me after many years of obscurity to greatness, is not extinct. My sister's daughter (it was in the year of Catiline's conspiracy) bore a son, Octavian, and I have made him my heir. He is a boy of outstanding ability, ambitious, sensible and utterly ruthless. Unfortunately his health is weak, but so was mine at his age. If he lives he will inherit, grasp and maintain power.

With the notable exception of myself, there have not been for many years any males of great distinction in the Julian family. My father never attained the consulship. But my mother Aurelia was known everywhere, except in violent or dissipated circles, for her integrity, her charm and her considerable intellectual powers. She was ambitious for me and used to stand beside me in every crisis of my career, loyal even when she was most disapproving. And indeed not everything in my career can be approved by those whose principles, if liberal, are strict. Yet I like to believe that my mother, in her woman's way, understood the fact that principles, however sincerely held, must be, if they are to be effective, adapted in some measure to events. The tragedy of our times and, in a sense, my own tragedy consists in this : that remedies have not been able to keep pace with the disease, that accident, that dead weights of tradition, interest and stupidity have continued to impede my liberty and speed of action, so that what has been accomplished has been the necessary rather than the good. On the other hand it must be observed that not many people are capable of doing even what is necessary, still less of influencing, to some degree, the forces of necessity itself. For recognising some necessities and for acting with the speed and confidence required to ensure that out of two or more possibilities one in particular becomes an event I shall deserve the respect of posterity. It is probable, however, human nature being what it is, that I shall be both admired and detested for the wrong reasons. The doctrinaire and antiquarian spirit of Cato did not die with him at Utica. It will often be found sufficient to call me " King " or " Dictator," or to inflate beyond any possible meaning such words as " liberty " in order to make me appear as a calamitous phenomenon, one who, out of personal ambition, deprived other men of their rights and their opportunities of free development. And there will be people also who, as many do to-day, will admire me to the point of worship simply because they themselves are unfitted for responsibility. Such people will always adore the powerful even when power is used directly contrary to their own interests or imagined beliefs. Their adulation springs from natural servility and, though a factor in every situation, is not valuable. I should not like to be described as either good or bad. It would be true to call me necessary, brilliant and, whenever possible, well-meaning.

I should imagine that my mother thought of me in this way, though in my childhood, as is natural and proper in education, the words " good " and " bad " were frequently employed. Not only my mother herself but many of her relations were what might be described as " high-minded." There was, for example, my mother's uncle, Rutilius Rufus, who followed the Stoic philosophy and, unlike Cato, followed it with sincerity and a complete lack of ostentation. He was in real fact what is called " a Roman of the old type " ; indeed he was one of the only examples of this type whom I have ever met. His persecution by Roman capitalists of the new type taught me one of my first lessons in politics. Then there were my mother's brothers, the Cottas, two of whom have since held the consulship. In particular I remember Caius Cotta, one of the best speakers of his day and a man of most enlightened views. He and the majority of his friends were keen students both of Greek literature and of Greek political theory. Not that they imagined, as some earlier reformers had appeared to do, that the political structure of one society could be imported wholesale and imposed upon another; but they were well aware, long before it became apparent to everyone, that the constitution and theory of Roman government, admirable as they had proved themselves to be in the remote past, were now inadequate, out of date and dangerous. So in their conversations, to which even as a small boy I was often allowed to listen, they would debate the merits of democracy, oligarchy and monarchy, quoting from Thucydides, Aristotle, Plato and from philosophic popularisers of the day. I was an eager listener, being fascinated partly by politics themselves and partly by what I considered the great intellectual distinction of my mother's family. My uncles and their friends were kind enough to take an interest in me and to encourage me in my early and lasting enthusiasm for Greek literature. Once, I remember, I startled them by venturing, in the course of one of their discussions, to quote from Euripides a verse upon which I have often had occasion to reflect :

> *If wrong must be, then, best to do it for the sake*
> *Of supreme power, and in other things be always good.*

My Uncle Cotta, then a young man only just beginning his career at the bar, applauded me for having read and remembered Euripides ; but he deplored the sentiment as illiberal. Of course he was right ; but he was incapable of understanding what is meant by necessity.

I was proud of my mother and her relations. I was proud, too, and have been profoundly influenced by another family relation of an entirely different kind. To-day only personal friends or specialists in history remember the Cottas; but my Uncle Marius will always be remembered.

It is difficult to understand how this formidable and tremendous character was ever permitted to marry into our family at all. His own family was totally obscure and his parents, it seems, actually earned their living by the work of their hands. He and they were dependents of the powerful and often arrogant clan of the Metelli, but, so I was told, Marius himself, at a very early age, claimed complete independence for himself and showed his independence by going out of his way to insult the consul Quintus Metellus, who had given him his first opportunity to show his military abilities. Marius had no money, no gift of eloquence and, once he had offended the Metelli, hardly any support in powerful circles. Yet, solely on the strength of his great gifts as a soldier and of his enormous popularity in the army, he managed to attain the consulship. All this happened before I was born and it was before I was born that he married my father's sister, my Aunt Julia. It was a strange match, since Julia was very greatly the superior socially, and Marius himself never paid the slightest attention to rank. Had he wished to make an alliance which would be useful to him politically, he would probably have approached some family other than our own, since at this time our family, in spite of its great antiquity, was neither wealthy nor in command of much political influence. Perhaps Marius and my aunt were in love, difficult though it is to imagine. Certainly in later days my aunt would always speak of her husband with respect and would constantly refer to his great exploits in youth and early middle age. This was natural enough, considering the appalling savagery which marked the last stages of his life.

To me, in my early childhood, he was rather a legend than a real person. His name was constantly with me in the conversation of nurses, tutors and school children, and his name, whether one approved of him or not, was for many years the greatest in Rome. The most splendid of all his many victories had been won in the year after I was born. In this year he totally annihilated the great host of Germans who, but for him, would certainly have laid waste Italy and Rome herself. Soon afterwards, as I learned later, he made some foolish mistakes in politics. He was trapped by his enemies into performing an unpopular act and, for a time at least, he was discredited among his friends. But at no time did people stop talking of him. There was something in his personality which led to fable, even to romance. Perhaps it was the very intensity of his self-assurance; for in reality he was as far as possible from being a romantic character, and he was quite singularly devoid of all charm.

Like most young children, I was delighted with stories of prodigies and miracles. There were many of these concerning Marius and many are told to this day. In particular I remember having been impressed by the story of how, before each of his great victories, two vultures would appear and accompany the army on its marches. These birds could always be recognised, since on one occasion the soldiers had caught them and had put collars of brass around their necks. And so, ever afterwards, whenever these great birds, with the gleam of yellow behind their heads, could be seen on their broad wings sailing over the marching columns, the soldiers, whatever the odds against them, would grow impatient for battle and become certain of victory.

In my early childhood I believed this story implicitly and loved to dwell upon it. It was only as my mind developed that I grasped the obvious point that great though the range of the vulture may be, it could not possibly be so great as the range of Marius's armies. Later I questioned my Aunt Julia on the subject and discovered that what Marius did was to have with him on each campaign some six or eight vultures in cages and equipped with their brazen collars. The birds were procured and looked after by one of Julia's slaves, and Marius himself used them most prudently, never giving the order for their release until he was confident that, provided his soldiers showed the necessary resolution, a victory was inevitable.

Though for a short time I was somewhat disappointed to find that a rational explanation existed for what had seemed to me a direct intervention of the gods, I soon realised that the true story did more credit than the false one to my uncle's abilities as a commander. Certainly he, like the greatest of his subordinates, Sertorius, had the art of combining every force upon his side, including the considerable force of superstition. Men are prepared to believe almost anything, so long as the belief can give them pleasure, excitement or confidence. This is a fact known to all who, like Marius, can genuinely join in the feelings of the people and can win, as a result, not only respect but, even against all probability, confidence and affection. More intellectual characters (my Uncle Cotta, for example) believe, as of course we all do, in the power of reason; but they believe it to be more powerful than in fact it is.

Marius, being entirely uncultured, was superstitious himself; but his native shrewdness was such that every superstitious belief which he held was adapted to serve his own interests. In his old age, for instance, he was in the habit of relating an event which, according to his own account, had occurred in his early childhood. While he had been walking in the country, he said, he had caught in his arms and in the folds of his toga an eagle's nest, containing seven young eaglets, which had been dislodged by a high wind from the cliffs where it had been built. His parents had immediately consulted the augurs who declared that the meaning of the omen was that the young boy was destined to become the greatest man in the world and that, before he died, he would seven times attain the supreme position in the state. This was a story which Marius was particularly fond of relating after his exile and before his seventh consulship. There had been, it appeared, several versions of it. After his second consulship, for instance, he used to state that the number of eaglets in the nest was three.

I myself, being fourteen or fifteen years old at the time, first heard the story from Marius in its final form. I immediately knew it to be untrue. I was interested in natural history and was aware that the eagle never hatches more than two eggs. I even ventured to remind Marius of this fact, a daring thing to do, as could be seen from the expressions of horror which passed over the faces of all who were in the room at the time.

Indeed I was myself somewhat alarmed by the angry glare which the old man directed at me from beneath his shaggy brows, and at the sight of the great knotted muscles bulging on his stiffened arm. Soon, however, he smiled cunningly and then laughed, making a hoarse rattling noise that was peculiarly disgusting. "Boy," he said, "for Caius Marius the gods could make a hundred eaglets."

Evidently he regarded this remark as being not only final but, in its own way, clever. Of course it was neither, since the question was not whether the gods, supposing them to exist, are omnipotent, but whether, so far as we can observe it, they ever transgress the bounds of nature. I saw, however, that this was too fine a distinction for the old man to grasp and I forbore to pursue the subject. Also I was most reluctant to offend the great general who, at about this time, was beginning to take a considerable interest in me.

On the first few occasions when I had met my great kinsman, in spite of the kind of hero-worship which I felt for him and in spite of every effort on my Aunt Julia's part, I had won neither his attention nor his regard. He took, it seemed, particular exception to my personal appearance. For, partly from nature, partly from a desire to please my mother, I was, even in boyhood, very concerned with my dress and with my hair. As for my hair, I soon adopted a special method of parting it, allowing one lock to droop down rather low over the forehead. I would often find my school fellows laughing at me when they observed me, quite unconsciously, ascertaining with a forefinger whether the parting was in the right place. And I contrived to wear even the toga of boyhood in a manner peculiar to myself, paying attention not only to the texture of the garment, but to the elegance of its folds.

To Marius all this was just another example of the effeminacy which he expected to find among the upper classes. Moreover, so far from being impressed by my proficiency in Greek, he regarded this also as being in some way immoral. "Battles are not won with irregular verbs," he would say, omitting to observe that there are also irregularities in our own grammar, and he pronounced that, for his own part, he had no wish to study the literature of a subject race.

I myself, it must be admitted, was at first somewhat disillusioned when I met in real life this character who, in the gossip of childhood, had seemed to me so fabulously great. The stories which I liked to remember of him were not so much the miraculous ones as those which illustrated his energy in action, his toughness and the extraordinary hold which he had over his men. These stories were true. On active service, in spite of the severity of his discipline, he was capable of a kind of forbearance and understanding. His men would even tax him with over-caution—a sign that he knew well how to husband their resources for the decisive moment. He was abstemious in all his ways, merciless only to the cowardly and incompetent, just and upright with all, so that all loved him. But as soon as the time came for him to play any part in the life of the city his character altered completely. He was boastful and arrogant, rude and ungracious even to his friends, insolent and cruel to his enemies. Moreover, he was nearly always drunk and in this state would by his morose behaviour cast a gloom over the most festive gathering, or, when people had good reason to be either sad or serious, would interrupt their mood by his loud and bearish good humour, like the Hercules in Euripides, unseasonably revelling at a funeral feast. Though he always claimed to despise, and in a real sense did despise every grace of civilisation, this did not prevent him from living for long periods luxuriously and ostentatiously in a splendid villa at the fashionable watering-place of Baiae. Here, being totally incapable of appreciating any of the real refinements (the statues, the paintings, the porticoes) which he had bought at such vast expense, he would indolently spend his time in the indulgence of his brutal and enormous appetites for food and drink and for sexual relationships (if such a word can be used for a merely beastly coupling) with the lowest and least attractive types of women. He was singular, for a debauchee, in having no amatory desires for his own sex, and indeed regarded all homosexuality as decadent and effeminate, like the study of poetry and philosophy.

Naturally my Aunt Julia, my mother and other members of my family were shocked by his behaviour at this time; they were to be more shocked still before his life was over. I, too, could not help feeling a certain disappointment when I discovered that my idol was so little like what I had fancied. Yet I was able also to observe and to admire his real qualities. I used to blush for him when, as sometimes happened, I saw people laughing at the sight of him, waddling rather than walking, on his way to the athletic grounds. For even in advanced old age he would often join the young men in their exercises in the Field of Mars. But I was delighted when the laughter turned, as it always did, to expressions of wonder. Once he took up a javelin or a sword, he became transformed. The savagery in his expression was, for its very intensity, almost beautiful. There was even a lightness in those great limbs of his and a fine dexterity as well as strength in the management of his weapons. The legs which just now had seemed so inadequate to serve him stiffened in action, giving him a rock-like stability, and they, too, appeared beautiful, though one of them was covered with knots and nodules like an old tree trunk and the other (as the result of an operation) was deeply marked with dents and long incisions of the knife.

I noticed also in my uncle a quality which can only be called, though in rather an unusual sense, humanity. It was the humanity of blood, bone, courage, a kind of loyalty and endurance 'rather than the humanity which we associate with any moral or intellectual eminence. Indeed, from many points of view, Marius could be rightly described as both wicked and stupid. Yet in his simplicity (again not a moral quality, for he was cunning and vindictive) and in his strength there seemed to me something divine. Often I remembered him stopping in the street to address a word or two to some old soldier of his whom he had recognised in the crowd, but who had not dared to approach personally his commander-in-chief. Marius's words were seldom particularly gracious, and his behaviour was often that of an exhibitionist. He was fond, for instance, of showing his wounds, remarking at the same time that they were better titles of nobility than a collection of family portraits. Yet, whatever he said and however he behaved, to those who had served with him he remained an object of almost fanatical and quite personal affection. A man to whom he uttered some gruff sentence in the street would remember the incident (one could see it from his face) for the rest of his life, and would describe it, with embellishments, year after year to his friends, his wife, his children and his grandchildren.

I was capable of sharing in these feelings myself, just as later I was able to inspire them in others. I was therefore grateful when, towards the end of my childhood, Marius began to show that he had not only overcome his original aversion to me, but was actually interested in my future. I attribute this change in his manner to the fact that he once watched me give a display of horsemanship for the benefit of my mother and some friends. Even at an early age I was expert in the management of horses. I would amuse myself by riding at different speeds with my hands locked behind my back, and I had practised a style which, I had been told, was in use among certain tribes of Germany and of Gaul, who have cavalrymen trained also to fight on foot and who are able to mount and dismount when their horses are at full gallop. It seems that Marius, quite by accident, witnessed this riding display of mine and was profoundly impressed. He was amazed to find that a boy of my appearance was capable of such athletic prowess, particularly when he remembered that I was supposed to be good at Greek. He himself was now approaching the last and most savage period of his career, but during his final years he conferred several marks of distinction on me. Indeed there was a time when it seemed that I was about to enter politics under the best possible auspices. This, as events turned out, was not to be. Soon the best men in Rome, including the Cottas, began to shrink from every connection with Marius, and, as for me, the favours that he bestowed upon me nearly cost me my life.

Still I like to remember in Marius what was great, rather than what was brutish, boorish and savage. Marius was no idol for a child ; yet his tremendous shadow dominated my childhood. Sometimes I used to wonder whether it might be possible to combine together in one character his strength and vehemence and tough efficiency with those wholly different qualities of culture, moderation and political integrity which I admired in my mother's family. It still seems to me doubtful whether, in the circumstances of my day, this is a possibility, if, that is, one wishes to preserve one's life.

CHAPTER II

A STREET SCENE

THROUGHOUT MY life I have been either admired or blamed for my revolutionary activities. It is often forgotten that it was not I who began the revolution in Rome. The revolution had started before I was born; and, during the formative years of my childhood and early youth, day by day there were forced upon my attention the violence, the ferocity, the apparently irreconcilable antagonisms of the times. These antagonisms were, to a great extent, embodied or reflected in the important personalities of my Uncle Marius and of his enemy, Sulla. Only gradually did I begin to understand the real nature of the antagonisms themselves. As a child it was the personalities which impressed me, and, out of family loyalty, instinct and, it may almost be said, affection I was unreservedly on the side of Marius. I realised later that my choice, if a choice had to be made between two such savage extremes, was right; for Marius, with all his enormous faults, represented forces greater than himself, forces of flesh and blood, something capable of life, growth and expansion into history; while Sulla had a dead hand; his pride and ambition were of an icy and rooted selfishness beside which Marius's vainglory appeared almost as generosity; the forces which he represented were forces of contraction and ossification.

I must have been about nine or ten years of age when I first came into contact with Sulla; but of course I had heard much of him before then. Indeed, much as I liked hearing stories about the career of my Uncle Marius, I must own that I often became bored with the frequent repetitions of that particular story of events in which Sulla was concerned and which had taken place

some years before I was born. At this time Sulla had been a
junior officer under the command of Marius in Africa. Clearly
he was already showing the great military qualities which he
undoubtedly possessed, and in the course of the war, by a clever
piece of diplomacy, he succeeded in securing the surrender of
the native King Jugurtha, who for many years had fought with
success against Rome. The capture of the King meant the end
of the war, and Jugurtha was duly exhibited in Marius's well-
earned triumph, which he held just before taking up his even
more important command against the Germans. But meanwhile
Sulla and his friends had been spreading the story that Marius
was quite unjustly claiming for himself the credit for finishing
the war in Africa. Most of the work, they said, had been done
by his old commander, Metellus; and the final achievement
belonged to Sulla. There was a little truth in the story, but not
much. In any case the military reputation of Marius was firmly
enough based to be able to resist easily any attack that might be
made on it. A generous, or even a sensible man would have
paid no attention to such stories. But Marius, where his own
glory was concerned, was neither generous nor sensible. He
hated Sulla with a febrile and frightening intensity; and Sulla,
more poised, if possible more savage, and with a show of contempt that nearly drove Marius frantic, hated him in return. By
the time I reached boyhood this hatred, on both sides, had
become an obsession. I was, of course, personally prejudiced on
the side of my uncle and I was glad to find that my mother's
family also had few good words to say of Sulla. They distrusted
him, rightly, as an unscrupulously reactionary politician and they
were offended by his private life. They criticised him for being
an upstart, though in fact he came from an old, if impoverished,
patrician family, and accused him of having risen in the world
by a number of shady means, such as the wooing of rich and very
unattractive old women in order to receive legacies from them
at their death.

These latter criticisms, as I was to discover later, were somewhat unfair. Certainly it would not become me to criticise anyone
who has had to borrow money or, for some service or other,

acquire it in order to gain influence and power. Sulla, in spite of his aristocratic birth, started life in cheap lodgings; he was conscious of his own power and he took, reasonably, I think, what steps he could to secure liberty of action for himself. One cannot blame him for a rich widow or two. Nor were his extravagant pleasures altogether unusual or entirely revolting. What was displeasing was the contradiction between them and what one imagined to be himself. For Marius, in his brutality, his drunkenness, his strange generosity and toughness was all of a piece. Sulla seemed to be at least two people at once. In action he was ruthless, stern (except when he deliberately encouraged licence) and efficient; he was cultured and well read; yet when he relaxed into private life he became almost ridiculously affable. His favourite associates were not men of importance or culture, but the most disreputable characters—singers, ballet dancers and players. For one of these players, a man called Metrobius, he conceived a violent passion which lasted for many years; and indeed his love affairs were reputedly very numerous, comprising people of all classes, though particularly the lower, and of both sexes. Marius, who regarded his own excesses as being perfectly normal, would speak with horror and contempt of Sulla's way of living.

Personally what I found least attractive in Sulla was his physical appearance, in which there was something grotesquely flamboyant and exaggerated. Even at the age of forty-five (which was the time I first saw him clearly) he had a head of bright golden hair, which might have looked well upon another man, but which, though people affected to admire it, suited very ill with his other facial characteristics. His eyes were large, piercing, and of an unnaturally brilliant blue colour. When he was angry they could be, as I was to discover, very terrible; but this effect proceeded partly from an indecent incongruity. It was as though a lion were glaring through the eyes of a doll. His complexion also was indecent, for his skin was mottled with deep purple and white. Later one of the singers in a taverna in Athens made some verses on this subject, beginning:

A STREET SCENE

Sulla's face is a mulberry with oatmeal scattered on it,

and it is quite possibly true that these verses and others of a more
obscene character referring to his fourth wife, the distinguished
Lady Metella, influenced him when, in his eastern campaign, he
ordered the barbarous slaughter which followed his capture of
Athens. That would have been like Sulla.

There was something, perhaps, slightly ludicrous about my
own first contact with Sulla, and yet I learned from the incident
to know myself better. I was not more than nine or ten years
old at the time. It was in the year of Sulla's praetorship, and
Sulla had gained the office partly by extensive bribery and partly
by encouraging the hopes of the people that he would provide
them with unusually magnificent games and entertainments. All
this I knew from the gossip of my family. I was still too young
to know that in fact no candidate for office at this period was
likely to be elected without a lavish outlay of money, and,
secondly, that of all the candidates for the praetorship Sulla was
incomparably the most efficient. My hostile feelings, therefore,
were both prejudiced and irrational, proceeding solely from my
boyish notion of loyalty to my Uncle Marius, who was Sulla's
enemy.

I was also angered by the thought of the great numbers of
animals which were slaughtered in the Circus to afford entertainment for the people. The display given by Sulla was on an
unprecedented scale and indeed was not surpassed until many
years had gone by and the time came for the triumphs of Pompey
and of myself. From Africa, where he had great influence, Sulla
had succeeded in importing a prodigious number of wild animals.
What particularly attracted attention was a display in which a
hundred lions were matched against Numidian archers. I was
somewhat singular in being revolted by the thought of this
butchery of noble creatures. I have never enjoyed these bloody
exhibitions, though of course in later years I found that in order
to gain the people's favour, at least in times of peace, it was
essential to entertain them brutally and ostentatiously. Now
when I am forced to attend the games I only look at them for a

time long enough to make certain that they have been efficiently organised and for the greater part of the performance I avert my eyes and employ myself more profitably in reading or in dictating letters. My indifference to the people's pleasures does me no harm politically. Once the people have given a man their favour, as they gave it to Marius and have given it to me, they will not only tolerate but applaud any act which seems to them eccentric or original. Those who never forgive one for being unusual are invariably members of one's own class.

As it happened, Sulla, whose real passion was for the ballet and the theatre, was quite indifferent to that entertainment which is provided by the slaughter of animals, except in so far as the entertainment increased his own prestige. I did not know this at the time. I regarded him, quite rightly, as being both treacherous and cruel, but I was not aware that his cruelty was directed rather against human beings than wild beasts.

So on one of the days that followed some display or other given by Sulla, I went about the streets with a band of young boys who had come to look upon me as their leader, and, in a childish enough way, began to organise a kind of demonstration. I would keep shouting out in as loud a voice as I could manage such questions as "Who saved Rome from the Germans, Sulla or Marius?" "Who won the African war, Sulla or Marius?" And my small gang of boys would, of course, shout back the answer, "Marius." I would have liked to have demonstrated against the killing of the lions, but I realised that this would be an unpopular thing even with my own little band of supporters. As it was, the reiteration of the name of Marius and the mention of his victories delighted the crowd, partly because Marius, "the man of the people," still had a great hold over the affections of the ordinary Roman citizen, and partly because the sight of such young boys engaging in a political demonstration aroused a certain amount of amusement. Before long many others in the crowd began to join in the chorus celebrating the superiority of Marius over Sulla, and then I began to feel what was to me a strange and overwhelming excitement and satisfaction. I was finding that my own words and actions (for all this had been my idea) were spreading beyond myself into the minds and feelings of an expanding circle. This was, perhaps, my first experience of power. It was not altogether a worthy experience, but it was agreeable and significant.

Suddenly I observed, with a kind of dismay, that the volume of sound which had been following and greeting my shouted questions was first gradually and then very rapidly diminishing. I soon saw the reason. Sulla himself, attended by the tall figures of lictors with their rods and axes and followed by a lot of young men on horseback, was approaching. Even without the lictors, the golden head would have been unmistakable, and the upright bearing of the man. So, as he approached, the crowd fell silent, fearing him rather than loving him; for there was less applause than might have been expected for one who had so lavishly entertained them.

I noticed too that, while some of my own band of boys were looking at me as though for reassurance, others were glancing over their shoulders, evidently searching for a convenient side street down which to bolt. This threatened desertion infuriated me, but I mastered and disguised the feeling and, looking at them with a smile, I used my full voice (which at that time was quite untrained and must have sounded ludicrous), shouting out the words : " Long live Marius, who kills Germans instead of animals ! Long live Marius, the saviour of his country ! "

All the boys joined in with me—" Long live Marius, the saviour of his country ! " And now even some members of the crowd began to applaud.

They were immediately silenced by the strong voice of Sulla ordering his lictors to halt, and I noticed then how those who, in the narrow street, were closest to him began to back away as though they were in the proximity of some fire already singeing their garments. There was indeed something terrible in the look of Sulla's great blue eyes, a look not so much of anger as of domination and of withering contempt. For Sulla always despised people in the mass, of whatever class, unless they were the soldiers of his own legions, whose devotion he was careful to secure.

I, as leader of the demonstration, was standing elevated above the others on a small hand-barrow. Sulla slowly turned his eyes towards me. "Boy," he said, "you must learn manners, or else you will be made to feel *my* authority."

He gave a strong and particular emphasis to the word " my " and I can remember his voice to this day. But what I chiefly remember is my own intense nervous excitement and the surprise I felt at not finding myself in the least frightened either by the threat or by the man himself. There was a kind of lightness in my head as I shouted back at once, " We all know that it is *your* authority. Of course it is your very own. You bought it at the elections."

The remark was not particularly witty, yet in the circumstances it was accounted to be so, and a certain amount of laughter broke out among the crowd. As for me, as soon as the words were out of my mouth, I waited with resolution, but with some trepidation, to see what their result would be. If I had been more experienced I should have recognised that there was nothing to fear. Sulla, certainly at this stage of his career, was far too intelligent a man to involve himself in a public incident with a mere boy. He directed one look at me from his piercing and disturbing eyes. It was a look which I was to see once again, in circumstances of far greater danger. Then he went on and, as he went, the young horsemen behind him edged their horses into the crowd, forcing the people to scramble out of the way, jostling one against the other, cursing and swearing, and not for some moments recalling the incident which had just taken place.

Yet still the incident caused some stir and when I returned home later in the day I found that rumours of it had preceded me. I told the whole story to my mother and was severely scolded by her. Yet as she was scolding me she was half smiling and, as I discovered later, she took care that Marius was informed of this instance of his nephew's enthusiasm.

To me this incident, though trifling in itself, had some

importance and I would often reflect upon it. My reflections encouraged me to believe that it is possible to be, at certain decisive moments, entirely without fear and that this state of fearlessness confers a strange energy and resilience to the whole body and mind, qualities which can even, by a kind of telepathy, affect others as well.

CHAPTER III

INTRODUCTION TO POLITICS

IN THOSE days it was customary to impress on boys during their history lessons how wise, stable and flexible was the Roman constitution, how firm and at the same time generous had been Rome's treatment of her allies and of her enemies ; how, finally, the wealth and power which Rome now enjoyed were the rewards of the exercise, through the years, of the old Roman virtues— sobriety, patriotism, seriousness, endurance and a high sense of honour. I was encouraged to believe that in the senate we had evolved the most efficient governing body that had existed in the history of the world. It was a body whose membership was, on the whole, confined to my own class, though others of exceptional ability—my Uncle Marius, for example—had not only sat in the senate but had held the highest offices, thus becoming members of the nobility themselves. (What, in this story, was usually omitted, though never by Marius himself, was the fact that the nobility had done everything in their power to prevent him from rising to their ranks.) It was of course assumed that in course of time I, too, would enter the senate. I would first take my seat as a junior government official ; then, after regular intervals, prescribed by the laws, I would be entitled to stand for election to higher posts and, if I were to show the necessary ability, I might attain the praetorship or—the crown of a political career—the consulship itself. Praetors and consuls were indeed in a class apart. They were entitled to the governor- ships of provinces and the command of armies. Meanwhile I was called upon to admire the public spirit shown by all members of the nobility who devoted their lives to the service of the state in peace and war.

I was told to admire also, though perhaps not so much, that other powerful and influential class of gentlemen outside the senate who had grown rich either because of their financial transactions or as the result of their careful management of land and other property. These financiers and business men, not being members of the senate, could not of course hold any public office; but they still, it was pointed out to me, performed a number of important functions. All banking was in their hands and it was they who contracted with the senate for the collecting of taxes from the provinces. Also at this time they formed the juries in the courts of law.

Finally there was the Roman people, the whole citizen body which, organised in one form of assembly, voted for the election of the higher magistrates, and, in a different form of organisation, could approve of and even initiate legislation. It was customary among the nobility to assume that the people showed most wisdom when they followed the leadership and guidance of the senate; but some liberal theorists would point out that, invaluable as the expert guidance of the senate was, the last word in legislation always rested with the people. The people's representatives, the tribunes, who in fact were nearly always members of aristocratic families, had the power to intervene even in the senate and to veto, in the people's name, any bill that was proposed. They could also put before the Popular Assembly measures of their own which might be directly contrary to the will of the senate. But when this happened it was deplored by the liberal theorists, who liked to imagine a nice and reasonable balance of functions, a beautiful symmetry, efficiency, decorum, flexibility and goodwill.

It did not take me long to discover that this conventional picture of the Roman constitution was quite valueless as a guide to my own times. I learned from facts. Before I was fifteen two tribunes, both high-minded men and both friends of my family, had died violent deaths, and my mother's relative, Caius Cotta, had been tried by a summary court and exiled. And far worse things were to follow. Greed, ambition, envy and pure selfishness have been more evident in my time than have been the ancient Roman virtues. No doubt these qualities have always marred human nature, but there seem to have been some periods of history when the governing classes, at any rate, have been comparatively immune from them, at least for a short time. I have not been fortunate enough to live in such a period. In my day human society, if regarded from the point of view of morality, has compared unfavourably with any congregation of savage animals, such as a pack of wolves.

It was not easy in those days for a boy—indeed it was not easy for a grown man—to realise quickly and immediately how distracted, how centreless and pointless was the society into which he had been born. I was first disillusioned with what I had regarded as the equity of the Roman constitution by the affair of my great uncle, Rutilius Rufus. This occurred in the year after Sulla's praetorship, and I remember that at first we all considered it a joke when we were informed that an obscure character called Apicius, I think, was to prosecute Rutilius for allegedly corrupt financial practices. The charge was concerned with his behaviour in the province of Asia five years previously and was in every way ridiculous. Rutilius had been a great soldier, as even Marius admitted. He had, after studying the methods practised in gladiatorial establishments, introduced into the Roman Army a new system of sword-drill, a system which is still in use. He was even more famous as a jurist and as an orator. But above all he was known for his absolute integrity and incorruptibility. And these qualities had been especially evident during the short period when he had been administering the province in Asia. Here he had not only indignantly refused the bribes that were usually offered by the agents of Roman business men to provincial governors, but had been remarkably successful in preventing their illegal extortions from the inhabitants. The financial transactions of the tax collectors and of their employers in Rome were, according to his view, dishonest, disreputable and, considering the real interests of the province, unpatriotic. In curbing them he must have been aware that he was making enemies of a powerful class, but he could scarcely have imagined how powerful and how unscrupulous this class would prove to be.

I myself was at first puzzled by the conduct of these Roman financiers. I knew that they were not all wicked, brutal, irresponsible and crooked. Yet I observed them acting as though they were, in spite of the fact that among their number were men of great eminence, of considerable culture and even, in a sense, of principle. Principles, however, among the business community more often than not coincide with self-interest, and when money is pursued as an end in itself, rather than as a means towards some further object, it becomes invested with a peculiar sanctity. It is even possible that some of those business men who were active in the prosecution of Rutilius believed that they were performing a patriotic action. They had begun to deify such works as " Capital " and " Interest " and so conceived the notion that these words, quite abstracted from reality, had, as it were, rights of their own. Thus they were scarcely concerned with the fact that in ruining an innocent man they were committing an act of injustice and bringing discredit on the courts of law. They simply aimed at demonstrating their power, so that in the future members of the senate who were in control of provinces and who might, through motives of honesty or efficiency, wish to resist the demands of the capitalists at home, should know that this was an extremely risky thing to do. Their choice of Rutilius as a victim made their purpose quite clear. For if Rutilius, a man quite obviously innocent, were condemned, who could consider himself safe ?

As the day appointed for the trial approached it became clear to us that this was no joke at all but a dangerous and determined attempt to ruin this relative of ours of whom we were proud and to whom we had been accustomed to look up as a model. And Rutilius himself alarmed us by the intransigence of his own attitude. He had decided that it was right to confront naked injustice with naked innocence, and he refused to engage any of the leading lawyers of the day to speak in his defence. The only legal help that he would accept was that of his nephew, Caius Cotta, then at the beginning of his career, an excellent speaker, but with none of the prestige that he was subsequently to acquire. Nor would he follow the customary method of exciting the

sympathy of the jury by parading in front of them members of
his own family, mostly women and children, all dressed in black
and ready, with tears and lamentations, to appeal for mercy on
behalf of the defendant. A trial at law, he used to say, was not
concerned with the future of a man's family, but solely with the
guilt or innocence of the man himself.

In all probability Rutilius would still have been condemned
even if he had conducted his defence in a more orthodox manner.
The jury was packed with men who knew exactly how they were
going to vote long before the trial began. Certainly they would
not be tempted to change their minds when they found that
Rutilius, so far from imploring mercy from them, began in
court to act as though it was he who was the prosecutor. It
was the state, he said, and the whole legal system that was on
trial in this case; and he prophesied that, if he were found
guilty, it would not be long before the jury who had convicted
him and the state itself would feel the effects, inevitable to his
way of thought, of injustice. His prophecies were to be fulfilled
sooner than he could have imagined, but at the time they were,
of course, entirely disregarded. He was sentenced to pay a fine
much larger than could be paid out of his own fortune and, though
his friends offered him gifts and loans to make up the deficit, he
refused all their offers, preferring to live the rest of his life in
exile. He chose for his place of refuge the city of Smyrna in
Asia, one of those very cities which, according to the sentence
passed against him, he had defrauded and oppressed. He was
received by the magistrates and by the local population with
every mark of distinction. A house, a library and everything to
make life pleasant was provided for him and here, supported by
the grateful hospitality of those whom he was supposed to have
injured, he lived for many years, for he was as healthy in body
as in mind.

At the time, and subsequently, I used often to reflect on the
case of Rutilius and of course his fate was a frequent topic of
conversation in our family. Like everyone in Rome outside the
business circles we were agreed in our indignation at the injustice
of the thing; and indeed, as a result of the case, people began

immediately to agitate for a reform of the law courts. But I could not at once understand why it was that the senate, of which Rutilius had been so distinguished a member, had remained passive, if it were really, as I had been taught, a united and powerful body of statesmen, used to authority and practised in the guardianship of standards of justice. However, as I considered the character of Rutilius himself, I noted two points of interest. The first, an obvious one, was that virtue, unaided by material power, is seldom or never able to resist a well-organised attack, and, when attacked, can only be effective, if at all, through a kind of martyrdom. Secondly I observed that, though Rutilius had friends among the most distinguished men, these were his only friends ; he had no party of his own devoted by affection, propaganda or self-interest to his cause and consisting, as it would have to do if it were to be really powerful, of elements good, bad and indifferent. Such reflections as these must, no doubt, have helped me to reach my later resolutions : not to allow myself to become a martyr, unless (which no one can help) accidentally ; and, while remaining constant and loyal to my principles and to my friends, to admit a certain flexibility in the first and to encourage a great diversity among the latter.

I now began to listen with added attention to the frequent political discussions which took place at our house. I noticed in particular at this time a severe but certainly impressive friend of my Uncle Caius Cotta. This was Livius Drusus, who was elected tribune almost directly after the condemnation of Rutilius. Drusus was one of the most serious men I have ever met and indeed he must have been somewhat of a prig. He used to boast that he had never in his life enjoyed a day's holiday, and he was totally incapable of either making or seeing a joke. He was not perhaps unusual in his belief that, whatever subject might be under discussion, he himself was invariably in the right. " I have made a study of the question," he would say ; and that seemed to him an argument that could not be resisted. What was more uncommon was the fact that, on almost every subject of political importance, he did happen to be in the right. And what was characteristic of the dilemma of our times was that he failed to achieve anything at all.

There were two measures for which he would have desired to be remembered. He planned during his year of office as tribune to reform the law courts and to grant citizenship to Rome's Italian allies. Of these two measures the second, as events were to show, was incomparably the more important, but at the time I thought chiefly of the corrupt court which had condemned my great-uncle and I imagined, since I was still very inexperienced, that a court composed, say, entirely of senators would be less corrupt. Certainly it was recognised by everyone, except by those gentlemen outside the senate who now had the exclusive right of serving on the juries, that the courts needed reform. And those senators who had done nothing to help Rutilius had now become alarmed for themselves and at the same time were grasping eagerly at the opportunity of securing a monopoly of the lucrative and powerful positions of jurymen. They, without question, and in all probability the Assembly of the People also would have supported Drusus if he had proposed that only senators should serve in the courts. But Drusus had "made a study of the subject." His ideal was a united Rome and a united Italy. He planned rather to reconcile than to antagonise the classes. So he proposed that in future the juries should be mixed, containing a proportion of senators and a proportion of gentlemen of means who were not members of the senate. It was in itself an admirable proposal, but it pleased no one. Each party wanted everything; neither would be content with a compromise.

Having lost the support of the richer classes, whether in or outside the senate, Drusus now turned his attention to the people. He tried to win favour with them by the usual methods of gifts of corn, proposals for redistribution of land and the founding of colonies. Many of these proposals were admirable. They were also necessary, since without the support of the people Drusus would find it impossible to proceed to his really important measure of granting at least some of the rights of citizenship to Rome's Italian allies.

However, the very mention of a Land Law has always proved in my time a signal for bitterness and violence. Many members of the senate now began to go about saying that Drusus was planning a revolutionary dictatorship. After they had uttered the words often enough it is possible that they even believed them. Armed bands of slaves and gladiators began to appear in the forum in order to break up the meetings addressed by Drusus. Soon there was street fighting every day and I remember the general horror when, on one occasion, the consul himself, who had been attacked by a supporter of Drusus, was carried away into safety with blood streaming from his nose. These undignified scenes were already evidence to prove that the Roman constitution lacked that serenity, flexibility and efficiency which had been attributed to it during my history lessons. I noted also how great was the difference between those calm and logical discussions on politics which I had heard and the actual procedure of attempted legislation. I was shocked to find that a wise, and, as it turned out, a necessary reform such as the proposal to grant citizenship to the Italians should never even be considered on its merits, but merely made into an occasion for ugly, violent and impassioned outbreaks. I was disappointed, too, to discover that this mixture of apathy and the wildest partisanship in politics was general. Even a great public figure like my Uncle Marius showed no knowledge of or interest in what Drusus was attempting to do. Indeed at this particular moment Marius was uniquely occupied with his quarrel with Sulla. Some statues had recently been set up in the Capitol illustrating the achievements of Sulla in the African war. The thought of these statues nearly drove Marius out of his mind with jealousy and rage. He openly boasted that he would tear them down by force and so make it plain to everyone that it was he and not Sulla who had won the war in Africa. Sulla was equally determined to resist violence with violence. So, apart altogether from the political conflict between Drusus and his opponents (though the conflict had long ceased to be conducted along proper political lines) it appeared that at any moment Marius and Sulla might plunge the city into a civil war in which no principles other than greed or ambition would be involved at all.

I was only eleven years old at this time, but was already becoming used to those scenes and expectations of violence which were at such variance with the liberal theories of my education. But I have never become so used to disorder and cruelty as to regard them with indifference. Certainly in this year I was profoundly shocked when we received the news that Drusus had been assassinated. Whether the murder was the work of some extremist in the senate or of a private enemy was never clearly established.

It was certainly made use of by extremists in the senate for their own narrow and vindictive purposes. Special courts were set up to try all those who had been associated with Drusus on the charge of having organised an armed rebellion of the Italian allies against Rome. Many eminent men suffered from this parody of justice and among them was Caius Cotta, who was driven into exile. The fact that he and the rest, so far from organising rebellion, had been taking the only possible steps which might have prevented the rebellion from breaking out was not even considered. As had been proved in the case of Rutilius, innocence and good-will were no defence. And the new law courts were as corrupt as the old.

In my own family we were, of course, chiefly concerned about the fate of Caius Cotta; but we were also disturbed at what seemed to be the imminent outbreak of violence between the partisans of Marius and of Sulla—all, apparently, for the sake of those offensive statues on the Capitol.

But this conflict was postponed. The armed rebellion of the Italian allies which Drusus had endeavoured to prevent now took place. For at least two generations the Italians had attempted to gain their rights by peaceful methods. Now the assassination of Drusus and the conduct of the senate in cancelling all his legislation made them realise that nothing except force could have an effect on the government at Rome. They went to war and fought with a skill and energy that very nearly proved overpowering.

CHAPTER IV

FIGHTING IN THE FORUM

I HAVE often wondered how Rome and Italy ever recovered from the disasters which succeeded one another throughout the whole period of my late childhood and early youth. Losses in manpower and in material wealth were prodigious. I have heard many estimates of these and believe that what appear to be the most exaggerated figures are probably the most accurate. But the moral damage was even greater. In every city of Italy during this period there were times when friends were betraying each other, when sons murdered fathers and fathers sons. The horrors of peace, in the short periods when peace was assumed to exist, were worse than the ruin of war. In all classes of society human nature showed itself at its very worst—cruel, rapacious, treacherous, servile, arrogant, without scruple, without loyalty, respecting nothing but superior force, yet jealous of any real superiority, subject to terror and anxious to inflict it. If any good appeared anywhere, it seemed in the nature of things doomed to extinction and defeat.

Anyone who grew up in and survived these years might be forgiven for adopting an attitude of total cynicism both with regard to nature, politics, and human beings. I myself have sometimes been tempted in this direction. I have read with admiration the great poem of Lucretius which, in spite of its archaic Latin, splendidly conveys what seems to me to be the probable truth—namely that the gods, if they exist at all, take no interest whatever in the affairs of men. But Lucretius was not quite sane. Though he writes magnificently of the great and beautiful force represented by Venus, my ancestress, it is evident that he was incapable of enjoying the pleasures of love. He respects, indeed he almost worships, the natural order which he finds in the universe, yet fails to observe that, if one leaves aside the stars, the ants and some other insects, the most imposing examples of order are to be found in the organisations of human society. Unless order prevails here, not only literature, philosophy and friendship, but life itself must become extinct.

It remains true, however, that this necessary order was, during the most formative years of my life, profoundly and continuously disrupted.

I was just twelve at the beginning of the war between Rome and the Italian allies and only dimly grasped the fact that this war, with all its wastage and savagery, a war that lasted for at least two years during which Italy was ravaged from north to south, was a war which need never have taken place at all. At the time I was chiefly interested in the military fortunes of my Uncle Marius, who, now approaching his seventieth year, again took the field, though not—to his intense disgust—as supreme commander. I remembered the consternation at Rome when the news arrived that the consul under whom Marius was serving on the northern front had, against the advice of Marius himself, led the greater part of his army into battle before they were sufficiently trained, how the consul and most of his troops had been destroyed and how the enemy were expected to move directly on Rome. And then, a few days later, there were the rejoicings when it was announced that old Marius, with the remnants of the army, had won a great victory and forced the enemy back. There was now strong popular feeling in favour of giving the supreme command to Marius, but even in these days of national danger the old political feuds continued. According to the friends of Sulla, Marius was now totally lacking in enterprise and too broken down in health to be capable of standing a prolonged campaign. Such gossip as this used to infuriate me and indeed it derived entirely from jealousy and political intrigue. I preferred to hear the story of how Marius, who would never risk battle unless he were certain of victory, had been surrounded by the entrenchments of one of the enemy commanders who in the end rode up to his camp and shouted out, "Marius, if you are really a great general, come out and fight." To which Marius replied, "If you are, make me."

However, in Rome the party of Sulla was in the ascendancy. Sulla himself had been serving with distinction on the southern front under the command of another uncle of mine, the consul Lucius Julius Caesar. After a number of defeats my Uncle Lucius wisely left the conduct of the war to Sulla and returned to Rome, where, in spite of his undistinguished military career, he at least showed some political wisdom. He passed a law giving a number of concessions to those Italians who would lay down their arms. There were some who complained that these concessions had been extorted from the government "under duress." This was perfectly true, and it was also true that without these concessions the war would have continued indefinitely, and that, had they been offered earlier, the war would never have broken out at all.

As it was, though my uncle's law was a step in the right direction, it did not go far enough. Though the total area of the war was somewhat reduced the fighting continued with increasing bitterness for another year and more concessions still had to be made before the end. In the second year of the war the new consuls took over the command in the north from Marius, who retired to Rome in a most furious and embittered mood. He became more furious still when he discovered that Sulla was retaining his command in the south and was likely to be elected consul for the following year. His one and only idea now was to secure for himself another important military command before he died, and one of the very greatest importance now became available in the East.

Here the King of Pontus, Mithridates, a man of enormous energy and insatiable ambition, had observed how Rome was weakening herself in this aimless struggle against her allies and had rightly seen that this was the moment to begin his long career of conquest and aggression. While Roman legions were tied down in front of Italian towns, his armies had overrun Asia Minor and his fleets were approaching Greece. This was shocking enough, but even worse news was to follow. On one day, by the King's orders, every Roman or Italian financier or tax collector on the Asiatic coast and inland was put to death. At least eighty thousand were murdered in this way. It was a thing which could not have happened if the home government had been able to inspire respect or if the officials on the spot had not made themselves universally hated. We were glad to hear that my great-uncle Rutilius had not suffered in this massacre. Even in such times the local population remembers its real benefactors. What was to be noted was that for one benefactor of our race they found, or imagined that they had found, eighty thousand oppressors.

The news of this outrage and of the spreading conquests of Mithridates affected everyone in Rome and not the business circles alone. Now, after so much blood had been wasted, it was recognised that it would be necessary to concede to the Italians more than all they had asked for through the peaceful mediation of Drusus. For it was essential that the war should be brought to an end so that Rome could equip an army strong enough to defend her interests in the east.

In my own family we were glad to find that necessities were being acknowledged and that, for a short time at least, some consideration was being paid to moderate opinion. Among the signs of this consideration was the recall from exile of Caius Cotta and of others who had unjustly suffered in the period of panic and reaction that had followed the assassination of Drusus.

Very soon, however, it became once more evident that moderation was bound to be ineffective and that unanimity was illusory. All were agreed that the war with the Italians must be ended and that an army must be sent to the east. But opinions were as sharply and bitterly divided as ever on the question of who should command the army and on the desirability of keeping faith with the Italians.

These questions had, it seemed, to be decided in the year of Sulla's first consulship. In this year I reached the age of fourteen. I was well placed to observe the facts and was now old enough partially to understand them, though in the excitement, rapidity and horror of the times understanding was not easy.

Before the year began people's nerves were already on edge, as can be shown from the number of prodigies which were reported. The fact is that prodigies occur every year, but people only look out for them and discuss them when they are either in danger or apprehensive of it. At this time, for instance, thunder was once heard from a clear sky. Those who heard it, instead of using the word "thunder," described the sound as being that of a tremendous trumpet and, on consulting the Etruscan sooth-sayers, were informed that the prodigy meant the end of one age and the beginning of another. In this the soothsayers were not far wrong, though they were right for the wrong reasons.

It was, in fact, a year of tremendous and final importance ; for, though history is a continuous process, this process is marked from time to time by culminating and decisive events which, once they have occurred, constitute, as it were, either barriers or flood-gates for what may be imagined as the general stream. After such events have taken place, nothing will be the same again ; certain processes will have become irreversible, certain tendencies and ways of thought permanently obsolete. So, before I reached the age of fifteen, the whole fabric of my early political education was torn before my eyes demonstratively into shreds.

The year began with a decision of the senate so mean and inept as to be almost incredible. They had been forced to grant Roman citizenship to the Italians ; but now they discovered a means for making this concession absolutely meaningless. By a system of reorganising block votes in the Assembly it was to be arranged that the new Italian voters, however numerous they might be, would always be heavily out-voted by the existing citizen body.

This shameless and obvious piece of trickery was designed to win for the senate the support of the Roman people who have never been anxious to share their privileges with others. But its effect, quite clearly, would be to prolong the war in Italy and to weaken Rome still further just at the time when her interests were so seriously threatened in the east. Sulla, of course, supported the senate's proposal, though he must have known how dangerous it was. But he was consul; he confidently expected that the senate would give him the command in the east and he wished by this cheap means of gratifying the people to make sure that no agitation in favour of an alternative commander would have a chance of success. So long as he received this command he was, at least for the time being, indifferent to the fate of Italy.

At the time I no doubt believed that the opponents of Sulla and the senate (and particularly those of them who were connected with my own family) were actuated by the highest motives of patriotism. This, of course, was not true. No party has ever had a monopoly of greed, arrogance and selfish ambition. But this does not mean that there is nothing to choose between one party and another. In decisive periods of history such as the present, changes in the structure of society and in the organisation of government are not only desirable but absolutely necessary. The necessity would not be altered even if it were true that good men try to resist change and bad men try to promote it. And of course such a proposition as this is no more true than would be its precise opposite. In my boyhood the great protagonists, Marius and Sulla, could both with reason be pronounced bad men. Yet all my life I have preferred one to the other, and this is not simply because Marius was my uncle or because I was later to find his name and reputation useful to me politically. It was, I think, because Marius represented, however imperfectly and, as it were, without design, life, whereas the world of Sulla was a dead world.

In this particular year of Sulla's first consulship the opposition to the senate, while it centred round old Marius, was directed by the tribune, Sulpicius. Had Sulpicius been in the end capable of holding power he would now be remembered more kindly. As it is, the common view of him is that he was an unscrupulous demagogue, a monster of savagery, an enemy to the whole structure of society. The same things have been said about me and they are true neither of myself nor of Sulpicius, whom I remember well. He was one of the best speakers of his day;

there was great dignity in his bearing and grace in his gestures ; his voice was strong and clear ; and, though he spoke rapidly, he spoke precisely and to the point. In politics he had begun by being a man of the senate, but, like Cotta and like Livius Drusus, he had become disgusted with the narrowness and incompetence of the senatorial government of his day and, since he wished to oppose it, took the only course open to him, which was to appeal directly to the Assembly of the People.

There was nothing unconstitutional in this ; but Sulpicius had learned from the recent past that the senate had no intention of allowing the constitution to work. He therefore equipped himself so as to be able to meet violence with violence. He went about with a bodyguard of some six hundred young men belonging to the moneyed class outside the senate and used to refer to them as his anti-senate ; and apart from them he could call out at least three thousand less reputable characters— gladiators, personal dependents, ex-slaves—who could be used to protect his own meetings and break up those of his opponents. For these precautions of his he was, of course, bitterly attacked as a revolutionary and as a subverter of law and order. In fact it would be more just to blame the revolution on those whose actions in the past had made these precautions necessary. Yet here again a precise judgment is not easy. There is still some justice in what may seem the hypocritical verdicts of history which exalt the successful revolutionary as a liberator and con- demn the unsuccessful one as a malefactor. I have seen a number of unsuccessful revolutions in my time and they have invariably done more harm than good. They disrupt one order without substituting for it a new order and they lead to counter-revolu- tions which, as happened in this case, may postpone for years the doing of necessary things. But it is difficult to blame Sulpicius. He had, to all appearance, made certain of success by accepting the logic of the times and by confronting force with superior force. Had he been dealing with anyone except Sulla, he would have been successful ; and at this time Sulla had not yet revealed the full ruthlessness of which he was capable.

Everything, it seemed at first, was going well for Sulpicius and for Marius who supported him. Their propaganda was skilful and violent, consisting chiefly of perfectly justified attacks on the senate for its handling of the war with the Italians and on its muddled policy in the east. In any attack made on the governing nobility the name and presence of Marius were invaluable. He had, as it were, risen from the ranks himself; he had begun his career by quarrelling with members of the great families; he had, without question, saved Rome from the German invasion, and had held more consulships than anyone else in history. He could thus be held up to admiration as "the man of the people," and his rough strength and humanity could be contrasted with the greed, exclusiveness and inefficiency of the governing classes. The picture was not accurate. Marius was as greedy as Sulla and Sulla, at this time, was more efficient than Marius; yet still the picture corresponded to something in reality.

Certainly the people accepted the picture at its face value. I used to notice with pleasure how every day the statues of Marius in the forum were garlanded with fresh flowers and leaves. The speeches of Sulpicius, in which he cleverly combined the unpopular theme of doing justice to the Italians with the popular proposal for giving the command in the east to Marius, were rapturously applauded, while his opponents could scarcely obtain a hearing at all. As for Marius himself, it was, in some ways, amusing to observe his conduct in public. With the best will in the world it was impossible for the old man to appear gracious. He was, in fact, much more frightened of crowds than he had ever been of enemy armies. His speeches were rambling and incoherent; when he attempted to ingratiate himself by a smile, his face would take on a peculiarly forbidding expression. Yet for all this the people seemed to love him the better. There were many who could remember how after the German victories in their feasts at home they had poured out grateful libations—"To the gods and Marius." To them he was still almost a god and yet one of themselves. He was helped, too, by the presence at his side of his son, Young Marius, who possessed most of the graces which his father lacked. Indeed this cousin of mine was one of the handsomest men in Rome and might, had things turned out differently, have been a good commander as well. Even at this time he was known as "the son of Mars," though, because of his numerous love affairs, his enemies preferred to call him "the son of Venus"—not a very telling criticism, since, as has been amply proved by my own career, there is no necessary incompatability between these two deities.

So, as the days went by, it became a matter of certainty that the Assembly of the People would vote for everything that Sulpicius proposed. But the consuls, one of whom was Sulla, and the senate were not prepared to submit. They issued a proclamation declaring that all public business was indefinitely suspended, on the grounds that the situation was too tense to admit of calm and reasonable discussion. The effect of this declaration was, of course, to make the situation far more tense than before. Even had he wished to do so, Sulpicius would no longer have been able to control his followers, and when the consuls were unwise enough to show themselves in the forum surrounded by their armed supporters, their appearance immediately provoked some of the worst rioting that had ever been seen in Rome. My mother succeeded in keeping me away from these scenes of violence and bloodshed ; but all Rome was full of the story of this day. Long afterwards I remember discussing it with my third wife (not a very satisfactory one). She was a small girl at the time, the daughter of Sulla's colleague in the consulship. One of her earliest memories was of this day, and of how her elder brother's dead body was carried into the house. He had been killed in the riots, and her father, the consul, had only narrowly escaped with his life.

Sulla also escaped, though in the strangest possible way. He was driven back by the crowd along one of the side streets and found himself cornered in the very last place which he would have chosen—the entrance to the house of Marius. Here he was forced to ask for refuge and here Marius received him.

What precisely happened next it is impossible to say. In later years Marius himself was almost unintelligible on the subject, so great was his rage with Sulla for the events which took place shortly afterwards and so bitter was his regret that he had not then and there made an end of him. And Sulla, in his Memoirs, rather glosses over this incident, as indeed he might be expected to do if, as many people say, he had been forced to beg for his life on his knees before his old enemy. But I do not think that at this time even Marius would have contemplated the killing in cold blood of a consul of the Roman people; and, even if he had contemplated such a thing, his advisers would have dissuaded him, since it appeared that now his party were having things entirely their own way.

What is certain is that Sulla, whether as the result of threats or persuasion, left the house of Marius escorted by Marius's own followers and proceeded directly to the forum, where he proclaimed that the ban on public business was at an end. There was now nothing to prevent Sulpicius from proceeding with his programme, and in the course of the next few days his proposals were put before the people in a more or less orderly manner and became law. In particular the command of the army for the east was taken from Sulla and conferred on Marius. Meanwhile Sulla, pretending that his life was in danger, had slipped out of the city and gone to join his troops.

In our family we deplored the rioting, but were relieved to find that, as it seemed, there was no likelihood of any such trouble in the immediate future. It did not occur to anyone as a possibility that a Roman army might march against Rome, since this had never happened previously in the history of the city, and it is hard for people to expect what they have never even imagined.

CHAPTER V

THE FALL OF ROME

OUR UNEASY confidence in the future lasted for less than a week. Looking back on this time, it is difficult to see how we could have felt any confidence at all. There was the obvious arithmetical fact that, whereas Sulla had six legions in the south of Italy, Marius and Sulpicius had no troops at all. Yet throughout the whole of Roman history the government in Rome had, so far, been obeyed, and when some senior staff officers were sent south to take over Sulla's army in the name of its new commander, Marius, it was generally assumed that they would carry out their mission without difficulty.

People were shocked and horrified when the news reached Rome that these officers had been stoned to death by Sulla's soldiers; but even then this event was regarded as evidence of mutiny among the troops rather than of rebellion on the part of the general. It was not until some days more had passed that it was clearly established that Sulla was marching northwards. Officers from his army who were sympathetic to Marius and Sulpicius deserted and came to Rome with the news. At the same time friends of Sulla were constantly leaving Rome on one pretext or another and hurrying southwards to join him. So, almost before the possibility of the rebellion of a Roman general had been accepted, people were acting on the certainty that this precisely was what was happening. On both sides, it may be said, action was preceding theory.

So far as Marius and Sulpicius were concerned, their actions were ineffective. They put to death a certain number of Sulla's friends and acquaintances—a measure which merely encouraged the defection of the rest. It was too late for them now to raise an army, but they could still control the senate, even though the majority of this body was secretly on Sulla's side. By a decree of the senate the praetors, with their rods of office, and their purple robes, were sent out on what was meant to be a dignified and impressive mission, with instructions to order Sulla to halt. When they reached Sulla's advancing army, their lives were spared (for Sulla could easily control his troops if he wished to do so); but their rods of office were broken in front of them, and their purple robes stripped from their backs. I remember the mood of dejection which settled on the city when these praetors, so humiliated, returned. Something undreamed-of now suddenly became a possibility, a probability, a certainty— Rome would be forcibly occupied by a Roman general.

And indeed it soon was. The last messengers sent out to delay Sulla's advance by promising him all kinds of concessions had only just returned with the comforting news that he had consented to camp outside the city, when his troops began to break their way in. On this day my mother kept me inside the house with my sisters, my tutor and other members of the family. From time to time someone would arrive with news of one kind or another, true or false. We were told that Marius had offered freedom to the slaves and was preparing with their aid to resist Sulla's advance in the very centre of Rome. This news shocked us and we did not immediately realise that it was untrue. In fact Marius was experienced enough as a commander to know that Sulla's legions could only be resisted by trained troops, and of these he had none. As we found out later, both he and his son had already, and very wisely, fled from Rome. Then we were told that Sulla had been checked at the outskirts of the city and that his men had even been driven back again to the wall by the unarmed citizens themselves, who had hurled down bricks and tiles at the soldiers from the rooftops. This had indeed happened, but by the time the news reached us the situation had changed again.

The change was made evident to us by the noise of voices from the streets—shouts, cries, groans, sounds both human and animal, expressive of misery, excitement, panic, indignation or mere hysteria. In the course of my military campaigns I have often heard this sound—the multifarious outcry of a population which sees with various emotions, among which terror predominates, the imminent destruction of what it has been accustomed to think of as an established order. Now I heard the sound for the first time, and I heard it in Rome.

We went out into the street and soon saw what had occasioned this outcry. In the direction of the Esquiline Hill long columns of black smoke were curling into the air. The noise of shouting and crying was indescribable; it echoed from street to street; and every now and again above the general clamour would rise a clear voice crying out in amazement some obvious fact—"Rome is burning" or "Sulla will kill us all if we resist."

Resistance, in fact, was at an end. In no case could it have been effective. Sulla had only hastened the inevitable by setting fire to the houses on his route, destroying, incidentally, the property of his friends as well as of his enemies and so revealing openly for the first time his quality of utter ruthlessness. In this ruthlessness of his he differed from Marius who, though savage and blood-thirsty to the extreme, respected, in his rough way, some decencies. Sulla respected nothing that was an obstacle to his immediate aim.

By the evening Rome was occupied by his troops. The streets, I remember, were unnaturally silent and the troops behaved better than might have been expected. It may be that, now that they had attained their objective, they were impressed by the gravity of what had taken place. Dimly, perhaps, they were aware that their action had altered the whole course of our history. The Jews have a myth which describes how the first parents of mankind fell from a state of primeval innocence into vice and dissatisfaction through eating some kind of fruit which had the effect of making them able to distinguish between good and evil. Many other such stories are current in the East and are, of course, interesting to any intelligent man. Modern civilisation, however, is the creation of the West and it is in our own contexts that I am reminded of the Hebrew myth when I think of Sulla. Our civilisation has never been innocent, but it has been most innocent, most fruitful, most enjoyable and efficient when it has rested upon generally agreed principles of law and order. There have been moral, religious and, it may be, sentimental sanctions for these principles. The law and order have sometimes been oppressive ; many of those who have most sternly asserted the principles have often been the greatest hypocrites. It is thus necessary for our health that these principles should be continually criticised, and that there should always exist in our society a revolutionary factor. Yet revolution itself, if it is to be valuable or efficient, must depend, in a certain degree, on the very principles which it appears to be attacking. It is disastrous to fight against government in the name of anarchy, or, however unjust the proceedings of one's opponents may be, to deny that such a thing as justice exists. Above all it is important to disguise the terrible truth that, in the last resort, what counts is physical co-ercion. This truth is terrible because it is a half truth. Pure and naked force can certainly dominate and transform a particular situation, but can do nothing to solve the problems which gave rise to that situation. Indeed once men have seen force used irresponsibly, and, to all appearance, effectively, the fabric of society is split ; all order is imposed and, beneath the imposed surface, there is primeval chaos, corruption, weakness, indecision, greed and jealousy, and a lack of articulation. This state is, paradoxically, one of hope ; for surely life would not be worth living if it were possible to force all men permanently and without regret into the framework designed by one man's will. Yet still something of the sort must, with infinite tact and patience, be attempted once the necessary bonds of human respect, principle or, if you like, superstition have been broken. Men cannot live without government ; they cannot live well unless they enjoy a government which deserves respect and in which, so far as they are able, they share. In my days the government, until I took it over myself, has not deserved respect ; but Sulla was the first to show that it could be treated with contempt. It was he who finally destroyed the fabric of the past and made it a certainty that the course of the future would be along the paths of civil war.

In the excitement and horror of the moment all this, of course, was not immediately evident. We ourselves thought first of Marius, of his son and of other friends who had been closely associated with him. We were outraged when, a day after he had entered the city, Sulla called a meeting of the senate and received its authority for pronouncing the death sentence on Marius, Sulpicius and others of their party. That rewards should be offered to any slave or criminal who could bring in the head of Rome's greatest general was something which shocked public opinion generally ; to me it seemed an almost personal affront and humiliation.

Marius, fortunately, had escaped, though no one knew what had become of him. Sulpicius was betrayed by one of his slaves and was killed without any pretence of legality. Even those who had most disliked Sulpicius were offended by this action. To kill a tribune in the course of street fighting seemed to them reasonable and honourable enough ; but to see a magistrate of the Roman people butchered in cold blood on the information of one of his slaves was something which horrified them. Their attitude may seem illogical but it was not really so. They had grasped, however remotely, the fact that Sulla's own logic was ruthless to the point of indecency and that without decency civilised life is impossible. In a characteristic way Sulla attempted to efface the bad impression which he had made. He first freed the slave who had betrayed Sulpicius and then immediately had him arrested and hurled down to his death from the Tarpeian Rock. This over-subtle piece of morality impressed nobody.

I myself, who hated Sulla, was glad to observe that my feelings were shared by most people in Rome. I observed with great pleasure that Sulla was now faced by difficulties with which he had not reckoned. It was true that his legions controlled Rome, but they were urgently needed in the East, where Mithridates was going from success to success. The whole revolution had been carried out in order to give Sulla the command in this war, and if Sulla did not set out immediately the war might well be lost. On the other hand, once he withdrew his legions from Rome, there would be no security either for his friends or for his own policies. This was made quite clear by the result of the elections, in which Sulla's nominees were rejected. One of the consuls for the next year, a superstitious reactionary called Octavius, could be regarded as safe; but the other was Cinna, a leader of the Popular Party and a bitter opponent to the whole method, character and aims of Sulla. I admired Cinna greatly, though I did not know that before long I was to become closely associated with him and I had scarcely seen Cornelia, his daughter, with whom I was to enjoy so happy a married life. At the time, no doubt, what I chiefly hoped for from Cinna was that he might annul the death sentence that had been passed on my Uncle Marius and might recall the old man to Rome. For, though no one knew where Marius was, it appeared certain that he had escaped from Italy. I used to pray daily for his return and would be constantly discussing the subject with my sisters or anyone else who would listen to me. That Sulla's actions should be allowed to go unpunished seemed to me monstrous and I was vexed with those members of my family who acquiesced in the present state of affairs and who would defend their attitude by saying that anything was better than civil war. "We have had enough of that already," they used to say, and neither they nor I knew that the civil war was only just beginning.

All of us, I think, felt an immense relief when, before the end of the year, Sulla left Rome and marched southwards to embark for the east. Before leaving he had induced Cinna, in more or less public circumstances, to swear an oath that he would remain friendly to him personally and would not subvert the existing régime. But he could not have expected that Cinna would keep this oath. In fact even before Sulla had left Italy, Cinna was instituting legal proceedings against him and was talking of bringing forward again the proposals of Sulpicius for doing justice to the new citizens.

We would, I remember, frequently and eagerly discuss these proposals (which were indeed excellent) and other political measures which Cinna was supposed to be sponsoring in opposi-

tion to his colleague Octavius and to the majority of the senate.
Among those with whom I used to hold long conversations at
this time were the two Cicero brothers—Quintus, who was
nearer my own age, and Marcus, who was four years older than
me and had even seen a little military service. Their family was
quite undistinguished, but the two boys had received an excellent
education and their father, who had made his money in trade,
was exceedingly ambitious for his sons. What first interested me
in them was the fact that they came from Arpinum, the birth-
place of Marius, and were proud to have done so. They would
talk about my uncle with almost the same enthusiasm as I showed
myself, and so it was easy to become friends. Quintus was the
more robust of the two and, in spite of his hot temper, the easier
to get on with. He would at least listen to what one had to say,
whereas his brother Marcus was, even at this age, one who
preferred to express his own opinions than to consider those of
others. He was, however, exceptionally brilliant and, in spite of
certain gaucheries, had a peculiar charm. I both liked him and
admired him. Particularly I was impressed by his learning.
He had already translated some of the works of Xenophon into
Latin and had written a heroic poem on the subject of Marius,
which had been much admired by some of the leading critics.
He could recite most of Ennius by heart and much of Homer.
Moreover, when one got to know him he showed a friendly
disposition and was capable of making the most witty remarks,
so long as he was with an audience which appreciated him.
With strangers he was inclined to be either too shy or too out-
spoken. He was acutely conscious of the mediocrity of his birth
and though in his epic on Marius he had exalted the merits of
the people as opposed to the aristocracy, he was himself somewhat too readily impressed by the very idea of inherited nobility.
He was, for example, almost indecently delighted when, as the
result of his precocious learning, he was invited to attend some
of the receptions given by Scaevola, the Chief Pontiff. However,
when the receptions were over and he was back again with his
friends, he would often declare that the day of the great nobles
was over and that the state could neither survive nor progress

without new blood. He would one day become consul himself, he used to say, and the name of Cicero would be as famous a name as that of Scaurus or of Scipio. We used to laugh at this, particularly as " Cicero " is in fact a somewhat ridiculous name, meaning " chickpea " ; but even at the time I admired the young man, since I could see that he spoke not from vanity but from conviction. The vanity was to come later.

I noticed, too, even at this time, a quality in Cicero which has not changed with the years. It would be untrue, or almost so, to say that he lacks the courage of his convictions, though he has often given this impression. Nor would it be true to say that he lacks convictions. He is and was full of them, though they have always been of a very generalised kind. His trouble has always been, I think, that in order to act or even in order to define his thoughts he has felt it necessary to secure for himself in advance the approval of those whom he regards as the respectable classes. This timidity or shyness of his may be ascribed to his consciousness of his inferior birth. Certainly he has always been something of a snob. But this explanation does not fully account for the facts. He is a man of genuine principle and he is not a coward. Perhaps it would be kinder to set down his weakness to the fact that he has always been pre-eminently a literary man whose attachment to history has been sentimental rather than vital. He has demanded from human affairs a kind of accuracy and style which is not to be found except in works of art. A mistake, certainly ; yet how curious to reflect that Cicero's own art, the art of oratory, could never have been developed by him to such perfection if Cicero himself had not taken part in the events of a history which he scarcely understood. It was not only through timidity that he clung to the past and to a fancied respectability. He, like many men, looked for perfection and wished to find in this period of utter and necessary revolution the balance and dignity and organic structure of his own prose.

As for me, I saw more clearly than ever Cicero did the full squalor, the confusion, the hypocrisy, the savagery, the demeaning beastliness of political activity. Indeed no time could have been more propitious for making these discoveries than were the most impressionable years of my life, those from the age of fifteen to that of twenty.

Now, in beginning to recall these years, I see that I must often have miscalculated and misinterpreted much. Some of my mistakes I realised at the time and others later. Yet if in this period I was made aware of the fallibility of judgment, the unpredictability of events, the clear distinction between life as it is imagined and as it is lived, I was made aware also of something else—of a kind of truth unlike that of literature, of art or of mathematics—the truth, indeed, of fact. This is the kind of truth which can be like a barrier or brick wall, against which one may run one's head in vain ; or like a knife or searing hot iron with its immediate incision or impress upon the flesh. It is what forces one to recognise necessity and to be humble. And next, when this lesson is learned, it will encourage agility ; for many barriers can be circumvented and many thrusts parried. And there is a higher and more important use for agility than merely comfort or self-preservation. Those whose temperaments are by nature creative and who possess (for this is something that cannot be learned) the power to control the feelings and desires of others will go farther and will attempt to introduce into life a principle, not precisely of art, but of order. Hard facts, they will know, cannot be altered ; but they can be manipulated, rearranged and, to that extent, controlled. Nor is it degrading to work in this medium of human life, passion, cowardice and revolution. A life, certainly, is more transitory than a poem, but a principle of order, a new direction discovered, will continue to the end of time and is, unlike poetry, translatable into every language.

Not that it is necessary to defend the exercise of creative activity in human affairs. There are times, such as those in which I have lived myself, when, in default of this activity, civilisation will come to an end and the very basis for art and poetry—for that different perfection—will cease to exist. At such moments the task before one cannot be denied, so urgent it is and so delightful are the discoveries one must make in carrying it out. For of course the creative politician, like the artist, has no clear-cut prescription by which he works; theory and practice must go together, each modifying each from time to time. Yet both the politician and the artist, if really creative, will be marked by a particular and individual style. The work done by each will be recognisable and easily attributable to its author; for the work will be the result of a particular insight, a particular force, a particular agility or technique.

I was too young at the time when Sulla sailed for the East to have reached these conclusions and, if I had reached them and had imparted them to the Ciceros, Quintus, I think, rather than Marcus, would have been the more likely to have understood them. As it was we talked much of literature and much of what Cinna would do next; we speculated upon where Marius could be and whether he would ever return. None of us, except possibly Marcus, thought that things could remain as they were; but none of us imagined how terrible, savage and profound was the change that was already taking place.

CHAPTER VI

THE RETURN OF MARIUS

OUR DISCUSSIONS on the immediate political situation could not, in fact, have lasted for very long. As soon as Sulla had left Italy, Cinna openly brought forward again the proposals of the dead Sulpicius. Fighting in the streets broke out at once, but this particular street fighting has not left a deep impression on my memory. It was less surprising than the fighting which had preceded it and less appalling than the slaughter which was to follow. Still, much blood was shed before the consul Octavius and his supporters, who included the majority of the senate, succeeded in driving Cinna and his partisans out of Rome.

For Cinna this apparent defeat was a positive advantage. He still had the prestige of a consul and, unlike the other consul in Rome, he could count on the support of the Italians whose rights he had championed. He was thus in a better position for raising troops than were his enemies in Rome and, as had recently been demonstrated by Sulla, it was physical force which, in the last resort, determined which of two parties was to hold power. Cinna therefore began to raise an army. Here he was immeasurably helped by having on his side a man who was, without doubt, one of the greatest military geniuses who has ever lived. This was Quintus Sertorius, of whom at the time I knew little except that he had been a trusted and brilliant officer who had served under Marius, that he had one eye, and that even Marius, who was not apt to praise others, spoke of him certainly with respect and almost with admiration. Later I studied the career of Sertorius with great attention and have learned, I hope, much from the study. He was the most intelligent commander of his day and, apart from myself, the only one who combined both military and political ability of the highest order. He was as tough and unsparing of himself as Marius, but he was also gracious in his manners, honourable, a good judge of character and a man of wide interests. The extraordinary rapidity of his actions and his ability to make full use of every kind of material are, no doubt, the qualities which will be remembered by historians of the art of war. But Sertorius escapes from ordinary categories by the vigour and unpredictability of his imagination. It was my loss that I never knew him intimately, since he and I alone seem to have understood the history of our times.

So, largely because of the skill and energy of Sertorius, Cinna very soon had a considerable force at his disposal. Meanwhile the consul Octavius in Rome had done little or nothing to counterbalance this force. Though a great stickler for preserving the precise forms of the constitution, he had secured from the senate an entirely unconstitutional decree depriving Cinna of his consulship and declaring him a public enemy, and, without even the formality of an election, he had appointed a conservative senator, Merula by name, to be consul in his place. Merula held the position, an influential one in the priestly colleges, of Flamen Dialis, or Priest of Jupiter. I had no idea that, before the year was out, I myself was to become Merula's successor as Priest, but I knew enough of the office to know that it was one most singularly unsuited for a consul in a time of civil war ; for among the many superstitions and taboos which surround the Flamen are two which must make him wholly ineffective at such periods : first, he is not allowed to look upon a corpse, and secondly, he is not allowed to come near an army.

But the jokes which we made about Merula and our feelings of mingled apprehension and excitement as we spoke of the impending action of Cinna and Sertorius soon gave way to an excitement of a more personal kind. It must have been about the time of my fifteenth birthday when we received the news that Marius was not only safe, but had landed in Italy. From that time until I was able to see Marius myself I used to go con-

stantly to my Aunt Julia's house and she would often allow me
to listen to the messengers who came secretly to her with news
of her husband. The full story of his exile we heard in detail
later, but we heard enough then to make us wonder whether
the sufferings which he had been through might not have disturbed the balance of his mind. He had been chased hither and
thither in Italy like a runaway slave; he had gone without food
and drink, yet still persisted to live, though all his companions
had given up hope; he had been dragged naked out of a pool
of muddy water where he had hidden himself and had then been
condemned to death, in accordance with Sulla's orders, by the
magistrates of the nearest town. Somehow he had been pre-
served by his own greatness. A German mercenary soldier who
had volunteered to put him to death had been unable to bear the
sight of the old man's blazing eyes as he lay in a darkened room.
He had dropped the sword at his feet and run out into the street
crying out, "I dare not. I dare not kill Caius Marius," and,
seeing this, the townspeople had felt ashamed of their previous
decision, had given Marius a ship and done all they could to
help him on his way. More hardships had followed before he
had succeeded in reaching Africa and making contact with his
son, young Marius, and the rest of his friends who had fled with
him from Rome. Still Marius remained firm in his conviction
that once more in his life he would be consul and, as he told us
later, he succeeded in numbing pain and in conquering exhaustion
by concentrating upon the names and faces of his enemies, on
all of whom he was determined to be revenged.

Now, we were told, he had landed in Etruria with his son
and with a small force which he had raised in Africa. This small
force soon became an army, for Marius had no hesitation in
promising their freedom to slaves who would serve with him or
in enrolling among his troops labourers, herdsmen and all sorts
of discontented or impoverished workers who were glad enough
to leave their employers and often to massacre them before
leaving. He was shrewd enough, however, to attempt in some
sense or other to legalise his position. One of the first things he
did was to send a messenger to Cinna acknowledging him as

consul and offering to serve as an ordinary soldier in the ranks of Cinna's army. The offer was, of course, only made for reasons of propaganda. Marius was quite determined to have an independent command; but the gesture was characteristic of him and deceived many people at the time, including myself.

It did not deceive Sertorius, however, and I was shocked to hear that he had bitterly opposed the idea of bringing in Marius as an equal partner in the alliance between himself and Cinna. I attributed this opposition to the basest motives of jealousy and ambition. In fact Sertorius was not the man to be swayed by such feelings as jealousy when important decisions had to be taken and his estimate of the situation turned out to be entirely correct. He had pointed out to Cinna that their forces were already irresistible and were still growing; what was important was that, once they had established themselves in Rome, there should be a period of peace, order and good government during which they could so strengthen themselves as to be able to deal with the armies of Sulla in the East, since Sulla would certainly not acquiesce in the new régime which they designed. All this, Sertorius said, could easily be done by themselves; but to put Marius into power would be to take a tremendous risk. He knew the man and could guess how he would behave. It would be in a manner that would weaken their party politically without greatly strengthening it from a military point of view.

Sertorius found little enough support for his views and, since he had never held high office, he lacked the necessary prestige to make his views effective. Cinna was an honest and well-meaning man, but he had no conception of the forces now about to be let loose and he showed no ability later in attempting to control them. He resented as ungenerous any idea that Marius should be kept in the background. I was delighted to hear that he had treated him with all the marks of distinction due to a pro-consul and had associated him in the supreme command of the combined forces.

Meanwhile in Rome the situation was rapidly deteriorating. The consul Octavius had indeed secured the support of Pompeius Strabo, who had been in command of a considerable army in the north and who, cruel, corrupt and unpopular as he was, could at least claim to be a competent general. Serving with him was his son, young Pompey, later to be called "The Great." Some idea of the morale of Strabo's troops can be obtained from the fact that young Pompey had to make use of his great personal popularity in order to save his father from being assassinated by his own men.

Indeed, what resistance there was collapsed very quickly. Marius, who had used his fleet with great skill, occupied the port of Ostia, thus cutting Rome off from all supplies. Meanwhile the main army under Cinna and Sertorius was converging on the city from different directions. It was already rumoured that the troops with Marius and in particular the large force of freed slaves whom he kept as his personal bodyguard were behaving with a singular and calculated ferocity.

I remember one day of conflicting rumours and the agitation into which we were thrown by what we saw and heard. Marius, who never liked to share any military distinction with anyone, was eager to be the first to enter Rome and, moving forward somewhat rashly from Ostia, did in fact occupy the Janiculan Hill. I succeeded in evading the supervision of my elders and went out towards the hill, wishing to see what I imagined would certainly be the triumphal entry of my uncle into the city. But when I got near the scene of the fighting I saw no signs of anything of the kind. Through the dense crowds of people who, like myself, had come out as sightseers, wounded men from Strabo's army were making their way to the rear. But those of them who were not seriously wounded were remarkably cheerful. They had defeated Marius, they said, and driven him back. Some even claimed that he had been killed. I listened to these rumours with consternation and as I pressed forward nearer to the Janiculan Hill I began to believe them to be true ; for there was now no sign of fighting. In fact, some cohorts who had been stationed in reserve were marching away in a different direction altogether. Not before sunset did we learn what had really happened. It appeared that Marius in his over-confidence had indeed suffered a reverse and that, had he been opposed by better generals, this reverse could have been serious. As it was he had been rescued from a difficult position because of the alarm caused by a diversionary attack made by Sertorius upon another part of the city's fortifications.

This was the last military action of any importance. Soon afterwards Strabo died of a sudden illness ; the troops, having no confidence whatever in the abilities of the consul Octavius, began to mutiny or to go over openly to the armies which now invested Rome on all sides. Octavius himself was advised by his friends to escape while there was still some possibility of doing so. But he had a childish faith in soothsayers and Etruscan prophets and Chaldaean calculations. According to these sources of information he was in no danger at all ; and so he remained in Rome while the senate, now in a state of utter panic, sent an offer of capitulation to Cinna, only begging him to guarantee that there would be no reprisals. Cinna replied that first the decrees passed against him must be withdrawn ; as for the reprisals, he said that he would be as merciful as circumstances permitted. So Merula, who had done little or nothing during his short period of office, was deposed and Cinna entered Rome as consul.

We had expected that Marius would enter the city at the same time and had made our preparations to meet him. The old man, however, had determined to make his entry into Rome in his own way. He sent a message to the senate in which, after a lengthy description of his achievements in the past, he went on to comment on the fact that he was now in exile with a price upon his head. Respecting as he did the Roman constitution and the freedom of the Roman people, he could not, he said, return to his own home and family until the Roman people itself had freely voted for his recall. Many of the people were, as Marius intended they should be, much impressed by this strangely legalistic talk, and the senate made arrangements immediately for the necessary voting to take place. Meanwhile an advance party of Marius's troops had entered Rome, marched directly into the forum and butchered the consul Octavius in cold blood. After the murder there was found on his person a Chaldaean document guaranteeing him a happy and successful life for many years to come.

This act of violence was indeed shocking but it was not, except by Octavius himself, wholly unexpected. Moreover, it was difficult at the moment to be quite certain about who, in fact, had authorised the act.

Next day Marius, at the head of his army, entered Rome. He was met by a large crowd, including his relations and friends, all eager to congratulate him on his safety and on his return. I myself was deeply moved by the prospect of this occasion. I put on the best clothes that I had and felt the keenest joy as I thought of how my uncle would be welcomed back with honour into the city which he had saved. I looked with interest and fascination at the faces of his troops and at him himself I looked with a kind of amazement, since I could hardly believe that he was indeed here, still robust in his old age, still unsubdued by every hardship. I noticed that he showed little interest in the speeches of congratulation that were being made ; all the time his fierce eyes glared about him, searching the faces of the crowd, and it soon appeared that he was looking, not for his friends, but for his enemies. His plan had long been made, and it was a simple one. He would not leave alive a single person by whom he imagined that at any time he had been injured. And he had fit instruments with which to work, for his army of liberated slaves, ex-gladiators for the most part or oppressed workers of the land, were as savage as their master and would obey or anticipate his commands.

The conventional speech-making was soon cut short. Marius had observed at the edge of the crowd an old senator who had once opposed him on some minor issue in the past, and, paying no further attention to a laudatory speech which someone was making, he pointed out this old man with his hand. In a second or two he was dragged forward and stabbed to death ; the head was then severed from the body and fixed, as a trophy, to the point of a lance.

There were some in the crowd feeble-minded enough and sufficiently disturbed emotionally to applaud the act ; and indeed wherever savagery becomes, as it were, authorised there is seldom any lack of so-called law-abiding citizens who will take their part in it and enjoy it. So now, though the better people of all classes withdrew hurriedly to their houses, there was still a considerable mob which followed Marius as he began to go systematically through the streets, dragging his enemies or those whom he believed to be so, out of their homes and having them butchered in front of his eyes.

I, of course, was not one of this crowd. I spent the day at home, shivering with a kind of fear and nervous exhaustion. Not only could I imagine what was going on, but every hour someone would arrive with more news of the horrors that were being perpetrated. I only hoped that they would end at nightfall.

This hope was not fulfilled. For five days and five nights the slaughter and rape and burning continued. The evidence of this savagery was everywhere. All senators who were killed (and there were at least fifty of them) were beheaded so that their heads could be exhibited in the forum as ghastly trophies of revenge. As for the others, mostly belonging to the richer classes outside the senate, their bodies were left in the streets to be eaten by dogs and birds. How many perished in this way it is impossible to say, but the number cannot have been less than a thousand. Soon the slaughter became almost indiscriminate. Some were cut down in the streets because they had failed to salute Marius as he passed, others because Marius had not bothered to return their greeting. Many committed suicide out of fear and many, who were not in personal danger, killed themselves in shame or in despair after seeing their possessions destroyed or their wives and children outraged.

During all this time Marius appeared to be, and indeed was, drunk both with wine, which, since he scarcely ate or slept at all, he took constantly to support him, and with the sheer lust for blood and for destruction. He was quite unapproachable and, though he would greet Cinna and Sertorius with a kind of ghastly good humour, he paid no attention to anything they said. Still less would he listen to his wife or other members of our family. Indeed he actually permitted Fimbria, one of the most brutal of his officers, to kill my father's brother, Lucius Caesar, and to display his head in the forum.

Finally Sertorius took matters into his own hands. He was the only man in Rome with the courage and ability to do so. There was a time when, from sheer weariness, Marius had temporarily desisted from slaughter and had gone to his house to rest. Acting with his usual rapidity, Sertorius brought up detachments of his own troops, who, alone among those who had captured Rome, had remained well disciplined and well behaved. With these men he surrounded Marius's bodyguard of ex-slaves and killed every one of them. It was an easy operation, but no one else at the time would have dared to undertake it. As it was, when Marius came to, he was too shrewd or else, perhaps, too exhausted from his excesses to attempt any reprisals. He actually pretended to approve of what Sertorius had done and from then on treated him with a curious kind of respect, almost as though he feared him and sought for his good opinion.

This, however, he did not enjoy; for in a few days he had accomplished exactly what Sertorius had feared. He had alienated all moderate opinion from the Popular Party, and, in so doing, had jeopardised, perhaps irreparably, the one hope which this party had of retaining power. Sulla would undoubtedly attempt to regain the position which he had lost and would now be actuated not only by ambition but by revenge; for his houses and property had been destroyed, his statues thrown down, his friends and some of his family murdered, while the rest of his family, the fortunate ones, had, after every kind of hardship and humiliation, escaped to tell him the story. He and his eastern legions could only be resisted by a united Rome and a united Italy. Marius, in less than a week, had made unity something so unlikely as to seem impossible.

On me personally these measures had an effect which, I suppose, has been indelible. Later there were to be other scenes of bloodshed more extensive, more deliberate and, in a sense, more cruel. But never again in my life have I seen anything so disorderly, so savage and so disgusting as was the conduct of Marius and his slaves. From it I learned beyond a doubt that there is nothing necessarily good, nothing which can necessarily demand our affection and respect, in human nature, which, once restraint is removed, becomes something too horrible to contemplate ; that all dignity, and with it the possibility of affection, comes from restraint, whether self-imposed or enforced from outside ; and that, of all the feelings of which the human heart is capable, the unworthiest is the passion for revenge.

CHAPTER VII

THE END OF MARIUS

ON THE subject of Marius my mind has always been strangely divided. This last period of his life was, for me, a period of horror and disillusion. I shrank even from his kindnesses—for, when he was sober enough to recognise me, he would show a particular interest in my future. Yet still I clung to that view of him which had filled the imagination of my childhood, and, I knew, moreover, that the view was not entirely false. What I saw now was a ruin, but it was the ruin of something great and powerful.

He died early in the year following his return to Rome and his death was, to me and others, a relief. At the beginning of this year he and Cinna had taken up their offices as consuls and Marius had signalised the occasion by having one of his enemies hurled to death from the Tarpeian Rock. This, however, was the last of his savage acts. The prophecies, real or imagined, had been fulfilled. He was consul for the seventh time ; but he died before seventeen days of his consulship had elapsed. The last period of his life was a miserable one. He suffered from insomnia and indeed from something worse than that ; for even his moments of uneasy sleep were vexed and made horrible by dreams, terrors and fantasies. Much of the time he was, to all appearance, out of his mind and the state of his sanity was not improved by the vast quantities of wine which he drank in order to numb his apprehensions and to secure some kind of besotted sleep. There were times when he would imagine that he was leading the armies against Mithridates, and then he would shout out in his terrible voice and, staggering about the room, would

seize on any weapon that came to hand and, as soon as his grip
had tightened upon it, miraculously it seemed, suddenly present
the appearance of a sober man, or at least of some inflexible
statue of a warrior. Soon, however, his fingers would relax,
letting the weapon fall, and Marius himself would, as often as
not, topple to the ground. Yet it was neither from sleeplessness
nor from excess that the old man died, though it seemed incredible
that any human frame could support so long the effects of either
of these. His last sickness was a pleurisy caused, the doctors said,
by a cold draught of air. It was a merciful disease for it enabled
Marius to relax and to die with dignity. He even composed a
speech in which, after enumerating his triumphs and his reverses,
he closed with the decent reflection that a prudent man should
trust himself no more to fortune. Those who heard him speak
in these terms knew that he had given up the struggle and were
glad of it ; for they could now think again of his past greatness
rather than live in fear of some new outrage or disgrace. Most
of his last few days were spent in sleep and he died peacefully.
Those who saw the dead body said that at the end the rough
features had become set in a strange nobility and an unusual calm.

I myself neither saw the body nor attended the funeral. I was
forbidden to do so by my religious duties ; for I had recently
been nominated by Marius and Cinna to the place among the
Flamens which had become vacant owing to the suicide of the
unfortunate Merula who, soon after the entry of Marius into the
city, had retired to the Temple of Jupiter and bled himself to
death.

I owed my appointment, of course, to the fact that I was the
nephew of Marius, though it is probable that the choice was also
influenced by the wish of Cinna and Sertorius to attract to their
party the Cottas and other friends and relations of my mother.
It was necessary too that the Flamen Dialis, or Priest of Jupiter,
should belong to a patrician family, and at the time there were
not a great number of patricians who could be relied upon to
support the present régime.

Nevertheless, it was an honour to be given at so early an
age so respectable a post and I took my duties seriously, though

I had to dissemble, as did many of my colleagues, some feelings of distaste for and disbelief in the religious ceremonies in which I took part. The sacrifices of animals and the inspecting of their steaming entrails have always been disgusting to me and, I cannot help feeling, must be equally disgusting to the gods, assuming them to exist. Then I had to wear, on official occasions, a peculiarly ridiculous hat, made of white leather and shaped like a cone. This hat, however, had one advantage connected with it. If it were to fall off during a ceremony the wearer was bound immediately to resign his office. There was thus always an easy escape available, though in fact I never wished to make use of it, partly because it is in any case indecorous to allow one's hat to fall from one's head, partly because I was perfectly content as I was. My position debarred me from any kind of military service, but I had no ambitions as a commander. I had associated the idea of command with the figure of my Uncle Marius and now I wished, so far as I could, to forget him and to forget those boyish imaginations or fantasies which I had once had and in which I seemed to see myself, like him, leading Roman legions into battle, perhaps in the east and perhaps in the undiscovered areas of the west. At this time my thoughts turned rather to a literary career. I have always, too, been something of an anti-quarian and I was genuinely interested in the knowledge which I was acquiring every day of the operations of Roman religion.

Most of our ceremonies have, of course, been handed down from a remote past and many of them have lost the meaning which they must once have possessed. Some of our sacred hymns and ritual formulae are completely unintelligible to those who pronounce them, yet we attach great importance to pronouncing these meaningless words in what is assumed to be the right way. At first I regarded all this as merely ridiculous ; for how can a god be expected to answer a mortal's prayers when the mortal does not even know what he is saying ? I soon realised, however, that this was a superficial view. Our system of religion has con-siderable practical advantages and in this age of intellectual and political transition, an age in which most people are apt to be hysterical or fanatical, it can be an important element of stability.

The prayers and sacrifices, however meaningless in detail, have a general object and a public effect. They were designed originally to propitiate rather than, as it were, to attract the gods ; and it is still assumed that if these ceremonies of propitiation are carried out with scrupulous correctness, the gods will not interfere with the necessary work of man in agriculture, war and other activities. Our state religion, paradoxically enough, is in a sense atheistic. It tends to keep the gods, always assuming them to exist, at as great a distance as possible from men, and, in freeing those who are naturally superstitious from their apprehensions, allows them to proceed calmly and confidently with the business of civilisation. There is the widest possible difference between this time-honoured and, on the whole, beneficial system and those Asiatic cults which even in my boyhood were becoming popular in Rome, particularly among the women, and whose appeal rests upon a real or imagined communication between the human and divine in some state of ecstasy which, very often, can only be reached by means of the wildest emotional excesses. No doubt in times of strain and stress and to people of hysterical and unstable dispositions these cults can offer definite advantages of a psychological character. Yet they are not without danger, since they tend to undermine the necessary belief in the duties which men owe to each other and to the state ; for in moments of physical or emotional intoxication these duties are not apparent. The priests of Cybele, for instance, after dancing themselves into a frenzy, encourage novices to castrate themselves in honour of the Great Mother. Catullus has written a fine poem on the subject which is extremely ingenious metrically. However, this practice of castration can obviously not be tolerated in a country which depends on a high birth-rate for the recruitment of its legions. We do, as it happens, permit the Phrygian worshippers of the Great Goddess to carry on their rites in Rome. Indeed, they have been established here for a long time, obviously because it was felt that the Great Goddess might correspond to something in reality and could be appeased. But quite rightly we do not allow Roman citizens to wear Phrygian dress or to take any part, except as spectators, in the processions.

Our religion, therefore, has solid advantages in so far as it tends to discourage unnecessary thought and undesirable emotion. As for the minority of people, a small one at all times, who are capable of and interested in thinking metaphysically, the whole of Greek philosophy is at their disposal. I myself, at the time of Marius's death, was only just beginning my studies in this subject. I enjoyed them greatly; but I observed that those who approach the subject with a certain modesty, even a certain scepticism, are more happy and often more accurate than the enthusiasts who are capable of believing that a prescription in words can fully explain or determine any really complicated process or event. Those who take to philosophy eagerly and single-mindedly, as to some Oriental religion which claims to embrace all things rather than as to an art which has its necessary limitations, tend on the whole to become narrow-minded, inconsiderate of others, stiff and awkward in their personal relations. This, certainly, was what happened to Cato and, in a sense, to a much greater man than Cato, the poet Lucretius.

I myself have always taken the keenest interest both in philosophy and in the various religious cults with which I have made myself acquainted both in the east and in the west. I have had agreeable discussions with Chaldaeans, Indians, Alexandrian professors and Gauls who have been educated in the discipline of the British Druids. But I have retained a practical taste for the religious ceremonies of my own country and even in the days of my first priesthood I would spend many hours in discussing them, particularly with some of the Vestal Virgins. The friendly relations which I cultivated with these ladies were to be of the greatest service to me later.

During these years of my early youth I was, however, by no means uniquely devoted to my studies and to my new official duties. I had already begun to show that zest for extravagant living for which I am, I fear, notorious and which is often an embarrassment to me, since, when I pass laws, necessary from an economic point of view, to limit the expenses of individuals on dinner parties, people are perfectly well aware that I do not propose to be bound by these laws myself. Not that I have ever been addicted to gluttony, as Lucullus was. Nor have I ever enjoyed those long drinking bouts which seem to appeal to a great variety of people—both to Antony, for instance, and to that perverse moralist, Cato. However, even in my very early youth I was fond of display. I liked my parties to be remarkable either for good taste or for splendour. I liked to possess horses which would attract attention from pedestrians in the streets. I was fond of purchasing rare books and works of art, and, in particular, I was most careful of my dress which, within the rather strict conventions of Roman costume, I used to vary as much as possible.

I soon began to run into debt and found that the only way of repaying the interest on loans was to borrow more and more money. Indeed, from the age of sixteen until I was well past forty my debts have grown and grown. They have always alarmed my family and my friends and have occasionally proved very embarrassing to me personally. It says something for the intelligence of Roman business men that I have been, on the whole, regarded as a good investment; for at any moment of my life until I had reached middle age I could have been utterly ruined if I had failed to discover people who were willing to make me loans, each one of which was bigger than the last.

My father, certainly, during the last years of his life (he died not long after Marius) was much worried by my extravagances. He suggested that I could do something to relieve myself and him of my debts if I were to marry a rich heiress, and I was forced to admit that there was some justice in his point of view. In the end, when I was seventeen, I followed his advice and contracted a match with a lady called Cossutia, whose father was a business man, not, of course, a member of the senatorial nobility, and who was glad to provide a considerable dowry to allow his daughter to marry into one of the patrician families. This match of mine was opposed by my mother and my Aunt Julia, both of whom wanted me to marry into one of the leading families whose support would be valuable to me in a political career. I myself, however, had not yet made up my mind as to what sort of a career I was fitted to pursue. Indeed, at this age I often contemplated the idea of becoming a poet or a dramatist. Moreover, Cossutia seemed to me not only wealthy but attractive. While I was not precisely in love with her, I was far from being indifferent to her charms. Indeed there must be few women in whom I am not prepared to be interested.

This marriage cannot be said to have been a great success, since it lasted scarcely more than a year. There were various reasons for this, some personal and some political. Among the political reasons was the fact that Cossutia's family soon began to think that, although they had married their daughter to a patrician, they had chosen a patrician with most dangerous connections and one who belonged to the wrong party. So, when a divorce was arranged, they were extremely reasonable on all questions concerning the return of the dowry.

There was some reason for the alarm felt by Cossutia's family. I was the nephew of Marius and I was known to be well thought of by Cinna. And by the time that I was eighteen it was becoming evident that the civil war would be renewed. The shrewdest observers, moreover, were already convinced that the party of Cinna would be on the losing side.

Personally I liked Cinna. I did not object to the fact that he had himself made consul year after year. As I have discovered myself, there are times when this kind of continuity in administration is absolutely essential. Moreover, though it later became fashionable to speak of " the tyranny of Cinna," Cinna's government was, in many respects, as good as it could have been in the existing circumstances. In particular the Italian problem, which had already caused so much unnecessary bloodshed, was now finally settled and, as a result, Cinna's so-called " tyranny " was more popular than any alternative government could have been throughout Italy.

Where the régime was weak was at the centre, in Rome itself. Here, as Sertorius had foreseen, the massacres carried out by Marius and his lieutenants had had a disastrous effect. Men of enlightened and moderate views, such as the Cottas, withdrew temporarily from politics, and they did this not from calculation (though, in fact, if they had not been inactive at this time, they would probably have lost their lives later) but from sheer disgust. And, if the more moderate members of the nobility were reluctant to associate themselves with the new government, the rest, who have always constituted the majority, among whom there were many who had some death or disgrace in their own families to avenge, were only waiting for the moment when they could make others feel what they had suffered themselves.

In the background was always the shadow of Sulla. News continued to arrive of his victories in the east. First we heard of his capture of Athens and of the appalling slaughter of the inhabitants that had taken place after the city had capitulated. Then came the news of two great battles in Greece which had resulted in the total defeat of Mithridates's best troops and most experienced generals. After this it was reported that Sulla was crossing over into Asia, but no one was under the illusion that he would remain there longer than was necessary for the reconquest of the province or that he would acquiesce in the government set up by his enemies in Rome.

The measures taken to deal with this threat were ineffective. An army under the consul Flaccus was sent to the east ostensibly to operate against Mithridates, but in fact, if it could be managed, to fight against Sulla. A number of the more notorious supporters of Marius served in this army, among them Fimbria, who had murdered my Uncle Lucius and who, at Marius's funeral, had nearly succeeded in murdering Scaevola, the Chief Pontiff. He had not been long in the east when he murdered Flaccus, his commander-in-chief, and took over the command himself. Here he seems to have shown considerable tactical ability, but he was unable to retain the loyalty of his troops. Sulla had taken care to see that Fimbria's men should be informed of how his own soldiers had grown rich on loot and how, when a battle was not in prospect, they were allowed to live easily, with all discipline relaxed, preying like locusts on the inhabitants of the towns where they were quartered. The rot soon set in and Fimbria's entire army went over to Sulla, leaving Fimbria himself to commit suicide.

It was soon after the beginning of my short marriage to

Cossutia that this news reached Rome and at about the same time came a despatch from Sulla to the senate announcing that he had reconquered the lost provinces and that the war with Mithridates was at an end. Sulla went on to complain of the ingratitude with which, after his great achievements, he and his friends had been treated. Now, he concluded, he proposed to protect his friends and to bring to justice all those who had taken part with his enemies. The tone of the despatch was that of one who had already entered Rome as a conqueror and was prepared to do so again. It was the characteristic tone of Sulla and it was effective in so far that it greatly weakened the authority and resolution of the senate, at least half of whom were secretly on Sulla's side, while many of the others thought only of how they could best avoid offending anybody. A pious resolution was immediately passed calling upon the consuls, who were Cinna and Carbo, to stop raising troops and offering to negotiate with Sulla once he had laid down his command. As an effort to prevent civil war this resolution was entirely ineffective. Sulla had no intention of disbanding his army, and Cinna, Carbo and Sertorius, knowing this, would certainly not leave themselves unprotected. But the motion of the senate was useful to Sulla, since it seemed to give him a certain legal position once he had landed in Italy.

During the months that followed the preparations for war continued. Cinna and Carbo planned to fight Sulla in Greece. The plan itself was a good one and might well have been successful if it had been ably carried out. As it was, it was made ineffective both by accident and by incompetence.

I myself was prevented by my duties as a priest from taking part, as I might otherwise have done, in the military operations which were now impending. Nevertheless, I took a keen interest in the movements of troops and in the prospects of the war. I was, in fact, rapidly growing up, and also was finding myself drawn nearer to the centre of power—very dangerously so, as it turned out, though at the time it seemed that I was beginning my career under the most fortunate circumstances.

It may be that the sudden death of my father, which took place shortly after my first marriage, had the effect of releasing in me certain ambitious energies. It was now to me rather than to anyone else that my mother and my sisters looked up, and I derived from this new attitude of theirs a new confidence in myself. I now began to plan for myself a political career and at the same time I fell in love with Cinna's daughter Cornelia and realised that by gratifying this love I would become the son-in-law of the greatest man in Rome. This was a prospect which particularly pleased my Aunt Julia who, as the widow of Marius, still had great influence and prestige among the families who had been associated with the Popular Party. It was she who approached Cinna and won his consent to the marriage. Here again I was helped, of course, by my connection with Marius, but Cinna himself, I think, had already formed a favourable impression of my ability.

I therefore divorced Cossutia and married Cornelia. She was a good wife and I remained married to her until her death some sixteen years later. The first months of our marriage were peculiarly happy. I was able to spend much time in my wife's company, since my religious duties kept me in Rome and I was delighted when it became clear that she was going to bear me a child.

Our pleasure, our tranquillity and my ambition were, however, very soon to be interrupted. I feared greatly for my wife's health when, before our child was born, the distressing news arrived that Cinna had been murdered. This had happened at the camp of the legions in Ancona who were waiting to be transported to Greece. There had been no question of a mutiny but only of some riotous behaviour among certain sections of the troops. Cinna had entered the camp inadequately guarded and inadequately prepared to deal with the situation. He had foolishly allowed himself to become involved in the rioting and, as a result, had lost his life. At the time I was so concerned with my wife's health (for the news had naturally been shocking to her) that I did not realise immediately the full implications of Cinna's death. These were important both militarily and politically. Not that Cinna was a commander of any distinction, but he was capable of taking the advice of others and notably of

Sertorius. The first result of his death was that Carbo, now left as sole consul, abandoned the plan of meeting Sulla in Greece and withdrew to Italy the troops that had already crossed over. This was a serious and might almost be said to have been a fatal mistake. Then, too, Cinna had been the unquestioned political leader of the party ever since the death of Marius. There was now no one in this position, though both Carbo and my cousin, young Marius, aspired to it and Sertorius, for his abilities, deserved it. So, while on the one side there was a unified command under Sulla, on the other side there were divided counsels, divided commands and shifting policies. That Sulla, in spite of this and other advantages, had to fight hard for nearly two years before he attained his object is some indication of the strength that was available to his opponents. Had this strength been organised and employed as Sertorius might have employed it, Rome would have been spared the most ghastly massacres in her history and the necessary revolution which, in later years, I myself have attempted, not without success, to guide, might have been brought about more smoothly, with less difficulty and less pain. But as things have turned out, hatred, even up to the present day, has led to more hatred, blood to more blood.

And as the time drew near for the birth of my first and only child, so approached the darkest days of the Roman republic, a period when it seemed that order could only exist in a reign of terror and sane thoughts could only occur to minds wholly exhausted by the excesses of passion.

CHAPTER VIII

SULLA'S VICTORY

FOUR YEARS had passed since the return of Marius when Sulla landed at Brundisium with an army of 40,000 veteran troops used to plunder, expecting more and devoted to their general. The usual portents were reported and many of them actually took place. For instance, one week before my nineteenth birthday the temple and statue of Jupiter Optimus Maximus in Rome was entirely destroyed by fire. Though the building had no great architectural merits, it had a certain antique charm, and the shrine itself was, in many respects, the holiest in the city. I myself, in my capacity as Priest of Jupiter, took part in an investigation into the causes of the fire, but these were never clearly established. It is quite possible, however, that it was the work of incendiaries in Sulla's party; certainly the effect of the fire served Sulla's purposes. People in Rome began to say that the gods themselves had turned against the existing government and the professional prophets quickly adapted themselves to the situation and went about foretelling disasters which were, in fact, impending.

Indeed, by the time of the fire Sulla, moving slowly northward, had already gained some successes and was beginning to receive substantial reinforcements from his friends and partisans in Italy. Of these the one most talked of in Rome was young Pompey, the son of the unpopular Strabo who had attempted to defend the city from Marius and Cinna. Up to this time Pompey had been known chiefly for his gracious manners, so different from those of his father, and for his great physical beauty. It was later, when he already had important military successes to his credit, that people began to observe a resemblance between him and Alexander the Great. In fact the resemblance was not striking. Pompey's face lacked the fire and the almost divine melancholy that can be observed in nearly all the statues of the great Macedonian. Nevertheless, he was singularly good-looking. He was also bold, resolute and, in spite of his gracious manners, could be as cruel and unscrupulous as was his father. In these days, however, I scarcely knew him, though like everyone else I was impressed by the extraordinary brilliance of his actions. He was only twenty-three years old when Sulla landed in Italy and, in the normal course of events, could not have hoped to command an army for many years to come. But in this period nothing was normal and from extreme youth Pompey was almost always in some command or other and almost invariably successful. Certainly no career can have had a more brilliant beginning. Acting entirely on his own initiative, Pompey raised three legions in the north and by the mere force of his personality convinced them that he and he alone was the man to lead them. Even at this stage he showed his rare ability for organisation; for his troops were not only enthusiastic but well equipped and well supplied. Though he moved fast, he did nothing in a hurry, and only began to march southward to join Sulla when he was satisfied that his stores of provisions and of arms, his numbers of baggage animals and wagons, were exactly sufficient to give him a balanced and independent fighting force. There were several actions on the way south and in all of these Pompey distinguished himself personally. But what most captured public imagination was the story of the extraordinary honour conferred on him by Sulla when, in the end, he joined forces with him. At their meeting Pompey had, as was correct, saluted Sulla with the title of "Imperator." Sulla, who was evidently immensely impressed by the sight of Pompey's army, so full of young men, so well disciplined and well equipped, had then dismounted from his horse and, speaking both to his own troops and to those of Pompey, had saluted the young man also with the same title. The cry of "Imperator" was taken up by both armies at once. Even with his long career of triumphs

Pompey can scarcely have known a more glorious moment than this. I myself was over forty before I first had occasion to be saluted in this way by Roman legionaries. Moreover, Sulla showed that in giving to this young man the title of " Imperator " he had meant what he said, for he immediately began to employ him in important enterprises and in independent commands.

There were other young men of ability, too, who followed Pompey's example of joining Sulla while the issue of the war was still undecided. Among these was Crassus who, in later years, was to be exceedingly useful to me because of his enormous wealth, his ambition and his almost morbid jealousy of Pompey, a feeling which seems to have originated at about this period. For Crassus, in spite of his disastrous end, was in his youth a very able commander ; yet neither his successes nor his rewards were as spectacular as those of Pompey. There were also occasions when, though Crassus had won a victory, Pompey, for some reason or other, received the credit for it. Thus Crassus, who was both ambitious and mean-spirited, began to feel towards Pompey much the same feelings as those which Marius had entertained against Sulla—though Pompey was a better general than Sulla and Crassus a very much inferior general to Marius.

As for me, I was still too young to take any important part in the war and in any case was debarred from service by my priesthood. My life with Cornelia was most happy. When our child Julia was born we used to amuse ourselves by predicting a brilliant future for the baby. It occurred to neither of us to suppose that she would ever become the wife of Pompey or that Pompey would be at that time indisputably the greatest man in the world.

Towards the end of this year a significant event occurred. Sertorius was sent out as governor of Nearer Spain. Here he was to have scope for his unique genius whereas in Italy the consuls in command of armies had continued to neglect his advice and had suffered in consequence. In Spain he was to do wonders, but in Italy the Marian party had, at the most critical moment of the war, lost the only one of their generals who might have been a match, and more than a match, for Sulla.

Early in the next year Sulla began to march up the Latin Way towards Rome. The consuls opposing him were Carbo and my cousin, young Marius, both men of determination and courage, but both self-opinionated and crude in military and political affairs alike. Young Marius still kept his good looks. He was perhaps the handsomest man in Rome, after Pompey. But he was now almost as savage as his father had been during his last days, and though he could certainly inspire loyalty in his troops, he lacked his father's ability to use this loyalty effectively at the right moment. It was on a cold wet day, I remember, that the news arrived that he had been utterly defeated by Sulla in the hills south of Rome and had, with what remained of his army, taken refuge in the fortress of Praeneste. Here, for the time being, he was secure and from here he ordered the evacuation of Rome, since the garrison was not large enough to defend the city. The troops were to proceed northwards to join the army operating under Carbo. But before the evacuation there was another massacre, carried out by the express orders of Marius. In this cruel and senseless butchery many senators lost their lives. Among them was Scaevola, the Chief Pontiff, who had narrowly escaped murder at the funeral of the elder Marius.

Sulla could now enter Rome unopposed. In the general apprehension we often discussed whether or not it would be wise for me to escape either to Africa or Spain or to the army in the north. However, I was most reluctant to leave my wife, my mother and my small daughter. I was aware, too, that, while my predecessor in the office of Flamen Dialis had been compelled to commit suicide, he had been, however ineffectively, a consul, whereas I, so far, had taken no part in politics. I therefore decided to stay and so saw for the second time Sulla's troops enter Rome as conquerors.

The panic of those days was, in any case, premature, since the campaign was not yet over. Indeed, at the very last moment Sulla very nearly lost the fruits of all his victories. Carbo, in the north, had despaired rather too soon of the situation and had fled to Africa. But in the vicinity of Rome there were still excellent armies of Samnites and Lucanians, operating under

their own generals, and still loyal to the memory of Sulpicius and
of Cinna, who had secured for these warlike Italian peoples their
proper rights. These armies had set out to relieve Marius in
Praeneste, where he was closely and very skilfully invested by one
of Sulla's officers, Ofella. Finding, however, that Sulla's forces
were ready to intercept them, they suddenly changed the direction of their march and moved rapidly and unexpectedly against
Rome, which had been left virtually undefended. Sulla was
forced to fight late in the day and after a long march in order to
preserve the city. The battle took place outside the Colline Gate
and was finally decisive. It was watched from the walls by many
of the citizens of Rome ; yet neither the spectators nor Sulla himself knew the result of the battle until the next day. Sulla, with the
left wing of his army, was utterly routed and forced to fall back
on the defences of his camp. Those who knew him said afterwards that in these moments of defeat, though he never lost
his nerve, he lost nearly all control over himself, It appears
that he used to carry into battle with him a small golden statue
of Apollo which, during his campaign in Greece, he had taken
from Delphi. Now he covered this statue with frenzied kisses
and cried out to it, groaning and weeping, " O Pythian Apollo,
you who in so many battles have made Sulla the Fortunate
great and famous, do not fail him now ! Do not let him perish
before the very gates of Rome ! " The prayer was, as it happened,
unnecessary ; for before midnight he received news from
Crassus, who had been in command of the right wing and who
had won a crushing victory over the majority of the enemy.
Next day Sulla joined him and together they surrounded what
was left of the Samnite force. Some of these, relying on Sulla's
promises of mercy if they did something to help him, turned on
their own companions. Finally, after much fighting among
themselves, they all surrendered to the number of six thousand.
It was in his conduct with regard to these prisoners that Sulla
first gave a clear indication of the way in which he intended to
behave. All six thousand were marched unarmed through Rome
into the Circus and there kept under guard. Next day Sulla called
a meeting of the senate in the temple of Bellona and began to

address the senators. Soon his speech became almost inaudible because of the noise of shrieks and cries and shouting which seemed to be coming from not far away. The startled senators, fearing something but not knowing precisely what it could be, began to interrupt, but Sulla, only slightly raising his voice, remarked, "I must urge you to listen to my words and not to be disturbed. The noise is that of some criminals whom I have ordered to be punished." The noise, in fact, was that of the slaughter in cold blood of all six thousand of his prisoners.

This act of cruelty was, like most of Sulla's acts, calculated. He intended by it not only to terrorise all who might still be in arms against him in Samnium and Lucania, but also to intimidate the senate, making it clear even to those of his own party that he was their master and not their servant. In these aims he was entirely successful, but the extent of his atrocities was far greater than that required to secure these aims, so that there was a kind of perversity even in the calculation of his cruelties.

The next to suffer were the garrison of Praeneste who, after the battle of the Colline Gate, had been forced to surrender. They, to the number of some ten thousand, were killed to a man. Young Marius, knowing what he had to expect, had previously killed himself. His head was brought to Sulla who, as he gazed coolly at it, remarked, "One must learn how to row a boat before one attempts to be the steersman."

But more terrible, because more unpredictable, than these mass executions were the murders which took place every day in Rome and indeed throughout Italy. No one, of whatever rank, who had had any connection with the party of Marius could consider his life his own. By this time it seemed necessary, and even reasonable, that all Sulla's personal enemies should be destroyed, but when so many others, for what appeared to be no good reason, were cut down in the streets, even members of Sulla's own party began to become alarmed and one of them, a Metellus, ventured to ask him in the senate whether he could allay public anxiety by giving some indication of how many others were to suffer, Sulla promised to consider the matter, and next day published a list of eighty names of those proscribed to die. On the following day another list, containing two hundred and twenty other names, appeared; and, at more or less regular intervals, further lists were posted in the forum. Rewards were offered to all who murdered or gave information leading to the murder of the proscribed persons. All property of the proscribed was confiscated and their sons and grandsons were debarred from holding any public office. Many were betrayed or murdered by their slaves and even by their sons, who in this way hoped to secure at least a share of their fathers' property. Others found the times appropriate for dealing in their own ways with their private enemies. Young Catiline, for instance, who later was to become a figure of some importance, first murdered his elder brother and then, to escape prosecution and to gain the reward, used his influence with Sulla to have his brother's name added to the proscription lists. It was said that these lists, before they ceased to appear, had contained the names of nearly five thousand people, but the deaths were much more numerous than this figure would suggest. And just as Marius, in the execution of his vengence, had employed a band of freed slaves whose savagery was as great as his own, so now Sulla did the same thing, but on a more extensive scale and in a more deliberately organised fashion. For out of the slaves who had belonged to the victims of the proscriptions he freed ten thousand of the youngest and strongest. These, taking the name from that of Sulla's own family, were called " Cornelii." Bound to him by gratitude and by interest, they were all the more formidable because they were at least to some extent disciplined.

Not that the word " discipline " can properly be used of these excesses, calculated as they were. And with regard to anything which was left which bore the name or could recall the glories of Marius savage anger as well as calculation entered into the account. Young Marius had been wise enough to kill himself; but his battered and bleeding head was carried in procession through the streets. Far more terrible was the fate of Marius Gratidianus, an adopted nephew of the great Marius and one of those who had been with him in his exile. Later he had twice held the position of praetor and had won very great popularity by a currency reform which had the effect of relieving debtors. Now, perhaps relying on this popularity and on the fact that his record had been that of a moderate man, he neglected to make away with himself. He was flogged and beaten through the streets of Rome with such violence and brutality that, before he died, the flesh was stripped from the bones and, as he lay dying, his limbs were torn piecemeal from the body.

Sulla's vengeance extended even to the ashes of old Marius, Rome's greatest soldier. His tomb was desecrated and the ashes were dug up and scattered in the river Anio. Every statue of him was thrown down, every monument of the victories which had saved Rome was destroyed.

In circumstances such as these I myself, with my young wife and child, not unnaturally lived in apprehension.

CHAPTER IX

MY ESCAPE

AFTER A LITTLE time, however, we began to fancy ourselves safe. It seemed that, if we had been marked out for death, death would have come to us in the first days of Sulla's terror. Moreover, in spite of my connection by marriage with Marius and with Cinna, it could not be said that I had taken an active part in politics. Sulla therefore had nothing against me personally, nor was I rich enough to be worth killing for the sake of my property. We noticed, too, that Sulla's savagery was not entirely irresponsible. It was part of a plan by which in the end there should be only one party in the state and, in order to build up this party, Sulla had already shown that he was capable of being conciliatory towards young men of ability whom he wanted to attract. If Cinna had been my father instead of my father-in-law or if I had been the son rather than the nephew of Marius, I should indeed have been debarred from ever holding any public office. As it was, I did not come under this disqualification and, if left alive by Sulla, might possibly be useful to him. Certain friends of our family were therefore able to approach some of those who might be assumed to have influence with Sulla and to try to gain his goodwill.

It might have been better for me if this attempt had not been made. Sulla was impressed by the accounts he heard of my abilities and of my growing popularity in social life. He decided that it was worth his while to secure my support for the régime and instructed the friends of my family to let me know that I had nothing to fear and indeed, if I acted correctly, might even hope for advancement. I was to be told, however, that I must first sever my connection with the past by divorcing my wife, the daughter of Cinna, in exchange for whom I would be given another wife to be chosen by Sulla.

There was nothing unusual in such a proposition. Even Pompey, who at this time stood very high in Sulla's favour, had been induced to divorce his wife, whom he loved, and to marry a step-daughter of Sulla's who, to play her part in the scheme, had first to be divorced from her own husband whose child she was about to bear. It was an unhappy arrangement, since she died in childbirth soon after she had moved to Pompey's house. Pompey himself, it was said, had been most reluctant to make this match, yet in these days so absolute was Sulla's domination that not even his friends dared to oppose his will.

As for me, when I was informed of the proposal made to me, I was filled once more and instantly with that determination to resist which I had experienced previously at the time when, as a young boy, I had confronted Sulla in the streets. In an intimate and personal matter to do the will of one who had murdered my kinsmen and disgraced the memory of Marius seemed to me an intolerable dishonour. Besides, I was in love with my wife. So although some members of my family and Cornelia herself (most loyally, if somewhat half-heartedly) urged me to do as Sulla commanded, I at no time felt the slightest inclination to submit.

It was obvious, of course, that in opposing Sulla's will, I was risking my life. I therefore hurriedly got together what money I could raise, left Rome secretly by night and went into hiding in the mountainous Sabine country north-east of the city. Here I lived for some weeks precariously enough. Even in this wild country there were large bands of Sulla's soldiers engaged in hunting down fugitives, and, though in some of the villages and small towns I had friends who could be trusted, in these times it was difficult to feel oneself safe from betrayal even in the houses of the best of friends.

At no other time in my life has my position appeared to be so abject, my future so entirely without hope. From Rome I received the news that orders were out for my arrest, that I had been deprived of my priesthood and that Cornelia's dowry had been confiscated. There was nothing to be surprised at in any of these measures, but when I heard of them I was forced to consider as a fact something which I had been reluctant to imagine—that in my own country there was now left to me no possibility of distinction. All I could hope for was to save my own life, and in order to do this I should have either to escape from Italy altogether or, which seemed a most unlikely thing, to secure a pardon from Sulla.

As it happened, my plans for escape were frustrated by illness. It was probably mental disturbance rather than any weakness of the body which caused this collapse in health. Certainly in later years I have endured far greater physical hardship than anything I was called upon to undergo at this period. But, whatever the cause may have been, I found myself, just at the time when I needed all my vigour and energy, shaking with fever and unable to stand upright. Nor could I receive proper medical attention. Sulla's troops were systematically combing the whole area, so that, though I was happy enough to have loyal friends, I had still to be constantly on the move, sometimes changing my lodgings twice in a single day.

As my illness made it necessary for me to be carried on a stretcher it was difficult to move inconspicuously, and so what I most feared took place. I and my small party were observed and surrounded by a detachment of troops commanded by one of the Cornelii, the ex-slaves chosen and appointed by Sulla for carrying out his work of extermination. Later I learned that this particular officer was notorious even in his own circle for his acts of savagery. It was fortunate, perhaps, that I did not know this at the time, since, in my enfeebled state of health, the knowledge might have had a depressing effect on my energies. The soldiers were standing around me with their swords drawn and it was with some difficulty that I managed to raise myself into a sitting position. I then hastily addressed the officer in as strong a voice as I could produce and with all the eloquence I could command. I pointed out that I had influential friends in Rome who were at that very moment interceding for me with

Sulla ; that, if I were taken to Rome and there condemned, then in any case Cornelius would receive the reward to which he was entitled ; that meanwhile I was in a position to pay him an equivalent sum, so that in any case he would not be the loser for showing mercy for the time being ; he might indeed actually double the profit which he expected. I spoke with an air of confidence and even of indifference, partly because these are qualities by which barbarians are impressed, partly to disguise the weakness of the argument I was employing. For there was really no reason why Cornelius should not make away with both me and my money and then subsequently claim a further reward from Sulla. In an attempt to distract his mind from working along these lines I made a few jokes about the state of his uniform, which was extremely dirty, and promised him clean clothes and a dagger that had once belonged to Marius if he brought me safely to Rome.

Fortunately Cornelius accepted the bribe. It was all the money that I possessed. I was taken under guard to Rome, and, in the time that intervened before Sulla had leisure to examine my case, I was allowed to return to my house. Here, under the careful nursing of my wife and my mother, I regained my health in a day or two. I could at any rate now die with dignity and in this anxious time it seemed likely that this was what I should have to do. My mother, however, my relations and my friends were indefatigable in attempting to influence the friends of Sulla and Sulla himself on my behalf. Among those who were most active were some of the Vestal Virgins, ladies of excellent family with whom I had become acquainted in the time of my priesthood and with whom I had enjoyed the most agreeable discussions not only on religious subjects but on life in general. Indeed, while it is always a pleasure to talk with intelligent people, in the case of women such conversations are even more delightful if one is not expected to make love to them.

It may well have been the intervention of these Vestal Virgins which finally turned the scale in my favour. Sulla was exceedingly superstitious and attached great importance not only to dreams, omens and soothsayers, but also to the ordinary conventions of religion. Had his temperament been different in this respect it is scarcely likely that I could have escaped. I was, after all, the only man in Rome still alive who had disobeyed one of his orders.

So, when the time came for me to appear before Sulla's tribunal in the forum, my wife and I parted from each other with tears on both sides. Though we did not express the thought it seemed to us both extremely unlikely that we should ever meet again. Other members of my family, including my mother, accompanied me to the forum, but it was considered unwise for Cornelia to attend, since the appearance of Cinna's daughter, even as a suppliant, would, in all probability, do more harm than good. I myself dressed on this day with particular care. I could no longer wear the toga with the purple border which I had been accustomed to wear while I held my priesthood, but I saw to it that the white toga which I put on was a new one and was carefully draped about my shoulders. Beneath the toga my tunic was loosely belted in a way which was then peculiarly my own, but later became fashionable among the young men. I had had my hair cut on the previous day and had used, in setting it, one of the most expensive perfumes that were obtainable.

So, putting the best appearance I could upon myself, I made my way to the forum accompanied by my mother, by the Vestal Virgins and by many persons of distinction who might be expected to have some influence with Sulla. Sulla himself was sitting on a raised platform with his guards about him. Outside the narrow circle which the guards kept clear was a great crowd of citizens of all classes, some prepared to denounce their neighbours, others attempting to secure justice or protection for themselves, others merely spectators. Our own party, which included several well known people attracted the attention and possibly the sympathy of the crowd who made way for us till we were admitted through the guards into the space in front of the tribunal.

Sulla was now a man of between fifty-five and sixty years of age. The debaucheries in which he had spent almost every night since his conquest of Rome had left their mark upon him; his face was even more blotched and mottled than before and there was something almost frail in the gestures of his hands when he turned from time to time to speak to one or other of his favourites (I observed among them both senators and ballet dancers) who were standing at his side. Yet the tremendous power of the man was as evident as ever before in the level stare of those great blue eyes of his which he kept fixed upon my face during all the time my friends were speaking in my favour. Feeling myself, as I did, so near to death, I was determined to preserve throughout a resolute and dignified expression ; but at the same time I watched Sulla closely, since I was curious to discover what was the effect on him of the words that were being spoken. In particular I hoped that a favourable impression would be made by the Vestal Virgins when they came to describe the conscientiousness with which I had carried out my priestly duties ; for Sulla was an admirer both of tradition (when it did not stand in his own way) and of efficiency. However, from the steady glare of his blue eyes I was able to deduce nothing whatever except, what I knew already, that my life was in extreme danger. When all had said what they had to say, he continued for some moments to gazed fixedly at me and still it was impossible for me to tell whether he had made up his mind already upon the verdict or whether even now some further consideration or some slight impulse might be swaying him in one direction or the other. Suddenly his eyes left mine and I felt it to be a release. He turned to my friends and spoke seriously—a fact often forgotten by those who regarded the remark which he was about to make as a witticism. "Have your own way," he said, "but beware of this young man. He wears his belt like a girl, but there is more than one Marius in his heart."

As I heard these words my first feeling, of course, was of immense relief. I was even prepared, as was polite, to express my gratitude to Sulla ; but Sulla had turned away, making it evident that he expected nothing of the kind. So, after I had embraced my mother and my friends, we returned home to the delight of my wife and spent the rest of the day in celebrating the occasion. In the course of these celebrations we would frequently refer to the words that Sulla had spoken, taking them lightly enough at the time.

In fact, the sentence was one of extraordinary prescience. As Sulla himself had suggested in his reference to my particular style in the wearing of my belt, there was nothing whatever in my appearance which resembled that of my uncle. Nor had I yet begun to envisage the possibility of re-creating the party and the policies of Marius. The very idea of such a thing, in those days, would have seemed an absurdity. No doubt it seemed so to Sulla himself and perhaps it was out of a kind of laziness that he spared my life. Yet it rarely happened that Sulla failed to act upon his intuitions which, as in this case, were so remarkably accurate that they amounted to what might be called second sight. It was this quality—something that looked like guess-work—rather than any outstanding tactical or organisational abilities which accounted for his victories in the field. Sulla was, in his own peculiar way, aware of this himself. He seldom boasted of his own great achievements but he regarded what he called his " luck " as something almost deserving of worship. In honour of it he adopted the name " Felix " or " Fortunate " and he had his two children, a boy and a girl, named " Faustus " and " Fausta," meaning " lucky." In this way while, in a sense, he was showing modesty, in another sense he was showing an arrogance unprecedented in Roman history. He was claiming for himself some supernatural power, some element of the divine, which set him apart from others. This notion of a ruler with divine or semi-divine powers is, of course, a common one in the east, and it seems to correspond, at certain periods of history, to the needs of the times. I myself am now worshipped as a god ; but it remains to be seen whether this attribution of divinity to the head of the state will remain valid and useful for the west after my death.

Certainly in my twenty-first year I was unable to imagine that I was to be the first of the Romans to receive officially such honours. It is possible, however, that Sulla, with his rare gift of intuition, may, during his long scrutiny of my face, have recognised the presence of powers of which I myself was unaware, and may, in his perverse and superstitious way, have respected them. Some such an explanation as this seems to be required to account for the fact that my life was spared.

I was, of course, happy indeed to have escaped. Soon, however, it became clear that, while I was safe for the moment, there could be little real security for me in Rome and no hopes of advancement. I was pleased, therefore, when, at the end of the year I was offered a post on the staff of the new governor of Asia, Marcus Thermus. The post did not seem likely to be particularly remunerative nor to offer any prospects of distinction. Yet it would at least ensure my personal safety and would leave me free for a time from the demands of my creditors. I regretted leaving my wife and family, but I had few regrets about leaving the Rome in which my childhood and early youth had been spent. When I sailed for the East, as I did early in the following year, I found myself suddenly, and delightfully, able to breathe freely.

BOOK TWO

CHAPTER I

THE KING OF BITHYNIA

I TRAVELLED to Asia by way of Greece and, though on this occasion my stay there was not prolonged, I was enchanted by what I saw and by what I imagined. I was aware that every grace and nearly all learning had come to us from the Greek cities of Sicily, the Greek mainland, the islands and the Asiatic coast. My studies, once I had learned the elements of our own still primitive literature, had been dominated by the greatness of Athens, Sparta, Thebes and Macedonia and by my delight in the literature, both ancient and modern, written in the Greek language. At this time nearly everyone knew Greek and though not everyone was as enthusiastic about the subject as, for example, Cicero or myself, there were now few indeed to be found, and those few the most notably stupid, who would reject Greek culture on the grounds that it tended to undermine those qualities of sobriety, unselfishness, piety and honour which were specifically Roman, and to which Rome owed her greatness. In the days of Sulla it was not easy to believe in the prevalence of these virtues and, for those who liked to contemplate them, better examples could be found in ancient Greek than in modern Roman history. Young Cato, for instance, who even then at about the age of fourteen was beginning to acquire a reputation as a moralist (though to me he appeared an ungainly, priggish and disagreeable boy) used constantly to pester his tutor with questions, extremely tactless at the time of Sulla's dictatorship, about how Harmodius and Aristogiton had, several hundred years ago, killed a tyrant in Athens. Both Cato and his tutor were ignorant of the fact, though it is plainly set down in

Thucydides, that this particular action had nothing whatever to do with Cato's conception of "liberty," but was prompted by passions arising from a homosexual love affair. But still it was always to the ancient Greeks that Cato would look for confirmation of his own singular ideas of Roman virtue. Later he became attached to the Stoic school of philosophy and made much, too, of the more puritanical aspects of Plato's writings, being quite incapable of understanding the rest, or even these aspects perfectly; for he had no conception either of the intricacy of the real world or of that beautiful kaleidoscopic quality which, in Plato's thought and style, reflects this intricacy so admirably. Yet if a narrow-minded egotist like Cato turned naturally to the Greeks for the limited intellectual fodder which he could absorb, it was more natural still that others, with keener intelligences and with more generous outlooks, should find in the whole range of Greek history and literature a continual joy, a challenge and an inspiration.

So as I travelled from Italy to the East, I was conscious that I was travelling in the direction of a civilisation older than my own and still immensely powerful. There were some certainly (and old Marius used to be among them) who claimed that the civilisation of the Greeks was now in a state of decadence or disintegration. Some evidence could be adduced to support this view. Athens, with its stupendous architecture and its schools of philosophy, still existed but was no longer a force capable of imposing itself on others except by intellectual means. Moreover, at this time it had not yet recovered from the recent disaster when it had chosen to take the side of Mithridates and had been sacked by Sulla's legions. Sparta was a negligible settlement. Indeed, all those city states, in whose republican virtues (though they were never republics in the Roman sense) Cato affected to believe, had long ceased to be powers in their own right. More adequate to deal with modern conditions had been the kingdoms set up by Alexander the Great and his successors; yet these, too, with the exception of Egypt, had succumbed either to Rome, to Mithridates or to the great eastern empires of Parthia or of India, though some of them (Bithynia, for example) retained, under Roman protection, a considerable degree of independence.

It was at this period of my life that I first began to be interested in the idea of kingship, an idea absolutely repugnant to Roman sentiment and one which used to be equally repugnant to the citizens of the Greek city-states. Yet I could not help observing that from the time of Alexander onwards whenever throughout the East government had to be organised on a big scale and over a wide area this idea of kingship has proved indispensable. There are certain conditions, it seems, in which people demand kings as a symbol of that unity and order without which all civilised life is impossible. I observed, too, that they would go further than this and would actually attribute divine powers to their monarchs, worshipping them with sacrifices. Was this, I wondered, a regression to a more primitive and superstitious past, or was it an enlightened recognition of the necessities of the modern world ? " Decadence " and " disintegration " would certainly be the words used by many Romans to describe these Oriental monarchies ; yet any Roman capable of using his eyes would observe that the same words could as aptly be applied to the Roman Republic itself at this period. For the Roman system had not only, as appeared clearly enough from the civil wars and the massacres, broken down in Italy itself, but had also shown itself to be most unfit for export. It had been the corruption and incompetence of Roman governors, the greed of Roman business men and the brutality of Roman taxation officers that had made possible the overrunning of Asia and Greece by Mithridates and the murder, by his orders, of all Italians in the Greek cities of Asia. Now for the moment Mithridates had been checked by Sulla, but no one imagined that the settlement was permanent. Moreover, as I saw with my own eyes, Sulla had done nothing to remedy the abuses of the past or to make Roman government acceptable to the provincials for the future. All the time that he had been in Asia his mind had been set on Rome. He was now settling the affairs of Rome in his own way. Asia, where he had made himself both feared and hated, remained on the whole disaffected after his departure. Just government and a show of military force were both necessary if Rome was to regain the position which she had once held in the East.

So far as just government was concerned it was still impeded by the activities of those Roman business men who had condemned my great-uncle Rutilius. Military force, however, was at our disposal and I myself took some part in these early actions which were intended to re-establish our prestige. The first task of my commander, Marcus Thermus, was to reduce and punish the Greek city of Mytilene on the island of Lesbos. We had every reason to deal severely with this city. Some ten years previously, at the time when Mithridates had been overrunning Asia, the leading Roman commissioner in the province (his name, I think, was Aquilius) had fled to Mytilene, but, with all the other Romans in the place, had been handed over to the troops of Mithridates. People still spoke of how Mithridates had used this surrender for the purposes of his own savage propaganda. Aquilius had been put on show throughout the province of Asia, either bound on the back of an ass or chained ignominiously to one of Mithridates's cavalrymen, a gigantic fellow whose great size, when contrasted with that of the Roman captive, was intended to provoke derision. Finally, as an indication to the provincials of what might be a fitting punishment for the greed of Roman capitalists, Mithridates had ordered Aquilius to be put to death by having molten gold poured down his throat. It was natural and proper that, after Sulla's victories, Mytilene should have been called upon to pay an indemnity. However, instead of paying it, the city was now standing out for her independence, relying on good fortifications and an excellent fleet. The Mytileneans hoped also for help from the Cilician pirates, at this time very powerful, and from Mithridates himself, who, they were sure, would renew the war with Rome as soon as he saw an opportunity of doing so with success. As it happened, Mytilene received no help from Mithridates and not much from the pirates. Yet her own fleet was powerful enough to give her command of the sea and to make the task of blockading the town extremely difficult. Thermus soon realised that he would be unable to carry out his plans unless he received naval reinforcements. These had been promised by Nicomedes, the King of Bithynia and an ally of the Roman people; but they had not arrived and it was suspected that they were not likely to arrive, since Nicomedes, who had already lost much in the war with Mithridates, was unwilling to risk losing more.

It was decided, before serious operations should begin, to send an embassy to Nicomedes demanding that the promised fleet should set sail at once. I was delighted when Thermus entrusted this commission to me. I owed the appointment, no doubt, partly to the fact that I was a person of some social significance whose manners were considered engaging, and partly to my proficiency in Greek; for Greek was the language of Nicomedes's court and the King himself, of mixed Greek and Thracian descent, was said to be an enthusiastic amateur of Greek culture. I naturally found out all that I could about this King before I set out and I learned more later. It was said that he had gained his throne in the first place by poisoning his own father, and this may well have been true. Though such a crime cannot possibly be condoned, it must be allowed that it was a common one in these Eastern kingdoms. Later, certainly, he put his brother to death; but his brother had usurped the throne with the aid of Mithridates. In recent years Nicomedes had again been driven from his kingdom by Mithridates's armies. He owed his restoration to Sulla and to the Romans and, this being so, had every reason for remaining on good terms with us. It seemed to me probable that the object of my embassy could be achieved quite easily, though I had no idea quite how easy it would prove to be.

I was, therefore, in a light-hearted frame of mind when with my few companions I began to travel overland across the northwest corner of Asia to the cities of Bithynia. The cities, the landscapes, the people, even the climate seemed strange, new and delightful. In Pergamum, for instance, near the start of our journey, were buildings far grander than any to be seen in Rome; the statues and works of art were more numerous, better displayed and better executed. Rome indeed had been adorned by much plunder from Greece and Asia, but it was evident that

those generals and governors who had sent back to Italy shipload after shipload of looted bronzes and marbles had been
people of very inferior taste, for what they had taken was greatly
inferior to what they had left behind. Here in Pergamum and in
other cities which I visited on my way, every style of Greek art,
sculpture and architecture could be examined and admired. And
even in household utensils, in clothes, in coins and all the ordinary
apparatus of living there was a grace, a delicacy, an unoffending
luxury most pleasing to the eye and to all senses. There was also
to be observed an enchanting variety in outlook, race, language
and religion. It was said that in these parts of Asia no less than
twenty distinct languages were in use, and, though the coastal
cities were Hellenised and proud of their Hellenic traditions,
even they had been influenced by the cults and customs of the
interior, where Hittites, Lydians and Persians had been for so
long established and where the troops of Alexander and his
successors, men of every race under the sun, had made their
settlements and introduced their own manners and religions.
I have always taken a keen interest in religion and I found here
a far more bewildering variety than that which I had already
noticed in Rome. It was not only that the more emotional cults
of the Great Mother Goddess, under her many names, were
practised more openly and with more abandon than would have
been permitted in Italy ; this was to be expected, though even so
it was difficult not to feel a certain horror at the sight (which was
also, in its own way, amusing) of the painted faces and mincing
gestures of the castrated priests who were very numerous and
urgent in their appeals both for converts and for alms. What
was more impressive than any manifestation of a particular
religion was the enormous range of religious emotion in general.
Here, for instance, it was normal for the Tyche or " Fortune "
of a ruler to be worshipped in a temple, sometimes by itself,
sometimes in association either with a known deity such as Zeus
or, very often, with some deity whose name and attributes were
entirely unknown to me and seemed imperfectly understood even
by the local inhabitants. One could also discover in the same town
not only a temple devoted soberly to the cult of Heracles or

Apollo, but also some vast establishment, immensely rich and equipped with some thousands of sacred slaves who acted as prostitutes in the service of some Syrian or Cappadocian goddess. Altogether religion was on a greater scale here than elsewhere. It seemed that it might be said with equal truth that either everything or nothing was sacred—a point of view which was fascinating to me at the time and which has continued to interest me, although I soon observed that, in the interests of good government and security, it was necessary that among all this welter and confusion and infinite variety there should exist some definite, strong, though not necessarily pretentious cult designed to emphasise the importance of the civic duties. Without such a cult as this people might be tempted, through enthusiasm, to neglect agriculture or to evade military service.

Again I noticed here not only the easy transitions that were made in people's minds between one god and another, but also how close to deity was, in the popular view, the King or even the distinguished man. There was, for example, a very beautiful coin, minted by one of the early Kings of Pontus, which came into my hands and which I kept for some time as a souvenir. The figure on the coin was that of a youth wearing a short cloak and either feeding or crowning a little stag with vine leaves. Above his head was a thunderbolt and at his side a crescent moon and some stars. I never received a satisfactory account of this figure. It was said to be Hermes, or the King's Tyche, or young Zeus (as would be indicated by the thunderbolt) or a son of Zeus called Aion and worshipped in the Far East. And, according to one account, it was not, in the proper sense, a deity at all, but a man, either shortly to be born or born already, who was destined to reform the world and finally to be received among the gods.

So in all this country through which I travelled to Bithynia I discovered ideas, sights, sounds and perfumes which up to then had been unknown to me. By now my health was fully restored and I accepted with delight every sensual gratification which I found in this land of profuse luxury, variety and excitement. The blood-stained streets of Rome, the terror of Sulla's armed bands were far away ; and far away also were the decent severities of family and of civic life. I was bound by no office and my mission, though important, was an easy one. I was free to talk and to act as I pleased, or as talk or action suggested themselves to me, and, for a few weeks, not to regard either the past or the future.

The welcome accorded to me by the King of Bithynia was most cordial and, indeed, affectionate. I responded readily enough to the King's evident desire for my friendship, partly because by doing so I would advance the interests of the Roman people, partly out of a genuine liking and respect for the man. Nicomedes had, it is true, certain characteristics which might be described as barbarian, but he combined with these a delightful kind of naïveté, a genuine respect for art and literature, a great sense of humour and a passion for the most splendid entertainments. On the evening of my arrival at the court I was placed next to the King at dinner and enjoyed what was, without question, the best and gayest meal that I had ever had. Later, certainly, such banquests as these were often held in Rome, where Lucullus, after his victories in the East, set a standard of luxury which can seldom have been surpassed anywhere in the world. But at this time nothing in Rome could equal the splendour of Nicomedes's entertainments. Nor did these feasts degenerate, as they often did at Rome, into occasions for mere gluttony. Flute-players, dancers, poets, singers and acrobats would perform in the intervals between the numerous courses. Particular attention had been given to the physical beauty and the artificial adornment of the youths and girls who carried round the wine ; and behind these admirable creatures stood, surrounding the banqueting tables, a hundred golden statues of young boys, each holding in his hand a torch to light the festivities. For hour after hour the feasting continued and I, sitting at the King's right hand, felt all the time a mounting excitement caused by the strangeness and brilliance of the scene, by the wine which I drank in what were, for me, unusual quantities, and in the curious sense of intimacy which I found to be developing between the King and myself. I have always been a good con-

versationalist, but on this occasion words and gaieties seemed
to flow from me with a more than ordinary ease and the King
not only flattered me with his loud applause or silent admiration,
but was quick to suggest to me even wilder flights of fancy, more
outrageous paradoxes, or, as moods changed and shifted, general
considerations of life which, at the time and place, seemed to
possess an extraordinary profundity.

How the evening ended I have never been able perfectly to
remember, for this was one of the very few occasions in my life
when I appear to have drunk myself into a state of insensibility.
It would seem that I was honoured by being escorted with
torches to the King's own bedroom. Certainly I woke next day
in a bed of gold, covered in rich purple coverlets and found, as
soon as I opened my eyes, slaves of an exceptional beauty standing
ready to satisfy my every need. Soon the King himself appeared,
ready to renew the intimacy of the previous evening and to
suggest enjoyments for the day. Much time was spent in agreeable walks through the royal garden or "paradise." These
"paradises" (a Persian word, since the Persians seem to have been
the first to have given attention to landscape gardening) I found
peculiarly charming in their mixture of art and nature. Again
the sight of flowers and trees unknown to Italy conveyed a feeling
of enchantment and of a delicious unreality. Then, too, there
were strange fish, kept either for the table or for curiosity in
great bowls of porphyry, or in ponds of transparent water.
There was also a most interesting collection of wild animals and
birds, including many panthers, bears and camels, and, perhaps
most remarkable of all, some specimens of the ostrich, a bird of
which I had read in Xenophon but had never seen.

As for the purpose of my mission, that was dealt with in a
few moments and, on the side of Nicomedes, with the greatest
charm. Indeed, he made rather too much of an insistence that
he was offering the fleet to me as a personal friend rather than
to the Roman people as an ally. In any case the fleet, it appeared,
would be ready to sail in a few days. Once this was established,
the matter was not mentioned again—nor, except in the vaguest
terms, was any military or political subject. Instead our talk was

concerned with the planning of entertainments for the few evenings and days which remained to be enjoyed. Here I found that my own inventive genius was matched and supported by that of Nicomedes. Both the King and I wrote verses in Greek, some, perhaps, not in the best of taste, celebrating the delights of easy and luxurious living. And together we planned a series of pageants and charades which again, perhaps, were sometimes more witty than dignified.

There was, for example, one evening when, having in a number of mythological sketches taken the parts of some of the more youthful gods, I finally threw off most of my clothing and gave an impersonation of Ganymede, the young cup-bearer to Zeus, whose part was taken by Nicomedes himself. There was possibly a certain indelicacy in the performance, though the dialogue, which we had carefully composed beforehand, was, at least in our own opinion, exceedingly amusing. Unfortunately there happened to be present at this feast a delegation of Roman business men who were travelling in Bithynia in order to secure contracts for themselves or their backers, and who had been invited by Nicomedes to attend the evening's banquet. These men, like many of their class, combined a very limited understanding with a limitless contempt for what was outside its scope. In particular they despised all foreigners, except in so far as they were wealthy. Nothing, not even the events of recent years, would persuade them that they were not, through the mere fact of possessing Roman citizenship, wiser, braver and, as they expressed it, " sounder " than all others who did not possess this qualification. These men, being naturally slow-witted, not only failed to appreciate the finer points of the charades in which I was acting, but were profoundly shocked to find a Roman officer and member of a patrician family conducting himself with such freedom and ease in a foreign court. Their reports, when they returned to Rome, did me, for the moment, a certain amount of harm and it was largely owing to them that I received the nick-name of " the Queen of Bithynia." Indeed, the scandal which was aroused by this friendship between Nicomedes and myself has lasted throughout my life. Though at the beginning the stories concerning this friendship were sometimes embarrassing, in the end they may have proved a positive advantage. For the people as a whole, however republican they may pretend to be, are as a rule impressed by any connection of one of their own leaders with royalty. Moreover, since my enemies tended to concentrate on this particular scandal, they placed less emphasis than they might have done on other scandals, both of an amatory and of a political nature, which, if cleverly enough misrepresented, might have proved much more damaging.

Certainly at the time I was either unconscious of or indifferent to the impression which I was making on my fellow Romans. I enjoyed every moment of my short stay in Bithynia and allowed the fleet to set sail for Lesbos without me, delaying my own departure by land as long as I decently could. Moreover, when I returned to the army and discovered that, owing to lack of siege equipment, there were bound to be further delays before operations against Mytilene could begin, I succeeded in securing leave for myself and went back again to Bithynia, accompanied by only one servant, and for some days was entertained there as richly and delightfully as ever. My excuse for going there was to repay a debt and, though my commanding officer did not believe in the excuse, he willingly granted the leave, since he was impressed by the success of my mission, not knowing how easy it had been.

So far from having repaid a debt, I returned to the army greatly indebted to Nicomedes, who had insisted on allowing me sufficient funds on which to live with dignity for the rest of the campaign. In the army itself there was naturally some comment on my newly found riches and on the stories, many of which were greatly exaggerated, about my behaviour in Bithynia. I found then, as I was to find later, that these stories were of the greatest service to me in winning the goodwill of the ordinary soldiers, once these men had realised that my supposed excesses were combined with those purely soldierly qualities which they most admired. It seemed that they would follow me all the more readily in battle for being able to call me " the Queen " behind my back. When, at the final storming of Mytilene, I won the decoration known as " the Civic Crown," an award given only to those who have saved the life of a fellow soldier in battle, the honour was welcomed more by the troops under my command than by myself; for I knew that, though in my own case the award had been deserved, these decorations are often distributed in a corrupt or haphazard manner.

CHAPTER II

RETURN TO ITALY

In this first period of my military service I was nearly three years abroad. Not that the military service itself was of much importance. The campaign for which I had originally volunteered ended with the capture of Mytilene and no further operations took place under Thermus. Though the civil life and administration of the province interested me and though I made many friends, some of whom were to be most useful to me later, in the Greek cities of the coast, I could not help feeling that I was wasting my time and in the end I secured an appointment on the staff of the new governor of Cilicia, Servilius Vatia, who was about to undertake an ambitious campaign against the pirate fleets and strongholds of southern Asia.

As it happened I took no active part in this campaign, but I did much work in connection with the planning of it. Servilius himself was a very competent commander and, before he left Rome, where he had shared the consulship with Sulla, he had discussed with Sulla himself the best methods of dealing with the increasing menace of these pirate fleets which were now beginning to operate all over the Mediterranean. Servilius had with him several young officers of marked ability and enthusiasm. Among them was Titus Labienus, a young man of my own age who was to become very closely associated with me later. Labienus indeed was the best general who has ever served under me and, up to the present moment, the only one who has ever betrayed me. In those early days I took a great liking to him and we used to spend much time in discussing both military and political affairs.

Our two main topics of conversation were Sulla's new constitution and the continued spectacular successes of young Pompey. With regard to the constitution it appeared that Sulla had acted with his usual ruthlessness and with considerable ability. In his view the disorders of the past had been due to the inability of the senate to exercise its proper authority. He had therefore determined to ensure its supremacy for the future. The power of the tribunes and of the Assembly of the People had been, to all intents and purposes, abolished. The control of the law courts was now once again exclusively in the hands of senators. Then, too, since Sulla can have had no illusions about the weakness and irresolution which the senate had shown in recent years, efforts had been made to increase its prestige and even to broaden the basis of its membership. Sulla himself had helped to deplete its numbers by putting to death at least a hundred senators who had been assumed to be his enemies. Now three hundred new senators had been enrolled, many of them from the richer or more able members of the business community. It was now possible also for young men of talent to enter the senate at the age of thirty, or after they had held the office of quaestor. Finally, a number of measures had been taken to subordinate commanders in the field to the central authority of the senate. Sulla knew well enough how he himself had gained power and he evidently wished to make it impossible for any general in the future to act as he had done.

Altogether the constitution looked well on paper. Sulla no doubt intended it to work. But what was required by the circumstances of the time and by human nature itself was something more progressive than this attempt to stabilise the present by invoking the dead past. Sulla seems to have been unaware of the fact that the senate, even as reconstituted, could not, simply by the inclusion of a number of business men, become as it were overnight an efficient instrument of government. It remained what it had been for two generations, a battlefield where, though noble and patriotic sentiments were often expressed, various bitter and conflicting oligarchies were struggling for wealth and power. Yet the necessary tasks of government were, through the growth of the empire and extension of the franchise, through the dangers of wars and the economic uncertainties of peace, continually becoming more complex and more urgent. They could only be dealt with at all by strong and consistent direction of affairs and by capable and honest administration. These were not forthcoming from Sulla's senate, and indeed were scarcely to be found anywhere in the political field of action. When large tasks had to be undertaken or quick decisions made it was still necessary, as it had been necessary in the cases of Marius and of Sulla himself, for one man to be given quite exceptional powers. Sulla had shown how such powers could be used and he was, no doubt, fully conscious of the danger to the state which they represented. Yet these exceptional commands still existed and Sulla himself, before he laid down power, was proved to have lost control over them.

The news which we received of young Pompey's extraordinary career demonstrated this point. When the campaign in Italy was over, he had been sent by Sulla to deal with the remnants of the Marian armies in Sicily and in Africa. At this time he was scarcely twenty-five years old and was, therefore, so far as the laws went, disqualified from holding any independent command at all. Sulla, however, wanted a quick end to the war ; he trusted Pompey ; and he was not one to respect the laws if they stood in his own way.

Pompey had rapidly made an end of the Sicilian campaign and in the course of it had acted in a remarkably high-handed way. Carbo, the ex-consul and colleague of Cinna, had been taken prisoner and Pompey, after subjecting him to a number of cruel and unnecessary humiliations, had, entirely on his own authority, put this distinguished statesman to death. This action and others like it earned him at the time the nickname of " the boy butcher," yet such actions were, I think, prompted not so much by cruelty as by an extravagant sense of self-importance. It was a quality which Pompey retained almost until the end of his life.

Pompey had next sailed for Africa, taking out a large force of six legions and a hundred and twenty warships. Here he was opposed by Domitius Ahenobarbus, who was, like myself, a son-in-law of Cinna and had got together a not inconsiderable army. Within forty days Pompey had defeated and killed Domitius, destroyed his army and, again entirely on his own initiative, deposed the King of Numidia and set up another one in his place. After these brilliant successes he enjoyed himself for some days in hunting lions and elephants and then returned to the coast. His intention was to go back to Rome and there to claim the honour of a triumph. Though he knew well enough that it was an absolutely unheard-of thing for this honour to be awarded to one of his age, he knew also that his victories and his command itself were equally unprecedented. He had already made his plans for importing into Italy four particularly large elephants which he intended to use to draw his triumphal chariot through the city gates, when he received a despatch from Sulla ordering him to disband his troops, except for one legion, and to remain in Africa himself until a new governor was sent out to succeed him.

Pompey, it seems, had simply disregarded these orders. Confident in the loyalty of his troops and in his own immense popularity, he had embarked for Italy with the greater part of his army. For a short time it had actually been supposed that he was in revolt against the government. Sulla had attempted to deal diplomatically with him. He had gone out of the city to meet him and, in an impressive ceremony, had saluted him by the title of " Magnus " or " the Great," a title which stuck and which Pompey ever afterwards was proud to use. After bestowing upon him this additional honour, Sulla might reasonably have supposed that Pompey would be content. However, this was not so. Pompey, supported by a devoted army which was now at the gates of Rome, insisted on his triumph. When Sulla pointed out to him how totally out of keeping with the new constitution such a thing would be, he had, it appears, coolly pronounced the astounding words " Allow me to remind you that more people worship the rising than the setting sun."

A year or two previously Sulla had put to death in the forum one of his own senior officers—Ofella, the commander in the seige of Praeneste—for having dared to stand for the consulship against his wishes. Now he showed himself powerless to enforce his will on young Pompey, and it must have been with the bitterest feelings that he had cried out in a loud voice, " Let him triumph ! Let him triumph ! " for here, just as he had finished with such care and skill his elaborate structure of a constitution which was supposed to last, he found himself confronted and over-ruled by the very force which had given him his own power and which, for the future, he had designed to check—namely, a popular general with a devoted army. Possibly, however, since he was a good judge of character, he may have consoled himself with the reflection that Pompey, being ruled more by vanity than by a desire for real power, was far less dangerous to the security of the state than either he himself or Marius had been. So on this occasion, once he had had his triumph, Pompey behaved with modesty and discretion, though he had allowed himself to show some annoyance when it was discovered that, because of the narrowness of the city gates, he would have to abandon his plan of having his triumphal chariot drawn by elephants. Instead he had had to make do with the conventional horses, though in the triumph itself there was nothing conventional ; for never before in our history had so young a man received so great an honour.

The news that came next to us from Rome was more surprising still and I followed the situation closely, since it began to appear that my own political prospects might not be so hopeless as previously I had imagined. Shortly after Pompey's triumph, Sulla had acted in a manner which still seems to me rather difficult to explain. After declaring publicly that the problems of the constitution had been solved and that the enemies of the state had been crushed, he had, to the amazement of nearly everybody, abdicated from his dictatorship and retired into private life, spending his time either in the writing of his memoirs or in the most luxurious and scandalous feasts and drinking parties with actresses, comedians, musicians and ballet dancers. I can only account for this behaviour of his by supposing that Sulla, with all his admirable qualities of efficiency, determination and intuition, was, in his heart of hearts, a character of almost incredible cynicism and irresponsibility—in other words, that he was wholly unfitted to be a statesman at all. It is impossible that he can have believed his own assertions about the stability and security of the state. Even I, with my limited knowledge of Asia, was aware that war with Mithridates might break out again at any moment; and in Spain Sertorius had, after his initial difficulties, defeated every Roman army that had been sent against him. It is possible that Sulla may have thought that, by depriving the tribunes of their power, he had permanently confirmed the senate in theirs; yet he must have observed that the senate itself was unworthy of this power and, without the force and ruthlessness of his own leadership, would be incapable of exercising it. I still think that in laying down his supreme power at this moment he was, in his own peculiarly cynical way, simply amusing himself. He had secured his place in history; he had exterminated his enemies; he had shaped the state in accordance with his ideas. That he might be remembered for evil rather than for good, that, so far from finding a solution to the problems of the times, he had merely impeded a necessary process, seem to him to have been matters of complete indifference. To him what was important was that his own will had found its own expression in his own lifetime. The future, so far as he was concerned, could look after itself.

So he abandoned himself wholly to his pleasures, and within a year of his abdication had died of a particularly disgusting disease. It was the news of the events which had followed his death which made me anxious to go back again to Rome. For indeed it seemed as though history were repeating herself. A situation had arisen which could not but remind one of the time when Sulla had sailed for the East and when Cinna and Marius had seized power. It seemed to me possible that now, just as had happened then, the whole work of Sulla might be undone, and, judging from the letters which I received from Rome, there were many others who held the same view.

The two consuls in office at the time of Sulla's death were

Catulus and Marcus Lepidus. They were as antagonistic to each other as had been Octavius and Cinna in the past. The father of Catulus had been the colleague of Marius in the German war and a life-long opponent of his in politics. He had wisely committed suicide when Marius and Cinna occupied Rome. His son, as might be expected, was a partisan of Sulla. He was also, incidentally, always an enemy of mine. That he should be elected consul at the time of Sulla's supremacy was natural enough. What was surprising was that he should have Lepidus for a colleague; for Lepidus was in open opposition to Sulla and Sulla had, it seems, used his influence to prevent his being elected. I was surprised to learn that at the election Lepidus had enjoyed the support of Pompey, for there was nothing in the career of Pompey to suggest that he was a revolutionary politician or, indeed, a politician at all. I imagine that on this occasion Pompey merely wished once more to show his independence of Sulla and to demonstrate the power of his own personal popularity, and it was no doubt because of this that Lepidus was successful in gaining the consulship.

Sulla had shown his displeasure with Pompey by ostentatiously leaving him out of his will. Every one of his other commanders had received honourable mention and substantial legacies. In spite of this, however, Pompey had soon dissociated himself from Lepidus and it had been largely due to him that Sulla had had a funeral at all. He had escorted the dead body from Cumae to Rome and had supported Catulus in his plans for doing it honour, whereas Lepidus had refused to have anything to do with the funeral and had wished to have the body buried or burned in as inconspicuous a way as possible. As it turned out, the funeral seemed to have been one of the most impressive that had ever taken place.

Lepidus, therefore, like Cinna before him, had lost the first engagement with his colleague. It immediately struck me as significant that he had not been able to retain so valuable an ally as Pompey and it occurred to me that he must have shown a lack of skill, of foresight or of tact; since, by all accounts, Pompey was extremely susceptible to flattery.

Nevertheless, I was much attracted by what I heard of Lepidus's intentions. My brother-in-law, Lucius Cinna, wrote urging me to come to Rome and to join him in what was evidently going to be a revolution against the existing régime. And so, after a little reflection, I decided, without as yet definitely committing myself, to leave the army and see for myself on the spot what was taking place.

I returned to Italy at about the time of my twenty-fourth birthday. The three years which I had spent in the East had done something, I think, to broaden my mind and to sharpen my wits. I no longer regarded Rome as the only city in the world and indeed saw much to deplore in her architecture and in the absence of those amenities which were common in the cities of Asia. Since then I have done much to remedy these defects. I had gained confidence, too, in myself and knew that, given the opportunity, I was capable of distinguishing myself as a leader of troops. It is curious to reflect now that no such opportunity did in fact come my way until nearly another twenty years had passed. At the time I imagined the possibility of acting myself as Pompey had acted at the same age. But first I had to examine the prospects of Lepidus and the character of the man himself. After the first pleasant reunion with my wife and family I addressed myself to this task at once.

I found that the measures which Lepidus proposed were excellent. In later times I have been instrumental in carrying out every one of them myself. He was basing himself firmly on the traditions of the Popular Party and it was gratifying to observe that Sulla, in spite of his ruthless use of terror, had been unable to destroy them. The most important of these traditions, from the point of view of internal politics, were the principles of state aid to the poorer classes (whether in the form of subsidised food, grants of land or encouragement of emigration) and of the extension of the citizenship itself. Both these principles had always been resisted, usually for selfish and short-sighted motives, by the majority of the senate, and what progress had been made in putting them into practice had invariably come by means of the action of tribunes dealing directly with the Assembly of the

People. Lepidus now proposed to give back to the tribunes the powers taken from them by Sulla. He promised the citizenship to the Italians living north of the River Po. He planned a regular system of free distribution of corn once a month to the entire citizen population of Rome. And he proposed, finally, to undo as far as possible the effects of Sulla's proscriptions. The exiles were to be recalled; the descendants of Sulla's victims were to be given back their political rights, and property was to be restored to its rightful owners.

Such a programme, quite obviously, amounted to a cancellation of everything that Sulla had ever done. Naturally it appealed to me, but I had to examine the question of whether it was practicable at the moment.

I soon saw that Lepidus had powerful assets on his side. He could count on the support of the great numbers of people who, in one way or another, had suffered under Sulla's dictatorship. He would be able to raise troops in the north of Italy, a district which is, as I was to discover myself later, the best of all recruiting grounds. Old officers of Cinna and of Carbo were ready to assist him, and in Rome itself he had, with his great wealth and influence, got together a party which was by no means inconsiderable.

So far as his friends in Rome are concerned, it is natural that I should think first of Servilia, who was then, as now, passionately interested and deeply involved in politics. It was at this time that I first became acquainted with her and I have known her for so long that it is difficult for me to remember whether she was then, as on the face of it would seem likely, at the height of her beauty. Beauty in men and women is in any case not an easy thing to assess. Youth certainly has its part in the reckoning, but many people, as they grow older, develop so much in charm and intelligence that they are amply compensated for the fading of that early bloom which is so exquisite in itself, which so profoundly and irresistibly rouses our passions, but which is often incapable of arousing them for long. Servilia is one of such people. The Queen of Egypt, probably, is another. I can imagine Cleopatra, who, I suppose, would be considered to be now at her most beautiful, being in ten years' time (since she has a most quick intelligence) as delightful as and more fascinating than she is at present.

Servilia is about my own age. She married young and, when I first came to know her well, young Brutus, her son, was already about six. I have always been fond of this boy, partly for his mother's and partly for his own sake, and I have done so much for him that some people have foolishly supposed him to be my son. I wish he were, though if he were, our relations might be even more difficult, since sons are particularly apt to disapprove of their fathers. As it is, though Brutus likes me and, in a way, admires me, I am quite aware that he disapproves of me. This is not, I think, because of my long relationship with his mother, but because he has come too much under the doctrinaire influence of his Uncle Cato. He would, in spite of his affection for me and of the loyalty he owes me, be quite capable of forming, on purely moral or theoretical grounds, some kind of conspiracy against my life, and it would not occur to him that, if his conspiracy were successful, the whole world would be plunged once again into disorder.

I had been acquainted with Servilia since my childhood. She was the niece of Livius Drusus and was unfortunate enough to have Cato as a step-brother. Even in these early days, when Cato was a mere boy, he used, I think, to dislike me intensely. But at that time I was less interested in him than in Servilia's husband, Marcus Brutus, who was deeply committed to the cause of Lepidus. He, Servilia and my brother-in-law, Lucius Cinna, all urged me to take part in the impending revolution, and, as I approved entirely of Lepidus's aims, I was strongly tempted to do so.

What made me, in the end, decide against their advice was the estimate I formed of Lepidus himself. It seemed to me that his character was unbalanced and his judgment haphazard and faulty. He was, for instance, devoted to his wife and yet was almost the only man in Rome who was ignorant of her infidelities. He was also, I thought, absurdly over-confident in his own resources and had not taken the trouble to make them, as he could easily have done, much greater than they were. He had already

lost the valuable support of Pompey and I was amazed to find
that no relations existed between him and Sertorius, who now
controlled the whole of Spain. The fact that Lepidus had made
no overtures to Sertorius was understandable; for Lepidus was
vain and appeared to think that his own wealth and great connections were sufficient for the winning of a civil war. But when
I discovered that Sertorius, after making a few inquiries, had
done nothing on his side to form any alliance with Lepidus, I
realised that, in the view of this great commander, Lepidus was
not worth having as an ally. I decided myself to have nothing
to do with him and, as events turned out, my decision was a
wise one.

CHAPTER III

FIRST STEPS IN POLITICS

EARLY IN the year following my return to Italy the expected revolution broke out and was crushed even more quickly than I had imagined possible. At first the senate had behaved with a timidity and lack of decision which revealed clearly how unfitted it was to exercise the powers given to it by Sulla. Later it had hurried feverishly into violent and, in some ways, unconstitutional action. This, incidentally, has been the pattern of behaviour of the Roman senate throughout my lifetime.

The revolution began with widespread disturbances, caused by the agitation of Lepidus, in which evicted landowners and other malcontents attacked the colonies of Sulla's veterans, determined to regain what they had lost or to acquire something for nothing. Though it was quite clear that Lepidus was behind these disturbances, the senate entrusted him and his colleague Catulus with the task of suppressing them. Both consuls were empowered to raise armies and—as pathetic evidence of the senate's weakness and irresolution—they were first required to swear an oath (for what it was worth) that they would not use these armies to attack each other.

So far the course of events had been strangely reminiscent of the times of Octavius and Cinna. No one was surprised when Lepidus, having raised large forces in the north of Italy, published the full programme of his demands, which included a second consulship for himself, and then began to march on Rome, leaving behind him in the north Servilia's husband, Marcus Brutus, to secure his bases and to recruit more troops.

It was at this stage that the senate began to act with a belated vigour, chiefly under the leadership of a distant relation of mine, old Marcius Philippus. He had been consul when I was scarcely more than ten years old and had been noted for his opposition to all kinds of reform. Later he had shown himself to be a great admirer of young Pompey. When people had commented on his affection for the young man, he had replied, " No wonder that Philip is a lover of Alexander," making a play on his own name and that of Philip, the father of Alexander the Great whom, at this time, Pompey was supposed to resemble.

Philippus now succeeded in persuading the senators that Pompey should be called in as commander in the field with Catulus. From a military point of view the decision was a good one, but it was obvious that to promote, over the heads of so many senators, a young man who, in spite of his deserved reputation, had never held any public office at all was a direct contravention of the constitution of Sulla and a clear indication of the weakness both of the senate and of the constitution itself.

Pompey marched northwards immediately and in a short, somewhat brutal, campaign deprived Lepidus of any hopes he may have had for ultimate success. His first action was to besiege Brutus in the town of Mutina and this action was decisive. Brutus must have been inadequately supplied, since he was soon forced to surrender. Most accounts agree that he was promised his life. Pompey, however, after having received the surrender in the most courteous manner, ordered a troop of horsemen, who were supposed to be escorting Brutus to a place of safety, to assassinate him as soon as he was out of sight. So Servilia lost her husband and young Brutus his father. It was an action on Pompey's part which cannot be defended, and, in spite of the brilliance of this short campaign of his, he was at this time more often spoken about in Rome as " the boy butcher " than as " Alexander."

Lepidus had now lost his bases and was soon defeated by Catulus outside the walls of Rome. With what remained of his army he crossed over to Sardinia, no doubt intending, too late in the day, to join Sertorius in Spain. However, he died almost as soon as he reached Sardinia. It was said at the time that his death was caused by a fever into which he fell after receiving in a letter certain evidence of his wife's infidelity, and it is quite likely that this news was indeed a contributing factor to a general collapse of nerve which followed upon the total failure of his ambitions.

It is interesting, though useless, to speculate on what might have happened to me if I had taken part, as I so nearly did, in this disastrously unsuccessful revolution. I should, no doubt, had I survived the fighting, have accompanied the other high officers and members of the nobility from Lepidus's army and gone to Spain to serve with Sertorius. I would give much now to have made the acquaintance of this great man, and I should, I think, have been of more use to him than were Perperna and the other refugees who, in the end, betrayed him. As it is, I have done my best to find out all I can about Sertorius. Not only the character of the man himself but the field of his operations has attracted me. For in my own life Spain has played as important a part as it did in his. It was in Spain that I first commanded a considerable army, and in Spain were fought the first and last great battles of the civil war.

As for Sertorius himself, I am convinced from what I have discovered about him that he had every quality which a good general ought to possess and many other good qualities besides. He was tough and resolute himself, commanding absolute loyalty and devotion among his men ; he was a master of every kind of stratagem, never acting in a way that could be predicted ; he could make use of all kinds of warfare and all varieties and nationalities in his troops ; he was an honest and capable administrator, able to conciliate subject races by his justice and good manners. He could deal with the future as well as with the present. He knew, for instance, that, in the end, a Roman way of life must depend on deep-seated habit rather than momentary enthusiasm, and so he founded a great college at the city of Osca, where the sons of Spanish chieftains were educated in Greek and Latin. He had, too, in the idiosyncrasy of his character, something of colour, imagination and humanity—the kind of quality which, in spite of his savagery, Marius had possessed and in which such excellent commanders as Sulla and Pompey were wholly lacking. And with this extreme efficiency and energy of his there was an unpredictable side of his nature which singled him out from others. I have met Spaniards who even to-day regard him as having been, in some sense, a god. They emphasise his human qualities—his daring, his loyalty, his sense of humour, his speed in action—with affection; but they revere him for his originality and for the fact that no one ever knew what he would do next. He seems to have been, for instance, unique among great generals in having a genuine dislike for war. In fact there was one occasion when, in a characteristic way, he very nearly abdicated from his place in history. This was shortly after his arrival in Spain, when, with his small army, he was forced by one of Sulla's generals to retire temporarily to Africa. Here he secured the support of some Cilician pirates and, with fresh troops raised in Africa, sailed up the Atlantic coast and landed near Gades. At this point he met some seamen who had just returned from what are known as the Atlantic Islands. They are also called the Islands of the Blest, and are supposed to be situated many miles out in the ocean. It is said that these are the islands celebrated by Homer as the last dwelling-place of Helen and Menelaus, that they have the most temperate and delightful climate, with no storms or snow, but only from time to time gentle rainfall sufficient to renew the luxuriance of the soil. As soon as Sertorius heard of these islands he had a passion to go to them and to live there for the rest of his life in peace and quiet, away from oppression, massacre and unending warfare. However, the Cilician pirates, who lived by war and rapine, refused to fall in with his plan and sailed away, leaving him without a fleet. So Sertorius turned again to war and, starting with a force which must have seemed to his opponents quite negligible both in quantity and quality, began to out-manœuvre and to defeat every Roman general who was sent against him. By the time that he was joined by the refugees from Lepidus's army, he controlled the whole of Spain and was in secret communication with many people in Rome who believed that in the end he was going to prove irresistible.

In those days, whenever there was alarm in Rome, it seemed to end in the securing by Pompey of yet another unprecedented command abroad. So on this occasion, and again on the motion of my aged relative, Philippus, Pompey was empowered to raise an army for Spain and given the rank properly belonging to a consul. He was to co-operate with the general on the spot, Metellus Pius, who had been one of the best of Sulla's commanders, but there was nothing in the proposal of Philippus to suggest that Pompey should be subordinate to Metellus, and Pompey himself evidently had no intention of subordinating himself to anyone. He raised his new army in forty days, crossed the Alps before the end of summer and, for the first time in his life, came into contact with a general who was superior to himself. Early in the next year he was out-manoeuvred by Sertorius and only narrowly escaped a disastrous defeat. This was not an experience which Pompey liked to recall in later years.

I myself, at the age of twenty-five, was now no younger than Pompey had been when he first equipped and led an army of his own. But I could see no prospects for myself in any kind of military activity. I was not an exile, and it would have been absurd to have left Rome for no good reason and to have joined Sertorius. Whether I had or had not any military ability was not a question that was to be tested for many years to come. And nearly another ten years would elapse before I could even enter the senate as an elected magistrate of the lowest grade. There was nothing, however, to prevent me from taking part in politics before this time and in winning for myself a certain name and reputation.

My course in politics was, on the whole, consistent and in accordance with the traditions of my family. I opposed the constitution of Sulla and supported every attempt to weaken it. Originally, no doubt, I thought in terms of simply undoing the harm that had been done, and, in particular, of restoring to the tribunes and the people the powers they had lost. It was only gradually and as a result of becoming increasingly involved in the intricacies of political manœuvres that I began to see that a mere return to the days of Sulpicius or of Drusus was not enough. Even now I do not know precisely how, in our state of affairs, liberty and authority can be reconciled. But I have always known that, essential as order is, no antique or doctrinaire form of order, such as those sponsored in such different ways by Sulla and by Cato, can ever be lasting or effective. I must not imagine, however, that in my early days I saw things as clearly as I do now—and even now I am disturbed by many uncertainties. In those days, too, I was certainly lacking in seriousness. To the distress of my wife and mother I became known for a certain profligacy in my private life. Not only were my extravagances as great as ever, but I indulged in a number of love affairs. I was also reproached, unfairly, I think, for trying to do too many things at once. I wrote much poetry, usually of an amatory nature, and I composed a tragedy on the subject of Oedipus. I was keenly interested in, among other branches of learning, astronomy and mathematics. These varied enthusiasms gave me among some people the reputation of a dilettante ; yet I have retained all these interests and have found them all not only enjoyable but actually profitable to me in my career.

The most normal way then, as it is to a lesser extent now, of attracting attention to oneself was to become a speaker at the bar. One ably handled case alone would be enough to raise a man from obscurity to distinction. I discovered indeed that, during the time when I was in Asia, Marcus Cicero had made a great name for himself in just this way. He had ventured, during Sulla's lifetime, to defend a client who was being persecuted in the courts by one of Sulla's most powerful ex-slaves, and his defence had been so brilliant that he had got the man off. I read Cicero's speech with admiration and I should no doubt have sought for his advice if he had been in Rome at the time when I decided to speak in the courts myself. But Cicero had gone abroad to study philosophy and oratory in Athens and in Rhodes. He had, it seems, suffered from complete nervous exhaustion after his great success. It may well have been also that, though in attacking Sulla's ex-slave he had been particularly careful to flatter Sulla himself, he had conceived the idea that he might still have incurred the dictator's hostility and so might be in some personal danger. This would have been characteristic of the man. Cicero has always been under the delusion that people are thinking and speaking of nothing but himself.

My own first attempt at public speaking was, in its way, as dramatic as had been the case in which Cicero had made his name. After the collapse of Lepidus and his party there was, as usually happens when a victorious party has suffered from a severe fright, a period of reaction. In the senate the old friends of Sulla imagined themselves to be more powerful than they were. They had forgotten that they had already exposed their weakness by giving in to the personal popularity of Pompey; and they were blind to the fact that, though the revolt of Lepidus had failed, the programme of Lepidus was a good one in itself and was widely recognised as such. I wished to make it clear from the beginning of my public career that I was not afraid of any man's power or influence and that, in particular, I would oppose the policies and the settlement of Sulla. It was for these reasons that I decided to prosecute Cnaeus Dolabella, an ex-consul, who had been one of Sulla's most prominent generals.

First I had to secure permission to bring the case at all, and I took great pains over the composition of the preliminary speech which I would have to make before the praetor in charge of the courts dealing with extortion. For, to be appointed official prosecutor it was necessary for me to convince the praetor both that the case was worth bringing and that I was the man to bring it. In this speech, as in all my speeches, I aimed rather at clarity, accuracy and force than at the more decorated and profuse style of eloquence which was popular at the time and which, owing to the influence of Cicero, has remained popular. In this clear direct style, known, rather misleadingly, as "Attic," I immediately won distinction. This first speech of mine before the praetor was regarded as a model of what such speeches ought to be. I am gratified to think that, long before I became a power in the state, it found its way into a number of text-books on oratory.

When the time came for me to present my case before the jury, it had already provoked considerable attention. Dolabella himself had made a foolish display of his feelings. He was angry at being prosecuted at all and particularly angry at being prosecuted by so young and comparatively unknown a person as myself. In various violent attacks which he made on me, both in the senate and elsewhere, he had a lot to say about my allegedly un-Roman conduct with the King of Bithynia and my revolutionary connections with the family and party of Marius. The insulting language which he used about me did me more good than harm. Indeed, a certain notoriety is always useful to those who are beginning their careers in politics. I have noticed many examples of this. There was the case of Marius, who, I have been told, first made himself known politically by the violent language which he used about the great nobles and particularly about his benefactor, Metellus. And in my own days there was the case of Clodius, one of the most disreputable characters I have ever known, quite fearless, and at one time as much loved by the people as I was myself. My own notoriety was of a different kind. I could scarcely attack the principle of aristocracy since I am an aristocrat myself. And though my private life may have been, in some respects, almost as scandalous as was that of Clodius and my language and actions nearly as violent, I differed from him in being, on the whole, consistent in my policy and reliable to my friends. People loved Clodius for his good looks, his recklessness and his charm ; they feared him as one might fear some sudden, unpredictable and destructive fire. They loved me for the same reasons ; but they feared me because it became gradually apparent that my actions were not irresponsible, that I planned to create rather than to destroy.

But at this early period of my life I was known simply for my charm, my daring and for certain scandals. The attacks made on me by Dolabella increased my notoriety and added to my popularity. And though, in the end, I failed to secure his conviction in the courts, my failure amounted, so far as I was concerned, to a success. What saved Dolabella was partly the corruption of the courts themselves and partly his own good sense in having

engaged for the defence two of the ablest lawyers of the day—
Hortensius, the great master of the florid " Asiatic " style of
oratory, and my own relative Lucius Aurelius Cotta.

The jurymen were now, of course, as a result of Sulla's legislation, all senators. They were exactly as corrupt as had been
that jury of business men who, in my childhood, had condemned
my great-uncle, Rutilius. The way in which Dolabella had
enriched himself during his governorship of Macedonia was
regarded, even by his friends, as having been somewhat dis-
graceful. However, his fellow senators were determined to
acquit him, some because they had been bribed, others because
they wished to enjoy the same impunity themselves either for
their past or their future actions. Even so I succeeded in pre-
senting the evidence so forcibly that it would not have been
easy for them, in the face of public opinion, to have voted as
they wanted to do had they voted on the evidence alone. As it
was, Cotta, in his final speech for the defence, made use of his
great learning to suggest that, owing to one imprecise expression
in the drawing up of the indictment, the jury were entitled, whatever they might think of the evidence, to vote for Dolabella's
acquittal. This they were delighted to do, being indifferent to
the fact that they were bringing discredit both on themselves and
on the Sullan constitution.

As for me, though in certain legal subtleties I had been out-
manœuvred by an eminent practitioner of the law, I had won a
name for myself and a position among that large party who still
wished to undo everything that Sulla had achieved.

Next year I undertook another prosecution, again against
one of Sulla's officers, though a less distinguished one than
Dolabella. Indeed Antonius Hybrida was distinguished for
nothing except rapacity—though this did not prevent him in
later years from becoming consul with Cicero. During Sulla's
campaign in Greece, Antonius had employed his time and the
troops under his command, not in fighting the enemy, but in
plundering Greek cities. I now undertook the case of these cities,
which were claiming restitution. I informed my clients that there
was not much chance of securing a conviction. Too many people

had made fortunes at about this time and in about this way for senatorial jurymen to set up a dangerous precedent by condemning even the most notorious of such offenders. Yet both from my own point of view and from that of the Greeks the case was worth bringing. The publicity which it would receive might have a deterrent effect on other officers in less troubled times. And I should have another opportunity of clarifying my own political position. As it happened, though, as I had expected, I lost the case, I gained much popularity from it. In particular I was able to make what was considered a daring attack on the way in which Sulla had handled his troops. I pointed out that he had been the first Roman commander in history who had bribed and pampered his soldiers and who had won the loyalty of his junior officers by encouraging them to loot. It was still unwise openly to mention the name of Marius, but when I contrasted the methods of Sulla with the methods of other generals in the past who had saved Rome from foreign invasion, no one could have failed to realise that it was Marius whom I had in mind.

It was not difficult in these years to win popularity by attacking the government. Though the revolt of Lepidus had been crushed, nothing else had been achieved. Sertorius was now at the height of his power in Spain, and Pompey, in spite of the large forces already under his command, had been forced into the humiliating position of writing to the senate to say that, unless he received much greater supplies both of money and of men, he could not guarantee the frontiers of Italy. Meanwhile in Asia Mithridates was threatening war and had concluded an alliance with Sertorius. And in Rome itself the price of corn had risen to an unprecedented height. This was due partly to governmental incompetence, but chiefly to the action of the large pirate fleets which, operating from bases in Cilicia, in Crete and other islands, now dominated the whole Mediterranean for many months of the year.

In these conditions the more reactionary elements in the senate were forced to keep quiet. In the year after my prosecution of Antonius, one at least of the consuls was a moderate and intelligent statesman. This was my uncle, Caius Cotta, and his consulship marked the first legal and accepted retreat from the Sullan constitution. True, the concessions were extorted by violence. Concessions usually are, when the governing body is weak but wishes to give the impression of strength. So, if it had not been for the fact that Cotta and his colleague in the consulship had been forced to run for their lives by a large and angry mob which attacked them in the Sacred Way, it is unlikely that any of Cotta's reasonable proposals for reform would have been accepted by the senate. As it was, Cotta, who was an excellent speaker, not only succeeded, when feelings had somewhat calmed down, in pacifying the mob, but had convinced the senate that mere words were not enough. What the people liked least about Sulla's so-called settlement were his measures against the tribunes. These had been deprived of most of their powers and, to make the office even less important, it had been decreed that no one who had held the office of tribune, was eligible to stand for any of the higher magistracies. This disability was now, by the action of Cotta, removed. It was a first step in a definite direction. Men of real ability would now offer themselves for election as tribunes and, once elected, they would remember the past and not be content with the minor role in politics which, according to Sulla's constitution, they were still expected to play. The next move would, of course, be an agitation for giving back to the tribunes all the powers which they had formerly possessed.

However, in this very promising situation, my energies were suddenly diverted from Rome.

CHAPTER IV

THE PIRATES

It WAS at about this time that I began to become sufficiently well acquainted with Crassus to be able to borrow money from him in large sums. As Crassus was the richest man in Rome and I was one of the most extravagant, this acquaintanceship was of great importance to me. I am glad to think that it was important to Crassus also. Certainly without my help he would never have reached that position of power for which all his life he had longed. Yet at first he must have regarded me as a rather doubtful investment. I must have appeared to him as an able, though frivolous, young man who had the great advantage of being able to make himself personally attractive to all sorts of people and who might thus be useful to a patron who would supply him liberally with funds. In the end Crassus realised, and realised with generosity, that I am not by nature a subordinate. By that time I had become indispensable to him and he continued to afford me financial support without which I should have been utterly ruined. For this I have always been grateful to him, nor indeed have I ever, as so many people do, turned against anyone who at any time and for whatever motives has been my bene-factor.

Not that any relationship with Crassus could be described as altogether easy. He had the faults as well as the virtues of the great money-maker. There was, in fact, something mean-spirited about him, as, I think, there must always be about a man whose whole life is spent in financial operations and in calculated invest-ments. Crassus's own financial interests were on enormous scale. He used to say, " I don't call a man rich unless he can raise, equip and pay an army out of his income," This is a sensible reflection ; but to Crassus it was the income, not the army, that mattered. However vast his undertakings were, he looked upon each one separately rather as a small tradesman might look upon a promising bargain. He was full of contradictions. Meanness was fighting in him with generosity. He loved display, and yet liked to keep himself in the background. He would favour and even initiate the most far-reaching and revolutionary policies, yet he would avoid, if possible, openly giving to these policies the support of his own name and influence. He would try to get them carried out for him by agents. And in his choice of agents he was remarkably, even pathetically, consistent. He mistrusted those whose character resembled his own. Those whom he financed for political reasons were always colourful and very often violent characters. They usually had some ability, but I was, I think, the only one who was both able and reliable.

Throughout his life Crassus suffered from a sense of grievance. Once I had realised this, I found him easy to manage. He was aggrieved even by the thought of his own success and did all he could, though quite unsuccessfully, to live down his deserved reputation for avarice. He would go out of his way to give lavish entertainments, but, as he was plainly not enjoying them himself, his guests would go away without any feelings of gratitude towards their host. Then he considered, with some reason, that he had been badly treated by Sulla. It was true that it was because of Sulla that he had acquired his enormous wealth. He had profited more than anyone else from the sales of confiscated property and had gone to all lengths to secure the most valuable assets for the smallest outlay. But he could never forget that though it was he, not Sulla, who had won the battle of the Colline Gate, he had not received from Sulla afterwards any command of real importance. Instead the whole glory of the war, so far as the younger officers were concerned, had gone to Pompey.

I soon discovered that it was on Pompey in particular that was concentrated all the deep sense of grievance that marred

Crassus's character. He was six years older than Pompey and he found the idea of Pompey's brilliant successes and great popularity something almost impossible to contemplate. Indeed his hatred and later his fear of Pompey were what a Greek doctor might call pathological. Nor did Pompey on his side do anything to mollify the ill-feeling. At no time did he make any secret of the fact that he regarded himself as superior to others, and, though he had a charm and dignity of manner in which Crassus was wholly lacking, he was also capable of behaving with a cool and studied insolence towards those who, like Crassus, appeared to be his rivals. In particular he used to speak slightingly of Crassus's ability as a soldier. This was unfair, since Crassus, in spite of his disastrous military failure in his old age, was a very fine commander indeed. He was therefore all the more infuriated by Pompey's easy assumption that no other Roman general existed except himself. I remember how delighted he was when the news arrived that Pompey had been defeated by Sertorius.

This antagonism between the two men was to develop further and was to be the dominant factor in my own early life as a politician. Now they are both dead and each was destroyed by his ruling passion—Crassus by the avidity with which he sought for a military reputation, Pompey by his intolerance of an equal, which led him to underrate my own abilities as a general and as a leader of men.

In the days when I first knew him Crassus was closely observing events in Spain and had not committed himself to any particular line in politics, apart from his persistent and not very successful efforts to make himself popular with all classes. He had financial interests everywhere and some of the greatest of these were in the East. It was in connection with these that I myself went out to Asia for the second time.

News had arrived that my old friend King Nicomedes was on his death-bed and according to some rumours he was proposing to bequeath his kingdom to the Roman people. This was a prospect which naturally excited the utmost interest among the financiers and Crassus, as usual, was one of the first to see in the occasion an opportunity for profit. He gave me credit for having some influence with the king and immediately suggested that I should sail out for the East at his expense and should do what I could to obtain from Nicomedes, before he died, certain concessions in Bithynia to which he attached a particular importance. As my mission was intended to be secret I gave it out that my intention was to go to Rhodes to study oratory under the famous Professor Apollonius, who had recently had Cicero as one of his pupils. I pretended that my failures in the law courts had convinced me that I needed further training, though in fact these "failures" had added immensely to my reputation. People believed the story and, as events turned out, they had no reason for not doing so, since I was prevented by unlucky circumstances from reaching Bithynia in time.

It was just off the Asiatic coast, near the small island of Pharmacusa, that my ship was sighted and captured by a force of Cilician pirates. Nothing could have been more disconcerting. There was no doubt that I would be kept a prisoner for at least a month while money for my ransom was being collected and this inevitable delay was likely to cost me everything that I hoped to gain in Bithynia. Moreover, these Cilician pirates were the most bloodthirsty ruffians to be found in the world and were quite capable of murdering a prisoner if, for any reason, they had to get away quickly from their base, or if they suspected that the ransom money would not be forthcoming.

I have discovered that when one is in danger from the rougher sort of people, whether they are Romans or barbarians, the best attitude to adopt is one of amusement mingled with contempt. It is above all things important that they should recognise one's superiority and realise that one is not in the least afraid of them. So on this occasion, when the leader of the pirates informed me that my ransom had been assessed at twenty talents, I burst out laughing and told him that he must be completely ignorant of Rome and of my social position there if he really imagined that my friends could not afford to pay a great deal more than that. I advised him to raise the figure to fifty talents and I demanded that, until the money arrived, I should be given comfortable quarters to live in and be treated with the distinction that was due to me.

The reaction of the pirates to this speech of mine was what I had expected it to be. They were amused at what seemed to them a boyish kind of boastfulness; they admired me for not being afraid of them; and they were impressed by my offer of more money. I soon saw to it that I was regarded by them not only as an object of amusement, but as one who was entitled to their respect. I could scarcely ask them to release me, but in all other matters I insisted on having my own way and in being obeyed promptly. I realised that my enforced stay on the island was likely to be a long one (in fact it lasted for nearly forty days), and I was determined to make some agreeable and profitable use of my time there. These pirates were brutal and uneducated characters, and lived a life of laziness when they were not actually engaged on their profession of rapine. They would spend their days together in eating and drinking and lying about in the sun, amusing each other with interminable stories of their own exploits, or singing in their harsh voices the most sentimental songs until far into the night. Within a very short space of time I succeeded in reforming their manners, at least to some extent. I organised regular athletic sports which took place two or three times a week, and since I competed in these myself and in many events habitually won the first prize, I soon found myself to be, among these savages, rather in the position of a leader than of a captive. For most of the period of my captivity I was alone, except for my doctor and one or two servants. The rest of my party had crossed to the mainland and were busy in raising the money for my ransom from Miletus and other Greek cities. So, being debarred from my usual enjoyment of intelligent conversation, I had to do my best with what material there was at hand. I used to assemble the pirates together and practise my oratory upon them, addressing them in set speeches on the various subjects which were then popular in the schools of rhetoric. At this time of my life, too, I used to write a lot of poetry and I arranged poetry recitals at which I would read my own work, or, when it was the case of a drama, I would take the main part myself and employ my doctor as a reader of the minor roles. The pirates, I found, were quite incapable of appreciating any of the finer points of style and many of them could not even follow a reasoned argument. I was often impatient with them when I observed their attention wandering during my speeches, or when one or other of them seemed to consider funny some passage in my poems which had been designed to express pathos. I used to call them dunces, ignoramuses, illiterate peasants and all sorts of other abusive names, all of which they deserved. For, though they were docile enough and would even stop their singing at night when I sent to them and told them to be quiet, they had, in fact, very few qualities which one could admire. In particular I disliked their boastfulness and the contemptuous manner in which they used to speak of Rome. They had already raided the coasts of Italy, they said, and before long they would be threatening Rome itself. Unfortunately there was truth in their claims, but this was not the sort of language which I liked to hear. I pointed out to them that, however numerous the pirate fleets might be, they could never constitute, what they were proud to call themselves, an independent power. So far from being a power, they were a disease ; for their whole existence depended on the destruction or squandering of what others had produced. In a civilised world, I informed them, they were quite intolerable ; and, though in recent years Rome had, because of her own troubles, slackly permitted them to grow in strength, a time would certainly come when every pirate ship would be driven from the seas. They regarded these remarks of mine as exceedingly amusing and when I added that, so far as they themselves were concerned, I proposed, as soon as I was released, to have the whole lot of them brought to justice, they thought this the best joke of all. Indeed their sense of humour was as imperfectly developed as were their intellectual faculties.

Finally the ransom money arrived and I proceeded immediately to put my plan into operation. Most of the money had been raised in the nearby city of Miletus, where I had many friends among the rich ship-owners and merchants whom I had met during my early period of military service in Asia. Ever since that time I had remained in contact with the most agreeable and influential of these men, partly because I valued their friend-ship for itself, partly because I was already beginning to make it a point of policy to leave behind me, wherever I went, the nucleus of a party on which, in any danger or difficulty, I might rely. Now, as soon as I was released, I went directly to Miletus, and, without wasting a moment, gathered my friends together and asked them for their help. I knew from my experience of the pirates that, now that they had received their ransom, they would be likely to spend the next few days and nights in feasting and carousing; their precautions would be relaxed, and they would not be a match for even a small force, if resolutely handled. At first my friends were sceptical of my suggestions. No privately organised expedition had ever before ventured to sail against a pirate fleet and even the operations of regular naval squadrons had seldom in the past enjoyed much success. How-ever, I was able in the end to prove that my plan was practicable. It could also be, I pointed out, very profitable since, if successful, we would not only recover the fifty talents just paid over to the pirates but would also come into possession of ships, of stores and of much other booty.

It was more difficult, once I had secured the promise of sufficient vessels for my purpose, to find crews willing to serve in them. The pirates were, very reasonably, feared by the seamen not only of the Asiatic coast but of every port in the Mediter-ranean. I had to employ much eloquence and make many promises. The sailors available were mostly Greeks from the islands and the mainland. Greeks, I find, will nearly always respond to appeals made to their national or local pride. By reminding them of their great seafaring traditions, I was able first to secure their services and then to inspire them with con-fidence and resolution. Within the space of a single day I had at my disposal a fleet which seemed to me adequate for my purpose.

We set sail before nightfall on an enterprise which was, in fact, rather more hazardous than I had suggested. It was not certain that the pirates would be off their guard, and it was always possible that they might have been reinforced by some of the numerous other pirate ships which from time to time would put in to the roadstead where they lay. However, on this occasion everything went as I had hoped. We found the men on shore, mostly suffering from the effects of their feast, and the ships inadequately guarded. There was very little fighting and among my own men there were no casualties at all. All the pirates, apart from a few who were killed on the spot, were taken prisoners and all their ships were captured. The booty was considerable. I was not only able to pay the crews the large sums which I had promised, but to retain a great deal of valuable property for the use of myself and my friends. As for the crews of my ships, they now believed that they were invincible and begged me to lead them against other pirate strongholds along the coast. I was aware, however, that in most circumstances the pirates were very formidable antagonists ; and besides I wished to go on to Bithynia without further loss of time. I was in any case too late to achieve my main purpose since Nicomedes had died during the period of my captivity and the Roman governor of Asia, Silanus, had already, it seemed, taken up his quarters in the King's palace.

With regard to my prisoners I thought that it would make a clean end to the expedition and would also redound to my own personal credit, if I were to have them executed immediately at Miletus, where already, as the result of my exploit, I was enjoying the greatest popularity. However, on second thoughts I decided that it would be more tactful to refer their case to the governor of the province, from whom also, it seemed to me, I was entitled to receive some consideration and some reward. So I brought the prisoners to Pergamum and left them there under guard. I myself went on as fast as I could to Bithynia by the same road as that on which, seven years before, I had first travelled to that country.

I found, on my way, and at my destination, everything changed and changed, from our point of view, for the worse. At the time of my first visit to Asia, Sulla's victories, though far

from having been conclusive, had re-established the prestige of
Rome. Since then, however, while our own governors had done
little or nothing to repair the damage of war and to insure good
administration, Mithridates had gathered strength. He had concluded alliances both with Sertorius in the far west and with the
leaders of pirate fleets operating from Crete and Cilicia. It was
obvious to anyone that, if he wished to retain his powerful
position in the Black Sea, he could not tolerate the Roman
occupation of Bithynia. In fact, his armies were already mobilised
and some contingents of them were being trained in Roman
methods by military advisers who had been sent to him by
Sertorius.

Against this obvious and increasing menace the Roman
government on the spot was, as I soon discovered, almost entirely
unprepared. The army was badly led, badly organised and
stationed in the wrong areas. Everyone appeared to be uniquely
interested in what profits could be made out of the new province
of Bithynia. The palace where I had enjoyed such agreeable
evenings with the late king was now full of officials and agents
of Roman capitalists, all looking for valuable concessions and
all blind to the fact that at any moment they were likely to be
swept out of the province altogether. Their conduct was, indeed,
exactly what Mithridates would have desired. They were neglect-
ing defence and at the same time making themselves hated by
their exactions, so that Mithridates himself would be able, when
the time came, to overrun the country without serious opposition
and also to represent himself as a liberator.

Notable among these fortune-hunters was the Roman
governor, Silanus. I visited him as soon as I arrived in Bithynia
and at once referred to him the case of the pirates who were still
under guard at Pergamum. I had expected that he would congratulate me on my action and would give orders, as was right,
for the execution of the prisoners; but, to my surprise and disgust, he merely looked somewhat embarrassed when he saw me
and, after a few half-hearted compliments, said that he needed a
little time to think the matter over. It was clear enough to me
that what he had in his mind was to negotiate through agents,

who were not hard to discover, with other pirate leaders and to enrich himself, at the expense of my reputation, by securing the release of the prisoners. I therefore took matters into my own hands. I knew that the commander of the guard at Pergamum was a man whom I could trust and so I sent to him secretly and ordered, on my own responsibility, that the prisoners should be crucified. As I hate causing unnecessary pain, I instructed him to have them put to death by hanging before the bodies were nailed to the crosses.

Not unnaturally this action of mine made me unpopular with Silanus. But there was nothing that he could do about it without bringing himself into the greatest discredit both with the citizens of the coastal towns who were delighted with my handling of the whole affair and also at Rome, where the government of Asia was already, and with reason, under attack. However, though he was unable to take any positive action against me, his attitude remained unfriendly and he lacked the intelligence to make use of the advice which I gave him. If I had received the slightest official recognition I was prepared to raise forces on my own account and to operate either against the pirates by sea or against Mithridates by land. I had influential friends in Bithynia and, with their help, would have found no difficulty in equipping either a fleet or an army. Moreover, unlike the governor, I had definite ideas of how to use them and of how also to dispose the regular forces available to meet the coming danger. Silanus, however, was interested solely in making as much money as possible for himself before his term of office expired. He neglected my advice and, out of a kind of jealous anger, refused to give official sanction to any of the projects which I was ready to undertake. Nevertheless I determined to keep my eyes on Asia in the hope that later on there might be some opportunity of taking an important part in events. So, instead of returning to Rome, I withdrew to Rhodes in order to attend lectures in rhetoric and philosophy; though, before doing so, I did manage to achieve something worth while in Bithynia. I possessed myself of a number of valuable objects which had been left to me personally by King Nicomedes and I successfully defended the rights of a number of old friends in the country who were in danger of persecution from Roman officials. This task I was most glad to perform, since I have always valued friendship above all things.

CHAPTER V

RETURN TO ROME

RHODES IS perhaps the most beautiful island in the Mediterranean. And apart from the natural beauties of the place—the
bright flowers, the mountains, the sparkling sea and the per-
petually enjoyable climate—I observed in the architecture and
amenities of the town—the porticoes and public buildings, the
drainage system—a splendour and a graceful ease of life which
compared most favourably with anything of the sort to be found
at this time in Rome. Here, too, were the most famous professors
of philosophy and rhetoric. I followed their lectures with the
keenest interest, learned much from them and, in less disturbed
times, would no doubt have been anxious to learn more. As it
was, however, my attention was distracted both towards the
nearby coast of Asia and towards Italy.

In Asia, as was now obvious to everyone, a new war with
Mithridates was on the point of breaking out. And in Rome,
just as had happened at the time of Marius and Sulla, there was
bitter competition for the honour and the opportunities of the
command. The consuls for this year, in which I reached the age
of twenty-eight, were my Uncle Marcus Cotta and Lucius
Lucullus. Each of these used what influence he could to secure
the command for himself, and there were others who strongly
supported the claims of the praetor, Marcus Antonius, the father
of that Mark Antony who has later been of the greatest service to
me and whom I count as my friend, though he has often been
a source of much embarrassment. This Marcus Antonius was,
like his son, a tremendous drinker. Unlike his son, he had no
charm and little military ability. Marcus Cotta, though ambitious

and courageous, also lacked the qualities required by a commander-in-chief. Lucullus was the obvious choice for the command, and it was indicative of the confusion of the times and the inefficiency of the senate that he had the utmost difficulty in getting himself appointed to a post which should have been offered to him at once. I have often attacked Lucullus in public, but I must admit that in many ways he deserves admiration. He was a loyal friend to Sulla and a loyal supporter of senatorial authority until in the end he discovered that his own loyalty was being repaid by treachery and he retired from politics altogether. He was a good scholar ; he kept the best table in Rome ; and, apart from one fatal defect—an inability to understand the psychology of his troops—he was as great a general as any in our history. He had important connections ; both his mother and his wife came from great families ; both, however, were peculiarly disreputable. His mother, from the family of the Metelli, was notorious for the immorality of her life at a time when such looseness of behaviour was less fashionable than it became later ; his wife Clodia was the daughter of Appius Claudius who had been consul in the year of Sulla's abdication. She and her sister, who bore the same name and who became immortal because of the foolish infatuation felt for her by the poet Catullus, were perhaps the most vicious women I have known. Both had incestuous relations with their brother Clodius and were known to be, to use a Greek word, nymphomaniacs. Their very zest for sexual action prevented them from doing as other women did and using their love affairs to promote their husbands' interests or their own. So in everything connected with his command Lucullus got no help from the powerful Claudian family and in the end he was deprived of the honour due to him largely through the intrigues of his brother-in-law.

In Rhodes I heard with interest of how Lucullus, much against his nature, had been forced to descend to flattery and bribery before in the end he received the appointment to the command against Mithridates. Cotta meanwhile was given a fleet with which to operate round the coasts of Bithynia and the Hellespont ; and Antonius received a far-reaching commission to deal with the pirate fleets throughout the Mediterranean. I learned, too that what had given a particular zest to this scramble for commands was the general feeling that before long Pompey would be back from Spain and, with the aid of his army, would be likely to claim for himself any important command that might be available. In Spain he had now built up an enormous force and, though where Sertorius was concerned, no military event could be predicted, it seemed that even Sertorius could not hold out much longer against such odds.

These were not times in which it was easy to pursue one's studies in tranquillity. I remembered the success I had had in my private action against the pirates and when I heard that Mithridates had already taken the field and that his troops, so far in small numbers, were penetrating into the Roman provinces, I determined to attempt some other action of the same sort, though on a larger scale. I crossed over to the Carian mainland opposite Rhodes, soon raised a force of light-armed troops and cavalry, and, as a preliminary measure, went from town to town in order to secure the loyalty of each to Rome and at the same time to raise subscriptions for the payment of my troops. I was acting, of course, in an entirely unofficial, indeed in an illegal, capacity, but I considered that an intelligent commander, like Lucullus, would recognise that my action was valuable.

In fact, this was an adventure which came to very little, but I still think of it with some satisfaction and can see clearly in my mind's eye the brown hills of Caria and the marching columns of my men—a mixed force of Greeks, Carians, Rhodians, and a few Romans, all enthusiastic and all willing to fight for honour as well as for the plunder we hoped to gain. On this short campaign which I commanded myself I learned more than I had learned when under the command of others ; though the action was so short as scarcely to merit the name of a campaign. After securing the allegiance of the cities along the coast I marched inland and made contact with advance elements of Mithridates' army. In some cases these troops of his were well disciplined and well led by military advisers who had been sent to him from Spain by Sertorius. In a short time, however, I was able to make my own small army into a very reliable force. We fought one general engagement with the enemy, routed them and drove them out of Caria. However, while I was planning my next move, I received news from Rome which made me decide to give up any further thoughts of military operations and to return to the city. I was informed in letters from my mother and my friends that I had been nominated for a place in the College of Pontiffs and, after some reflection, I decided that I should not miss the opportunity of taking up this post. As one of the fifteen Pontiffs I should not be, as I was when priest of Jupiter, debarred from political and military life. In fact, nearly all members of the College were men of great political importance. The chief Pontiff has always been one of the most influential men in Rome and the holder of the office at this time was Metellus Pius, the colleague of Pompey in Spain. Other members included the distinguished orator and ex-consul Catulus, son of that Catulus who had been the colleague of Marius in the German war and had later been compelled by my uncle to commit suicide. There was also Servilius Isauricus under whom, in my early youth, I had served in Cilicia. Indeed, as my mother pointed out in her letter, I was remarkably fortunate to be offered at my age a place of such distinction in the state, and my mother was all the more anxious that I should take it because the vacancy in the College had occurred owing to the death of her eldest brother, Caius Cotta. This uncle of mine had been distinguished both in peace and war. He had been one of the leading orators of his day ; his consulship had been remarkable for wise and moderate statesmanship ; and after his consulship he had carried out successful military operations in Cisalpine Gaul for which he had earned the right of a triumph. It was while waiting outside the gates of Rome before celebrating his triumph that he had died of the effects of an old wound. No doubt it was because of the fact that Cotta had been so generally respected that I, his relative, had been nominated to fill the place left empty by his death. No other explanation seems to account for my being honoured in this way, since my career in politics so far had not been of the sort that would commend itself to the majority of the members of the College who, on the whole, represented the most conservative interests in the state. It may be that, by offering me so respectable a position they were hoping to win over to their own way of thought a young man whom they knew to be talented and whom they feared might prove subversive. If these were their calculations, they were mistaken in them.

It was with great reluctance that I abandoned my plans for further military operations in Asia, but I saw at once that my mother's judgment was right and that, in the interests of the honour of our family, I should return to Rome. I am sure now that the decision was a correct one. Even if I had joined Lucullus with an army of my own he would not have employed me except in some very subordinate capacity, since he had a strictly legalistic outlook on the question of giving promotion to those below the proper age and, as he was to show later, was most reluctant to delegate responsibility to others.

My return journey to Italy was not without danger. Before I left Asia I received the news of how Mithridates had invaded Bithynia and, as I had anticipated, had easily swept aside the inadequate defences organised by Silanus. Meanwhile my uncle, Marcus Cotta, had arrived upon the scene. He had been foolish enough to risk a general engagement in which he was totally defeated and as a result of this had lost his entire fleet. He was now blockaded with the remnants of his army in Chalcedon, hoping to be relieved by Lucullus, who was operating from the south. So it appeared that at any moment the land routes across Asia might be blocked, and as for the sea, I wished to entrust myself to it for the shortest time possible. After Cotta's defeat, there was scarcely a single Roman warship in eastern waters. The pirates were operating on a larger scale than ever and I knew that, if I were captured again, I should not be given the opportunity of even offering a ransom. The final stage of my journey was the most dangerous of all, and for the passage from Dyrrhachium to Brundisium I engaged a four-oared rowing boat, hoping that the smallness of the craft might escape detection. Certainly I was alarmed as I seldom have been when, in the early morning, after many hours on the open sea, the steersman announced that the masts of ships were visible on the horizon. I slipped off my clothes, fastened a dagger round my waist and prepared to plunge into the sea. Here at least I would have a chance of escape if our boat was stopped and searched ; and, if I was in danger of capture, I would kill myself rather than submit to the kind of death which, as I knew from my conversations with those pirates whom I had crucified, I should be certain to suffer. It was soon discovered, however, that the supposed masts of ships were only the long lines of trees on the Italian coast. I have rarely felt so relieved ; for, though I have often risked my life in battle, in street fighting and even, once, in front of an infuriated senate, I could not bear the humiliating death of a prisoner, or, for that matter, of one of those hunted men of whom I have seen so many in the days of Marius and of Sulla. I would much rather be assassinated, as, I suppose, it is possible that I may be. And against assassination, in spite of what my friends tell me, no decent precautions can be taken. One cannot even, I know, rely, as one ought to be able to, on the loyalty of friends or the gratitude of those whom one has spared. Envy or even a perverted intellectual or moral theory can prove stronger than the warmer and more generous human feelings. So, I remember, it happened, a year or two after this return of mine to Italy, in the case of Sertorius.

It is a story which, even now, I find most painful to recall and it affected me greatly at the time. For Sertorius was murdered by those who should have been his friends. After ten years he was still undefeated in the field and though his military difficulties were increasing, he was one used to difficulty and his future, like his past, must be regarded as incalculable. He retained the devoted loyalty of his Spanish troops and was destroyed by his fellow countrymen, the exiles from armies of Marius, of Carbo or of Lepidus who had joined him and been treated well by him. These men seem to have been actuated by no more worthy feeling than that of mere jealousy. They could not forget that Sertorius came of a family less distinguished than their own families in distant Rome, and the evidence of his immensely superior abilities, both military, personal and political, stirred in them envy rather than admiration. Their leader was Perperna, an ex-consul, and an old companion of my cousin, young Marius. No doubt these conspiracies have to be planned and in the planning of them there is, I think, always something indescribably disgusting. On this occasion the conspirators invited Sertorius to a banquet and, while they were reclining at the table, exerted themselves to behave with more than their customary grossness of manner. They knew that Sertorius himself was fond of intelligent talk and, at his own entertainments, promoted that sense of civilised ease which can only come from good order. When, as had been expected, he turned his head aside in disgust from their deliberately coarse and boring conversation, Perperna, as an agreed signal, dropped the cup which he was holding, and another of the conspirators first plunged his dagger into Sertorius's back and then pinioned his body as he attempted to rise. Now they all thrust their daggers into his face, his eyes and his body, and so died the man who, of all those who had resisted Sulla in arms, was incomparably the most able, the most daring and the most far-sighted. The horror of such an assassination is, I think, in the fact that it is against the whole course and trend of nature. It is a debasement of nature to envy the great, and the whole of human nature is seen to be debased when a combination of inferiors succeeds in destroying by treachery one whom they would be ashamed to challenge as individuals and would not dare all together to confront in war.

Why is it, I wonder, that I found and still find the mere imagination of this murder of Sertorius so moving? When first I heard the story I was myself in no position at all comparable with his; and now, when I am undoubtedly the object of envy to many people, I take no precautions to prevent for myself the same fate as that which overtook him. So, when first I heard the story, I did not anticipate assassination and now I do not fear it. It is not, therefore, a story which by any process of imagination I associate with myself or with a fate which might befall me. I am disturbed, I think, by more abstract considerations— a hatred of ingratitude, a contempt for the passion of envy and an abhorrence of waste. And sometimes I have been led into despondency by the reflection that if, as the evidence shows, human nature is always apt to destroy what is greater than itself, then all one's labour may prove useless and life itself may be regarded as something to be tolerated with as much equanimity as possible rather than as something to be used with energy in the pursuit of an aim. This was the view of Epicurus, whose doctrine in general I accept and it is a view that has been admirably expressed in verse by Lucretius in my own times. To avoid ambition and to avoid love are his important prescriptions for happiness, since neither ambition nor love can ever be satisfied. Yet I am inclined to believe that such philosophical statements are nearly meaningless. Love and victory may be momentary but they are not partial satisfactions and happiness seems to proceed rather from the exercise of the spirit in action than from any kind of abstinence. It is true, of course, that one likes to regard one's life as something more emphatic than a mere exercise of one's faculties. One looks for results ; one aims, even, at a kind of permanence or immortality. I myself have, I suppose, in some sense achieved this aim, and I am glad to have done so, even though I have many more aims in front of me and am far from satisfied with what I have accomplished already. My supporters claim that I was born into a world of chaos and have succeeded in introducing a principle of order. This is true, but it is not the whole or the best truth. Sulla might have claimed to have introduced order ; but I should not like to be put in the same category as Sulla by historians of the future. Indeed, I should much prefer to be compared with Sertorius who, in desperate situations, was not content with conventional or out-of-date expedients, who understood his fellow-men and who, so far as it was possible, acted with honour, moderation and foresight. Perhaps what moves me most when I think of his assassination is the fact that his splendid gifts, so brilliantly exercised, were, by a kind of accident, doomed to result in nothing permanent except (and this is certainly something) an example and a record. As for myself, if I were told by some divine power that I was to be assassinated to-morrow, I should deplore the stupidity of my assassins more than my own fate. No doubt if such a conspiracy were formed against me, it would be done in the name of liberty and under the auspices of the dead Cato. The movement would be antiquarian and unrealistic. My death would merely plunge the world into a renewed civil war and at the end of it those methods of administration which I myself have devised would be found to be the only ones adequate to deal with the problems of our times. No doubt I should continue to be worshipped as a god. So far my success is secure. But if I were murdered by my own friends, my ghost (if one may assume that such things exist) would, I think, hunt down my murderers to the remotest corners of the earth. For in every sense they would have been acting against the nature of things—not only against friendship and gratitude but against the necessary order of society which I have established. So I should pity myself less than I pity Sertorius, who is not worshipped as a god simply because the precise opportunity suited to his genius never came his way. I must own that it never came to me either until late in life.

CHAPTER VI

POMPEY AND CRASSUS

AFTER TAKING my place in the College of Pontiffs I remained in Italy for five years on end. During these years Pompey concluded the campaign in Spain, Lucullus overran Asia and Armenia, advancing farther east than had any western conqueror since the time of Alexander; and Italy itself was ravaged from end to end by armies of revolting slaves. It is curious to think that I took no part whatever in any of these military events.

Instead, so far as my public life was concerned, I gave my whole attention to politics. Here I took up, with more consistency and precision than before, the line which was traditionally that of my mother's family, of the reformers I had known in my boyhood, of Cinna and, in a sense, of Marius—if one can credit Marius with having had a policy at all. The main elements in the programme of reform remained the same as in the past. We demanded freedom to act against the restrictions of the senatorial oligarchy and saw that this freedom could only be exercised constitutionally by means of support from the people and from the tribunes. We still favoured the extension of the citizenship to the whole of Italy as far as the Alps and encouraged the Italians north of the Po to press on with their demands for equal rights with those who lived south of the river. But since the time of Cinna Sulla had intervened with the precise intention of making the senate's authority permanent and absolute. Our first objective therefore was to destroy his constitution and the quickest and most effective way of doing this was to conduct a successful agitation for restoring their full powers to the tribunes.

I therefore supported to the best of my ability the tribune,

Licinius Macer, who was the most energetic popular leader in the year after my return to Italy. Macer was a man of culture, the author of a lengthy history of Rome. He was also, of course, well read in Greek history and, like many leaders of the Popular Party, had been much influenced by the ideals of the age of Pericles and looked forward, rather naïvely perhaps, to a state of affairs in which the people would elect magistrates to be their servants rather than their masters and would themselves be capable of initiating ideas and of controlling events. He had also reflected on those occasions in early Roman history when the plebeians had gained their rights by threatening to withdraw their services and he hinted that now the best way for the people to act in order to enforce their will was to refuse to fight in the wars that were only made for the profit and glory of a few. This, in the existing circumstances, was a dangerous proposition to make and was also somewhat unrealistic, since, in point of fact, one of the few profitable careers open to the poor was that of a professional soldier. Still the idea of the people pouring out their blood for the sake of the rich generals and capitalists was a useful one for the purposes of agitation and it contained at least some elements of truth. We were careful in particular to attack Lucullus, since he had been a friend of Sulla's and was far the ablest of those military men who could be counted on to defend the settlement made by Sulla. These attacks on Lucullus were to prove very profitable to the party, though the more or less pacifist views of Macer were not effective except as part of the general line of setting the poor against the rich. There was never in fact any great difficulty in recruiting men for the legions. What scared the senate much more than anything else were the violent speeches made to demand the restoration to the tribunes of all the rights which they had once enjoyed.

In putting himself at the forefront of this agitation, Licinius Macer was acting with courage as well as with conviction; for it was impossible to remember any tribune who had wholeheartedly set himself against the senate and who had afterwards escaped either death or exile or confiscation of property. And as it happened Macer was no exception to the rule. The senate did not forget its enemies and, seven years or so later, when this particular agitation had had its effect and had ceased to be the subject of talk, Macer was put on trial for extortion. He was, it seems, so convinced of his innocence that, before the case was over, he had left the court and gone home to put on a new toga and make preparations for a banquet to celebrate his acquittal. However, he was condemned and committed suicide shortly afterwards. At a later date still I, too, should have perished in the same way if I had obeyed the senate's decree and entered Rome as a civilian. As it was, they forced me into war.

No doubt Licinius Macer was aware of his danger, but he was supported in it by his very integrity as a doctrinaire. In emphasising the contrast and struggle between the poor and the rich he believed that he was working for what he called a " true " democracy. Thus he was more high-minded than Catiline was. Catiline's vigorous championship of the poor and the oppressed was motivated by personal ambition and by disappointed pride. As for myself, I saw that this agitation was necessary if we were to attain our aims, and in these years I gradually acquired a considerable influence and authority among the political clubs and among the poorer classes of the people. But I was careful not to give the impression of being a doctrinaire or a sentimentalist, and I was well aware that, in order to carry out any reforms successfully, it was necessary to have support not only from the people but from other elements in the state as well. I made my friends everywhere and in all classes. I believed that a combination of different interests could have at least one aim—that of efficiency—in common. And indeed this is a belief which I still hold, though events have forced me to modify it considerably. People cannot live without efficiency, but they are not prepared to die for it. On the other hand, they will gladly lay down or risk their lives for considerations of pride, ambition, envy, avarice or honour. Politics, in fact, must be adapted to passions as well as to events.

And in these early days of mine as a politician there were certainly times when I regarded all the speech-making in the forum, all the interviews and elaborate intrigues, as a kind of child's play. I had not forgotten my boyhood and my early youth. I knew, as everyone else did, that military force was the last word in politics. Yet still, I reflected, there were important differences in the way in which this last word could be uttered. Even military force, until matters had already gone very far, was not something necessarily or entirely brutal. It could be deployed effectively without even being put to active use. Also it was possible, I thought, for those who controlled military power to be bound together by personal and political ties strong enough to hold them back from civil war. Events, unfortunately, have shown that this theory of mine was mistaken.

In this period after my return from Asia, whenever, as frequently happened, the subject of military force and the possibilities of another civil war were mentioned in conversation, the first name always to occur would be that of Pompey. After the murder of Sertorius, Pompey had had little difficulty in dealing with the murderers. The loyalty of the Spanish troops had been rather to a man than to a cause and, even so far as the cause went, they saw in Perperna a most unworthy representative. Perperna, defeated and taken prisoner, attempted to buy his safety by producing all Sertorius's papers, which included correspondence from many people of importance in Rome who had, at one time or another, promised him their support if he would march on Italy. Pompey burned all this correspondence unread and had Perperna put to death immediately. He saw to it that these actions of his should be widely publicised in Rome, where they certainly produced a great effect. For, though the most reactionary elements in the senate were furious at having lost the opportunity to incriminate their enemies by means of the evidence which Pompey had destroyed, everyone else, and particularly those who were implicated in the correspondence, was delighted. Pompey's title " the Great " was on everyone's lips and it was now given a moral as well as a military connotation. His agents described him as a great and patriotic statesman, capable of acting above and beyond party in the interests of all. They even described him as merciful. And they made it clear that what he aimed at now, after his return and the triumph which was due to him, was the consulship itself. For this post he had, according to the constitution, none of the necessary qualifications. He was far below the age limit, and he had filled none of the offices of quaestor, aedile or praetor which, by custom and law, ought to have been held by all candidates for the consulship. It was an interesting situation and I saw at once how it could be used to further the aims of the Popular Party.

The situation rapidly became further complicated by the activities of Crassus, from whom all the time I continued to borrow money. But, as was to happen again in circumstances much more profitable to myself, the rivalry between Pompey and Crassus admirably served the purposes which I had in mind.

Ever since the battle of the Colline Gate, ten years before this time, Crassus had been looking for, but had failed to obtain, an important military command. He was now, in the year when Pompey was preparing to return from Spain, forty years old and held the position of praetor. He had been continually vexed by the successes of Pompey, a man six years younger than himself, and was particularly annoyed by the agitation in favour of allowing Pompey to stand for the consulship. However, he himself now at last received the opportunity for distinction for which he had been waiting. In a really critical situation with which other generals had failed entirely to cope he was given the supreme command against the large armies of revolted slaves led by Spartacus.

This Spartacus must have been a man of great ability. He had started his revolt with a mere seventy-four gladiators who, under his leadership, had escaped from the establishment in which they were kept at Capua. Within a year he had liberated slaves throughout the country and defeated two consular armies which had been sent against him. From his prisoners he had selected three hundred Romans and had forced them to fight in single combat for the amusement of his troops, many of whom had themselves been bought up by contractors to serve this very purpose of entertainment in Italian arenas. He was at liberty to march wherever he liked in Italy and he was credited with the purpose of actually moving against Rome. At this time people talked little of the victories of Pompey in Spain or of Lucullus in the East. The slave war was much too close to them and the war seemed to them merciless, dreadful and, in a way (since convention was so overthrown) obscene. How seriously the situation was regarded can be gauged from the fact that Crassus took the field with ten legions, a force as great as that with which, in later years, I conquered the whole of Gaul. And even with this enormous army he was not able to end the war easily or at once. Nor was this due to any incompetence on his part. In this campaign Crassus handled his troops with a skill and daring for which he has never received proper credit. The final battle, in which Spartacus himself was killed, was absolutely decisive. Crassus celebrated his victory with a singular and cruel ostentation. He had six thousand of his prisoners crucified and displayed at regular intervals along the whole distance of the Appian Way from Capua to Rome. I used sometimes to ride along this road and the sight of these bodies, first tortured and then rotting, was both appalling and, in a sense, instructive. They seemed to illustrate the horror of a war in which the conventions of society (in this case the obedience of slaves to their owners) have been destroyed, and the rottenness of a society in which so thorough a rupture of convention is possible. They illustrated, too, the massive and ruthless use of power which, in such circumstances, is alone effective.

Just before the final battle Pompey with his Spanish army had arrived in Italy. He was, as usual, eager for fresh honours and, with his immense popularity and prestige, had found it easy to get himself appointed as an associate commander with Crassus in the war against the slaves. By the time that he arrived anywhere near the scene of operations the war was over. He did, however, round up a certain number of fugitives and then issued the kind of proclamation which, more than anything else, might have been calculated to infuriate Crassus. " Crassus has defeated the rebels," was what he said, " but I have extirpated the rebellion." It was a foolish and untrue thing to say, characteristic of Pompey's irresistible vanity ; for he had no deliberate wish to make an enemy of Crassus. At the moment Pompey's one thought was his own glory and his only aim was to gain the consulship for the coming year.

Both he and Crassus now moved with their armies in the direction of Rome. The feelings of Crassus were not mollified by the news that the senate had decreed for Pompey a triumph because of his Spanish victory, and for himself the lesser honour of an ovation, because his own great victory had been won only against slaves. At this point Crassus also began to have his name put forward as a possible candidate for the consulship. As usual he acted with extreme caution, refusing to commit himself to any definite course; but he encouraged those members of the senate who were most opposed to Pompey to believe that his army could be used with the authority of the senate behind it in order to resist any illegal move that Pompey might make; and at the same time he was in communication, partly through my agency, with leaders of the popular party who, while somewhat frightened of Pompey, were chiefly concerned with breaking down the senate's opposition to the demand for the restoration of their rights to the tribunes.

There were thus three forces which had to be reckoned with —Pompey, Crassus and the senate, or rather that influential part of the senate which, for one reason or another, remained loyal to the constitution of Sulla and bitterly resented the idea of a young general, with no political or legal qualifications, becoming consul. I saw at once that no single one of these forces was strong enough to enforce its will, but that a combination of any two of them would prove irresistible. It was, naturally, in the interests of my own party that such a combination should be directed against the senate, and so we worked for an alliance between Pompey and Crassus. The situation was remarkably similar to that which arose nine years later, just before my own first consulship, though of course on that occasion I played a much greater part myself in the negotiations and as a result of them attained everything that I personally desired. If on either of these occasions the senate had shown an intelligent flexibility, the whole course of history would have been altered. Pompey was a commander of almost the first order, but as a politician he was inexpert. By nature he was conservative; he was very open to flattery; he could have been flattered and then used. However, the course of history at this period has been largely determined by the fact that the senate has been wholly blind both to the needs of the time and to the possibilities of asserting power.

Personally, I have never formed an alliance with anyone whom I regarded as an enemy. I have felt admiration, respect and even affection for both Pompey and Crassus. They, however, were undoubtedly anti-pathetic to each other and, when they acted together, they acted entirely from motives of self-interest. And on this occasion each had much to offer. To begin with, each was in control of an army. Then, while Pompey was immensely popular with the ordinary citizen, Crassus had power and influence with the moneyed classes. These classes were already angry with Lucullus who, after his victories in Asia, was successfully restraining the greed and extortion of their agents; and Pompey, whose thoughts were already turning towards the East, knew that the support of these financiers and business men would be most valuable to him when the time came to appoint a successor to Lucullus in the eastern command.

So an understanding was quickly reached between Pompey and Crassus. Pompey, who had no political ideas of his own, was forced to adopt those of the Popular Party, at least for the time being. He announced publicly that, if he were elected consul, one of his first acts would be to restore to the tribunes all the powers which had been taken from them by Sulla. The announcement was greeted with enormous enthusiasm. Sulla was still hated, but people forgot that Pompey's whole career had been founded on his collaboration with Sulla. Pompey now became, as it were overnight, a defender of the people's liberties. The pressure of public opinion and the existence of two armies at the gates of Rome had their effect on the senate. Decrees were passed to give Pompey the privilege of standing for the consulship without a single one of the necessary qualifications which had been sanctioned by tradition and carefully re-established by Sulla. And in due course Pompey and Crassus were elected.

Their year of office was a revolutionary year, as had been Sulla's last consulship ten years previously, and as was to be my own first consulship ten years later. But the revolution was carried out calmly and peaceably. Everyone seemed to have some reason for being pleased. The people were delighted by the restoration of their old powers to the tribunes ; the middle classes felt their interests safe in the hands of Crassus and, before the end of the year, were gratified by receiving once more the right to serve on juries in the law courts. This reform was carried through by my uncle, Lucius Cotta, who was praetor this year. He provided that, for the future, the juries in public trials were to be mixed. Only one-third were to be senators and the remaining two-thirds of the places were to go to people outside the senate with qualifications either of property or of administrative experience. These juries proved no more and no less corrupt than the old ones ; but the law courts did cease to be in the exclusive control of one class. Even the senate did not, for the moment, react violently against what amounted to the destruction of that absolute authority which Sulla had put into their hands and which, as events had shown, they had been unable to exercise. No doubt the more ambitious members realised that the new order would afford more scope for their personal ambitions, and all were relieved to find that this revolution (for so indeed it was) was taking place quietly, with no proscriptions and even with a touch of antiquarianism. For, after a lapse of sixteen years, Pompey and Crassus revived the office of censor. The two censors appointed were respectable nonentities who could be relied upon to follow the instructions of the consuls, and they expelled from the senate about sixty of its more disreputable members, including many who owed their position there entirely to the patronage of Sulla. The very legality of this measure, so different from the massacres of Marius and of Sulla, was widely approved, and not least by those senators who retained their seats.

This was in every respect a year of sensation. There were spectacles more brilliant than any which had been seen before. First came Pompey's triumph and later there was a prodigious public banquet organised by Crassus at which ten thousand tables were laid out and supplied lavishly with the best food and the rarest wines. Such bounty is certain to prove effective, and Crassus gained a popularity which he never enjoyed again. Yet even so, to his intense disgust, he found that his own popularity lagged far behind that of Pompey who, though he cut rather a poor figure in politics and indeed only mastered with difficulty the obvious conventions of behaviour in the senate, was surrounded by crowds of admirers whenever he showed himself in public and was given the sole credit for many of the popular reforms which had in fact been initiated by Crassus. By the end of the year the animosity between the two men was greater than ever, and for ten years to come it was to be one of the most important factors in the history of the times and the chief factor in the making of my own career.

CHAPTER VII

FUNERAL SPEECHES

As it was, my own career, as I was unhappily conscious, was only just beginning. At the elections which took place in the year after the consulship of Pompey and Crassus I stood for the position of quaestor and was duly elected. I would now be able to take my place in the senate and, after the proper intervals, to stand for the higher offices of aedile, praetor and consul. In other words, I was proceeding, at the normal age and in the conventional way, along the ordinary road to political advancement. Neither the conventionality nor the slowness of this progress pleased me in the least. I was now thirty-three years old. At this age Pompey had already commanded great armies and Alexander had conquered the world. As for me, I had been, it seemed, frustrated partly by events outside my own control, but partly also by deficiencies in my own character. I now began to feel both with regard to myself and to the world around me an almost overwhelming dissatisfaction which, while perhaps unreasonable, was not unnatural.

In a sense I had been unlucky. If Sulla had been defeated in the civil war, I, the nephew of Marius and the son-in-law of Cinna, should have been near the centre of power and certainly would have had some opportunity for exercising those abilities which I thought myself to possess. Yet I was bound to reflect that, even with regard to the limited opportunities which had come my way so far, my achievements had not been remarkable. I had, with no difficulty at all, won the affection and esteem of the late King of Bithynia ; I had carried out a daring and successful action against a pirate fleet ; I was popular in social gatherings; I had shown a certain skill in the management of political clubs and was, indeed, already something of a favourite with the people; I had a fairly high reputation as an orator and as a literary man; I was notoriously extravagant and, in spite of my deep affection for my wife and daughter, had engaged in a number of love affairs. The record was that of a brilliant wastrel, and it could encourage, in itself, no hopes whatever for the future. To have compared myself with Pompey at this time would have been, as I knew, ludicrous. Even Cicero, who had started life with none of my advantages, had by sheer hard work and the consistent cultivation of his talents by now become the leading barrister of the day and carried more weight in politics than I.

When I considered what my assets were, I found them to be very few. I had a respectable place in the College of Pontiffs and I was known as a somewhat eccentric demagogue. The work I had done with Licinius Macer in agitating for the restoration of full powers to the tribunes had had its effect, yet the whole credit for it had gone to Pompey. It seemed to me on the whole that my chief asset was in my very wide circle of intimate friends who were drawn from all classes of society and indeed from many nationalities, since I had been careful to remain in contact with most of those whose friendship I had enjoyed in Bithynia, Asia and Greece. These friends, I knew, could be useful to me, but only if I first were to become useful to myself.

It was in the year of my quaestorship that I became urgently and almost feverishly aware of this fact. Perhaps the feverishness of my attitude may be excused; for while I thought that I had in me the powers that make for greatness, I seemed to possess none of the means for exercising them, being burdened with tremendous debts, and being, in the view of all except my closest friends, a character of more interest than importance.

During this year I was, from time to time, the victim of terrible nightmares in which I found myself to be associating sexually with my own mother. These dreams were later explained by some partial priests in the temple of Hercules at Gades as indicating that, in the course of time, I would possess the earth —the earth being the mother of us all; and, of course, in later years this story has often been repeated. Such an explanation could deceive no one of any intelligence, and certainly did not deceive me at the time. The dreams, terrifying as they were, may rather have been evidence of my own instability at this period, and of a desire, felt if not acknowledged by most people at some difficult moments, to return, if at all possible, to what must be the only security known to human beings—that is to say the irresponsible existence of an infant. Certainly dreams like these seem to occur at periods, such as that of puberty, when the individual is suddenly confronted with something outside his past experience and from which, in some part of his mind, he shrinks. And for me this was a time when I felt peculiarly isolated. Not only did my general ambitions seem to be on all sides thwarted by superior material powers, but I suffered, in the space of a few months, two losses from within my own family. The deaths were those of my old Aunt Julia, the widow of Marius, and of my wife, Cornelia, the daughter of Cinna. Each death affected me profoundly, though in a different way.

It was natural that my Aunt Julia should have wished me to undertake the arrangements for her funeral. I was one of her closest living relatives and ever since the time that the head of her son, Young Marius, had been displayed and insulted over in Rome as one of Sulla's trophies, she had shown a particular interest in me, in my wife and in our daughter Julia, who was now a girl of about fifteen. She had approved of my action when by refusing to divorce my wife I had offended Sulla, and she had watched carefully, though with mixed feelings, my subsequent career. Her death brought suddenly back into my mind the thought and the imagination of many things which, in the hurry and excitement of my social and political life, I had tended to forget. Now I remembered, almost with a shock, the real greatness of that savage old man, my Uncle Marius, and I recalled again the horrors of the civil wars in which my late childhood and early youth had been spent. I reflected also upon the fact that the conflict in which Marius and Sulla had been engaged was still unresolved. There were still two parties in the state with mutually exclusive aims and interests, two opposing attitudes to the problems of government. Since personal ambition and family

rivalry played so great a part in Roman politics, it would have
been an over-simplification to suggest that on one side was a
narrow circle of oligarchs, jealous of their own privileges, averse
from innovation, discredited by the misuse they had made of the
supreme power put into their hands by Sulla, and that on the
other side was the whole population of Rome and Italy, the
legions, and those provincials who were rapidly acquiring Roman
manners and Roman speech. Yet, if such a picture could not be
described as accurate, it was not by any means entirely false.
Absent, however, from the present scene were the leaders
capable of, as it were, embodying in themselves the tension and
divergencies of the times. For, in the end, Pompey represented
nothing except himself and could as easily have been a leader of
the senate as of the Popular Party ; indeed he had already served
each in turn. Crassus, in spite of his great gifts and enormous
wealth, lacked the abilities to command devotion and to excite
surprise. I fancied that these and others were abilities which I
myself possessed.

The funeral of my Aunt Julia provided me with an opportunity both of doing her honour and of expressing my own
feelings. First I obtained permission to deliver in the forum a
a public speech in praise of the deceased. This was not a thing
done commonly at funerals and some diplomacy had to be used
before permission was granted. In particular I was able to quote
the precedent of one of my fellow pontiffs, Lutatius Catulus, a
rigid conservative, who had, thirty years previously, made a
public speech in honour of his mother at her funeral ; it was
also possible to secure the support of one of the consuls for the
year, Quintus Marcius Rex, another extreme conservative and a
cousin of my Aunt Julia, whose mother had come from the
ancient family of the Marcii Reges.

Once the necessary permission had been obtained, I proceeded to organise the ceremony with the greatest care. The
procession which made its way through crowds to the forum was
an unusually large one and the musicians and singers of dirges
and laments were the best available. Last came the wearers of
the death masks of the ancestors. These were specially trained

performers, chosen for the dignity of their bearing and their skill in the kind of mime appropriate for these occasions. But what, of course, produced by far the greatest impression of all was the appearance in this procession of an effigy of Marius himself, for no effigy or sign of him had been seen in Rome since the day when, by Sulla's orders, his ashes had been disturbed and thrown into the winds and water and all his statues overthrown. Now it was at first with the utter silence of amazement that people gazed at the lifeless shape of the great commander making its way again through the streets of the city. The image was decorated with all the insigna of a consul and wore the triumphal toga. It was escorted by lictors and by other performers bearing the names of his victories and the titles of honour that had been decreed for him. What was remarkable was that even the lifeless mask and even the solid wood of which the statue was constructed somehow gave an impression almost of reality, inspiring awe as Marius had inspired it in his lifetime.

After the initial silence of surprise, a few voices from the crowd could be heard raised in protest, the voices perhaps of some whose relatives had been destroyed by Marius in his last days or merely of those busybodies who tend to give tongue immediately at the appearance of anything that may be regarded as illegal (and, of course, it was, strictly speaking, illegal to parade the effigy of Marius, declared by Sulla and the senate an enemy of the Roman people, in public). There was a moment when I felt or half-felt that in making this demonstration I might have miscalculated, and that I should have experienced even this moment of doubt is a sign of how agitated my nerves must have been at this time. The moment was soon over. Suddenly and with one accord the whole crowd began to cheer and to go wild with a strange joy which I noted especially, since it seemed to indicate not merely excitement at a bold gesture, nor even a sentimental reverence for a great man unjustly used, but something deeper still—a gratitude, a relief, a pleasure at finding that honour was being done again to one whom, however in some ways mistakenly, they believed to have been their benefactor and their friend. Old men, veterans of the German campaigns, thrust themselves through the crowds and, with tears streaming from their eyes, kissed the garments in which the effigy of their general was clothed. Women shrieked in a kind of hysteria. Even the young, who had never seen the living Marius or only seen him in the savagery of his old age, joined in the demonstration. So great still was the power of my uncle, and I myself was pleased and interested to note that in the passage of time the faults of Marius, at least among the people, had been forgotten and that now he was being glorified not even so much for his virtues as for something else which he seemed to represent. What precisely this was it would be hard to say. It was something which had not been represented either by Sulla or by Pompey ; for, though their triumphs had been celebrated with enthusiasm, that enthusiasm had lacked the quality of warmth and of personal affection which was now aroused by the sight of the mere lifeless statue of Marius. It would seem that the people still regarded him as one of themselves and one who, having raised himself to greatness by his own exertions and their help, had not forgotten them, but remained faithful to what was not only obscure but strong in his own origins. Thus his savagery, his prejudices and his total incapacity as a politician had been forgiven him, and he was remembered only as the great commander whose very harshness to his troops was a sign of his affection towards them, as a man among men, capable of supporting with resolution every kind of hardship, a symbol and example of that great force within the people itself which, though nearly always dissipated, misdirected, distorted or deceived, still exists and, in the last resort, controls events.

So great had been the success of this demonstration that many people expected from me an inflammatory speech when the time came for me to make the oration in front of the dead body of my aunt which was surrounded on all sides by the living wearers of the ancestral death-masks, and among these, the great statue of Marius himself. I remembered, however, the proprieties of the occasion and my own interest. The ceremony was, after all, in honour of my Aunt Julia, and if I had devoted the whole of my speech to an attack on the enemies of Marius and to a declaration that I myself, the nephew of the great man, proposed to pursue his policies and recreate his party, I should have been guilty of a serious error in taste. Besides, such declarations were not necessary. The effect had already been produced by means of the procession. And so, though naturally I alluded from time to time to the victories and triumphs of my uncle, I dwelt chiefly upon the virtues of my Aunt Julia and upon her glorious ancestry which was, of course, also my own. I reminded my audience that my aunt, on her mother's side, was, through the Marcii Reges, descended from Ancus Martius, one of the early kings of Rome ; and that, on her father's side, she was of the family of the Julii, who traced their descent, through the goddess Venus, from the immortal gods. The boldness of my words and the deference which I paid to the dead greatly pleased the people and certainly proved that those friends of mine had been wrong who had urged me on this occasion to make little of my own aristocratic origins and instead to dwell upon the connection by marriage which bound me, through Marius, to the people. As it was, I had observed that one of the secrets of Marius's own popularity was that he had never at any time pretended to be anything other than he was. I myself was, unlike Marius, an aristocrat by birth, and it would have been not only lacking in grace to dissemble the fact, but also both disrespectful to the memory of my aunt and, in the long run, damaging to myself. I was well aware that the people, in their present mood, would be rather delighted than displeased to find me appearing not only as the champion of Marius but also as the descendant of gods and of Kings. Nor was my performance, though it was regarded as somewhat over-bold, greatly disapproved of in other quarters. The consul, Marcius Rex, for instance, while being scandalised by the effect produced by the effigy of Marius, was delighted by the reference which I had made to his own family.

It was, therefore, not difficult for me to obtain again, and within a few weeks, permission to make another public oration at a funeral, this time in honour of my wife, Cornelia, who had died before reaching the age of thirty. Never before had so young a woman had the distinction, after death, to be publicly praised in the forum, and in arranging for the ceremony and in delivering an appropriate speech, I certainly won again much favour from the people ; my action was regarded as the mark of a gentle and a loyal disposition. Yet I myself, while not unaware of the effect likely to be produced by this public funeral, was merely fulfilling the duties which I felt I owed to myself, my wife and my affection. Cornelia was the first woman whom I had loved and, in spite of my numerous infidelities, which had greatly distressed her, I loved her to the end. A sign of this may perhaps be found in the fact that I have never risked life or fortune, or indeed put myself to any considerable inconvenience, for any other woman, with the exception, in later years, of the Queen of Egypt ; and, in the case of Cleopatra, it must be said that I rather allowed my judgment to be blinded, thus becoming the victim of one of the few military surprises of my life, than that I deliberately accepted danger, as I did when I refused Sulla's order to divorce Cornelia.

I have known a considerable number of women. My interest in them never, I think, proceeded from depravity and not greatly from lust or self-interest. It has been rather a question of curiosity, of a passion to understand and to be understood, and, almost most important of all, a devotion to humanity when this humanity is seen stripped of many of its affectations, so that, even through what is, as it were, incrusted, something generous and divine appears. I am naturally both enticed and, in a sense, enthralled by adornment and by grace of manner ; yet these, to me, are nothing in the end, unless they are the signs or else, perhaps, the disguises of something different—something firm and, if not predictable, at least honest. This respect for personality has prevented me from becoming very often the victim of illusion or of fantasy ; I have been spared the sufferings felt by, for example, the poet Catullus, since it would have been quite impossible for me to have seen the loose, grasping and lustful Clodia in the role of a goddess or heavenly creature ; nor have I felt what were perhaps the greater sufferings of the poet Lucretius, who seems to have been unduly distressed by the fact that human bodies cannot, in the nature of things, melt entirely, one into the other. In my love affairs there has usually been an element of friendship, and this element remains long after the physical passion has died down. Moreover, my interest in human beings is such that I have been by no means restricted in the objects of my affections by any particularities of person, character or age. For example, shortly after the time of my quaestorship (or it may have been a little before) I entered into a love affair with the wife of Crassus, who, though twenty years my senior, proved a most agreeable companion.

Yet on this sad occasion of my wife's funeral I was far from congratulating myself upon or analysing my career as a lover of other women. I thought naturally of the great love which had existed between Cornelia and myself in the early days, of the devotion into which it had ripened, and of our daughter who, I thanked the gods, was still alive. The speech which I made at her funeral was modest, affectionate and sincere. I dwelt on her private virtues rather than upon her family connections, and if, from time to time my voice came near to breaking, this was no expedient of oratory. Yet in my sorrow for her I felt also, as I had felt before at the funeral of my aunt, sorrow for myself and a profound nervous disturbance and dissatisfaction. For I would have wished Cornelia to have been able to see me as something different and something which I was not yet. Now her death, greatly as I deplored it, seemed curiously to have set me free, unloosening some bond which had tied me to infancy and early youth. Yet this was not a liberation into a state of peace, but rather into a world of conflict and hostility. From now on I began to plan my moves steadily and with care. While always ready for the necessary and sudden improvisation, I set myself deliberately to shape events and to use for my own ends the abilities and resources and discontents of others. It was in these years and not, as has been thought, at a later period that I took part in designs for revolution ; for in these years I was filled with an impatience (which I was careful, so far as possible, to hide) since constantly I was harried by the thought that, in the making of my life and the shaping of my surroundings, I had left things too late.

BOOK THREE

CHAPTER I

THE TEMPLE OF GADES

DIRECTLY after the funeral of Cornelia I set out for Further Spain, where I was to serve as quaestor under the governor, Antistius Vetus. I had to borrow heavily in order to pay off some proportion of my debts before I left Rome.

On my way to Spain I took the opportunity of visiting the cities and making friends with some of the leading citizens of Cisalpine Gaul. I was to get to know this region between the Po and the Alps much better in later times, since it was to be the main recruiting ground for my legions. But at this time I was chiefly interested in exploiting the political feelings of its inhabitants. At first sight they seemed a mixed lot. There were Etruscans and tall fair-haired Gauls dressed, most curiously, in trousers; there were Illyrians, a few Germans and numbers of Raetians who worshipped strange gods with unpronounceable and unintelligible names; and there were large numbers of Italians who had moved from the south into this rich and fertile area as settlers, traders, lawyers and officials. Even at this time the province was very largely Romanised, and many of the great towns compared favourably in architecture, wealth and amenities with the cities of the south. The children of the leading citizens, whether of Italian or local origin, received as good an education as was available in Rome. I found remarkable evidence of this when I was staying, for the first time, at the house of one of the chief men in Verona, a certain Valerius Catullus. This man's son, later to become the great poet, was at this time scarcely twenty years old. He was a charming boy and one of the most learned that I have ever met. I was amused to find that he regarded me as absurdly old-fashioned because I did not entirely share his enthusiasm for the Greek Alexandrine poets.

However, it was politics rather than literature which interested me during my short stay in Verona and in the other northern cities. I found everywhere and in all classes a discontent with the present status of the province and a demand for the full rights of Roman citizenship already possessed by the rest of Italy. It was natural for me to support this demand. I met many leaders of the agitation and I pointed out to them that the time might be appropriate for more definite action than the mere sending of deputations to Rome. The armies that had been raised for Spain and for the war with Spartacus had now been either disbanded or sent overseas to join the forces of Lucullus in Asia. It seemed to me that the mere threat of an armed uprising across the Po might, at this particular moment, be sufficient to force from the senate all the concessions that were desired. I went with some detail into the plans necessary for organising such a revolt, not with the intention of beginning a civil war, but rather of making the kind of demonstration which would be successful without bloodshed. I was of course aware that a success of this kind would be of the greatest value politically to me personally. Before going on to take up my appointment in Spain I arranged means by which I could keep in touch with my friends in the northern cities and promised that, if and when the situation demanded it, I would, later in the year, return and take part in whatever action seemed appropriate.

So I set out for Spain, a province which at all times has greatly interested me and in which some of the most critical events of my life were to take place. I was interested in the country partly because of the extreme contrast which it afforded, both geographically and in many other ways, with the eastern limits of the Empire which I knew already. In Spain at this time was to be found none of the luxury and little of the culture which pervaded the East; nor were the prospects in every direction so usefully extensive; for, though only a narrow strait separates Spain from Africa and to the north beyond the mountains were the various and still unexplored tribes of Aquitania and Gaul, the whole of the west faces that completely unknown ocean into which Sertorius had once planned to sail in search of the Islands of the Blest. Yet even here, at the limits of the habitable world, there were marks everywhere of the greatness of men and cities and of their power to stamp something of their own likeness on events and even on geography. There were the high walls of the Greek city of Saguntum which for some time had resisted Hannibal, and there were evidences, too, though most of them had been destroyed, of the occupation of the country by Hannibal himself. More immediately interesting and important was what still remained of the influence of Sertorius. I was able to speak to many who had known him well, whether as friends or enemies, and I gained the most vivid impression of this great man who, if genius alone counted for success, above all men deserved to have succeeded. Though I was profoundly interested in accounts of Sertorius's military career, of his methods of training troops, his personal relations with men and officers, his system of intelligence, his improvisations and his strategy, what impressed me even more at this time was the amazing political achievement of the man. For Sertorius, an alien in a foreign country, had from his devoted Spanish followers organised something very like a Roman state just at the time when he was at war with the Government in Rome itself. Thus he had strengthened not only himself but the province also. Moreover, the success of his policy had forced his opponents, when they were intelligent, to adopt or to pretend to adopt some of his own methods. Pompey, for instance, in his attempts to detach leading Spaniards from Sertorius, had offered them, among other bribes, the rights of Roman citizenship.

One of those who received the citizenship in this way was Balbus, a native of the city of Gades and a man of about my own age. I had already met him in Rome, where he had gone after the end of the Sertorian war, and had begun with him the long friendship which still exists between us. Balbus has always been remarkable for his intelligence. In these days he was remarkable also for his beauty and was soon to become remarkable for his wealth, since he was adopted by a rich Greek financier from

Mytilene, who left him his entire fortune. It was largely because of Balbus that, during this period of my service in Spain, I took a special interest in the great city of Gades. Though this city, in its age, wealth, prospect and diversity of cultures and manners, was interesting enough on its own account. It was said to have been founded a thousand years ago, when Rome was not even a village, by colonists from Tyre and even now the coinage is of a Phoenician type. Its great wealth came from trade not only in the Mediterranean but with the African coast beyond the Pillars of Hercules and with the northern islands which in later years I was to visit and from which the merchants of Gades imported tin and gold. It was from Gades that the great Carthaginian general, Hamilcar Barca, the father of Hannibal, had set out to conquer Spain and to build up the force with which his son so nearly conquered Rome. From Gades, not so long ago, Sertorius had planned to sail out into the unknown ocean in an attempt to discover the Islands of the Blest. Later it became the base for the Roman army under Metellus operating against Sertorius from the south, and from its harbour, in future years, I myself was to launch a fleet into the Atlantic. Moreover, the inhabitants, the architecture of their city, even the landscape itself seemed suitable to the richness and diversity of so long a history. The merchants, among whom, as was my custom, I made many friends, were most various in their appearance and outlook, of mixed Phoenician, Greek or Spanish stock. Their ideas were both firm and adventurous, befitting a race who for so long had held this outpost secure and strong, though surrounded by savage tribes, who had absorbed different civilisations, while still retaining the original impetus for exploration and for self-assurance. In their temples and perhaps in their religious ceremonies there was often something heavy and barbaric, a Punic vehemence, something capable of being appalling, as indeed might be expected in a place where, under the Carthaginian occupation and even later, human sacrifices had not been uncommon. An African glare and brutality seemed to mingle with something softer and more wise, perhaps an inheritance of Tyre and of the Asiatic east; nor were these the only elements to be noticed. There was also a stubbornness and, as it were, a realism that might proceed from the place itself and from its ancient inhabitants. And together with all this there could be observed, like a glow lightening a surface and giving radiance, traces of that only humane civilisation of which we know, the civilisation of Greece.

It was in Gades that I was confronted with one vestige of this radiance and also, it must be said, of something different and, perhaps, less beautiful, though also important, namely an absolutely outstanding glory. For in the temple of Hercules in this Spanish Atlantic town someone had erected a statue of Alexander the Great. The statue was not remarkable in itself, though, like most statues of Alexander, it was immediately recognisable, in its grace, lightness and in a certain tension in the muscles of the neck, for what it was. Here was a beauty more piercing than that of Pompey, more feminine, in a way, and much more intellectual. In contemplating it I was aware that here, in the furthest of all known cities in the west, I was gazing at the likeness of one who had led his victorious armies through Asia, Mesopotamia, Persia, Bactria and Sogdiana; who had carried the language and science and thought of the Greeks from Macedonia to beyond the Indus; who had founded cities and dynasties; who, through the oracle of Ammon, had been declared a god; who had accomplished all this, and died, before he had reached the age at which I myself now was.

The grace and beauty of the image, the rapidity, certainty and brilliance of the real man's achievement, all combined together to produce the most powerful effect upon my mind. Much later I have suffered occasionally from epileptic fits. On this occasion also I was conscious of the approach of some kind of convulsion, though it was in outward appearance more decent and ordinary than these attacks. I burst into tears and for some moments had to be supported by the friends and attendants who were with me. When I came to myself and was asked to explain my behaviour, I remarked simply that I had wept at the thought of the contrast between my own life, which had effected so little, and that of Alexander who, at my age, had conquered the world.

This was, in a sense, true; but it was only part of the truth. What had struck me with a force that was almost overwhelming was something harder to put into words than a mere comparison between myself, with little or no title to fame, and a man who, at my own age, had deservedly won an everlasting glory. For a moment I seemed to see in the recesses of history, in the imagination of the dead, something surprising and of extreme beauty. My emotion was not unlike that which can be stirred in us by certain lines, daring and appropriate, of poetry. Such lines will fill us not only with admiration and delight, but with a kind of love. They will bring space and time together; years and distances will be at the same time magnified and made intimate. So to me this figure of Alexander, an effigy on the Atlantic coast, represented the far strides and the precision of genius, its impact upon millions of men, on cities, on the thought and organisation of a world—a world, too, which existed, not in words, however perfect, but in flesh and blood. Certainly I noted with dismay the disparity between myself at this time and the great Alexander as he had been and was; yet what moved my tears was admiration and delight and love in the contemplation of what seemed to be a kind of perfection.

It was in this same temple of Hercules at Gades that the priests attempted to interpret those disquietening dreams which I had had of a guilty love with my own mother. Their theory that these dreams were an indication that I would one day rule the world was not logically tenable; yet still it fitted in with my mood. From this time forward I began consciously to aim at power. Not that I envisaged yet that absolute power which later was to become mine. I wished merely to be the first man in the state and to transform the state in the direction of my own ideas. I saw, too, that, in order to reach the height at which I aimed, I should have to act not only with resolution, but with a kind of duplicity. I should have to make political alliances with others richer and more powerful than myself and to be content still, for some years, to appear as a subordinate. Yet I would neglect no opportunity of coming forward with policies which could be called my own, and I would not be afraid of carrying them through by violence, so long as I was certain that any violent action which I took would be successful.

Indeed, before my year of service in Spain was over I obtained leave of absence and returned to Italy with the intention of organising an armed uprising among the people north of the Po. I had remained in close contact with my friends in those parts and also in Rome. The news I received from them made me convinced that the time had come for carrying out the plans which I had discussed earlier in the year with leading men in the northern cities. For Italy was now almost denuded of troops. Two legions were standing by, ready to embark for the east. Once they had set sail it seemed possible that a well-organised rising in the north might achieve its object with little or no difficulty. I knew that in the senate Crassus would support the claims of the Cisalpines to full citizenship and I thought that, with a little diplomacy, Pompey could be persuaded to support us also. But first it was necessary to organise the revolt in an efficient and orderly manner. I therefore proceeded directly from Spain to the northern cities, which I found already in a state of anticipation and ferment. I made many speeches and I also busied myself in concerting plans for a simultaneous rising in all the cities, for the immediate occupation of various strongpoints and for the taking of other measures that seemed necessary. The operation, in fact, was well planned. However, it was frustrated. On this occasion the senate, and in particular my relative, the consul Marcius Rex, acted with unusual speed and efficiency. As soon as they received reports of the successful agitation which I was carrying out, they cancelled the orders for the embarkation of the legions for the east and made it clear that they were holding them in readiness to deal with any trouble that might break out in the north. It was clear that our plans could now only be carried out by means of a civil war and that in such a war the odds would be very greatly against us. There was nothing to be done except to cancel the arrangements we had made and to continue the agitation for the citizenship by more constitutional methods in Rome.

CHAPTER II

POMPEY AND LUCULLUS

When I returned to Rome from Spain and the north I busied myself once again, as was necessary, in Roman politics. After the lapse of a year I should be eligible to stand for one of the higher magistracies and I proposed to stand for the curule aedileship. Holders of this office, with their responsibilities for organising games and festivals and for the restoration or development of public buildings, have excellent opportunities for increasing their power and influence in the state. I had no doubt of my own abilities to win distinction both by architectural improvements in the city and by the giving of splendid shows. Here my only difficulty would be lack of money, and I was prepared to borrow, if I could, as much as I owed already. Crassus would, I knew, finance me up to a certain point, but I needed other backers as well and, in order to get elected to the office at all, I needed the widest support that I could obtain.

It was partly for these reasons that, soon after my return from Spain, I married another wife. Here my choice surprised many of my friends, yet the marriage, if in the end not wholly satisfactory, had much to commend it. My new wife, Pompeia, was, in fact, the granddaughter of Sulla. Her father, who had married one of Sulla's daughters, had been consul with him in the year of the first march on Rome. Pompeia herself was young and attractive and, at least so far as the events of her early childhood were concerned, somewhat pathetic. Her brother had been killed by the supporters of Marius and Sulpicius in the riots that took place during her father's consulship. Soon afterwards, when Sulla had set out for the East, her father was appointed to

supersede Strabo, the father of Pompey the Great, in command
of an army. Strabo, however, rather than give up his command,
arranged to have his successor murdered. Pompeia, therefore,
grew up without natural protectors and some of the elder
members of her family who survived at the time I married her
were most averse to the match. Not only was I connected
with Marius, but my own reputation, in spite of my position in
the College of Pontiffs, was that of a popular agitator. Some of
my own friends, too, attempted to dissuade me from this
marriage by pointing out that it would weaken the basis of my
popular appeal as one who was attempting to recreate the party
of Marius. These arguments did not seem to me cogent. While
it was true that I hated Sulla personally and his whole policy, it
is ungenerous to extend such an enmity as this to those who have
nothing to do with the policy and no deliberate connection with
its author. I was already, for instance, a close friend of one of
Sulla's nephews. Moreover, though there was a sense in which
I wanted to become the inheritor of Marius, I had no wish at
all to be his precise imitator. I was more impressed by my
mother's objections. She, not altogether unjustly, regarded
Pompeia as an unreliable and inefficient character who would
need watching.

Nevertheless, I was attracted to Pompeia myself and I could
see solid advantages in the support which I was likely to receive
from her family once the marriage had taken place. Pompeia,
too, was very eager to marry me, partly from a genuine, if short-
lived, affection and partly from motives of unreasonable vanity
which induced her to want to be the wife of one so notorious for
his love affairs with other women. She had no conception of the
impulse which was now driving me in the direction of power.
What she admired in me was my reputation as a lover and as a
man of fashion; she was not even aware of the extent of my
debts. Nevertheless the union was, for a short time, agreeable,
and Pompeia's family loyally used their influence on my behalf
when the time came for me to stand as a candidate for the curule
aedileship.

Before this, however, the whole political situation had been transformed by the successful ambition of Pompey—the last, the most powerful and yet in some ways the least impressive of those great figures which in my lifetime, and until I took up the position myself, have occupied the centre of the stage of history. Indeed, from my earliest childhood events seem to have been centred in and reflected by great personalities—Marius, Sulla, Lucullus, Pompey, Crassus, even Cicero—yet there has been, as it were, an undercurrent of more final importance than those characters, and scarcely perceived by any of them. Some historians have been found to speak of " the necessities of history," and, in this instance, they may invent " a force " making towards monarchy. The words are not entirely meaningless, though these " necessities " and " forces " are nothing but a convenient way of expressing the little we know of that enormous complexity of individual and communal interests, ambitions, thoughts, needs, hopes and deprivations which constitute the life we live and form the conditions within which, from time to time, an exceptional person can in political life exercise a degree of freedom. Again it is a commonplace to say that this period is a period of transition, that our times are revolutionary. It is less easy to understand the times and to guide them in a profitable rather than in an unprofitable direction. All guidance is dangerous and a lack of guidance is disastrous. In these times efficiency and often survival demand a concentration of power ; yet the holder of this power is regarded more jealously than he would ever have been in other and happier times when his supreme authority was not absolutely necessary. He can scarcely be said to be safe unless he is with his army. I am not safe now, though in a day or two I shall be safe, since I have never commanded a soldier who would betray me. And in some cases the jealousy (though jealousy itself is an unworthy feeling) is not without reason. For there is nothing good in itself in holding power and nothing finally glorious in making a limited use of it. What is needed is not merely the solution of a particular and pressing problem ; it is the transformation of the whole scene into something different. Such an aim, if one examines it closely, may well appear to be an impossibility. However the scene is changed, the actors will remain much the same ; nor would an intelligent man even desire to alter habits overnight. If one has any respect for one's civilisation (and without that one would not act at all) one must, up to a point, insist upon its continuity. And indeed a revolution so thoroughgoing as to constitute quickly a complete break with the past can only be accomplished by means of massacre on an enormous scale. This was the plan of Catiline, who wished to assassinate the entire senate except for a very few, amongst whom Crassus and myself were to be included. Such a plan is not only inhumane, but inefficient. The senate is a venerable institution, and though it is true that throughout my lifetime it has almost invariably adopted mistaken policies and resisted necessary measures, it still contains even now the vast majority of those who possess any real experience of administration or of leadership in war. I have no doubt that the senate must continue to exist as a school for statesmen. But it must be a disciplined school, as it was in the remote past when it was faced with obvious and compelling danger. To-day the dangers are less obvious ; no Hannibal exists. But they are more compelling than ever. The economic, military and administrative problems of our empire cannot be handled by rival cliques or divided interests. Yet still the central power must admit liberty and be responsive to human passions, though certainly some passions must be restrained and the name of liberty must not be accorded to the irresponsible play of personal ambition.

All this may appear perfectly obvious, although no one will pretend that it is easy to carry out in practice the essential aims of combining liberty with authority, revolution with continuity, discipline with initiative. Yet hardly a single statesman of my time seems to have ever made these obvious reflections or to have attempted to estimate the needs of the times and the conditioning factors of our situation. Crassus, I suppose, showed some understanding of them ; Catiline took an exaggerated and partial view of them ; Cicero a view that was, on the whole, literary and sentimental ; while Pompey, in spite of his enormous influence and outstanding administrative ability, had no notion of them at all.

The quite extraordinary luck which followed Pompey almost until the end of his career is not, therefore, an argument that can be used by those who like to believe in the existence of a beneficent Providence. Had the gods been interested in preserving Rome, they would not have put such enormous power into the hands of a man who was, on the whole, incapable of using it except in the most conventional way. Yet so remarkably did events seem always to play into Pompey's hands that it was natural for people to believe that he had been in some way miraculously chosen as a deliverer.

For the two years since his consulship Pompey had been unemployed, and during these years Lucullus in the east had gone from victory to victory. It was reported that at Tigranocerta in Armenia he had killed a hundred thousand of the enemy at the expense of five Roman wounded and two dead—an unlikely story, but it was believed. Certainly it is incontestable that Lucullus was, in all respects except one, a commander of supreme genius. He was also an admirable administrator and had, in the reconquered provinces of Asia, done much to relieve the population from the crushing oppression of Roman tax collectors. By so doing he had made himself hated by most of the powerful business interests in Rome. Since he had been a close friend of Sulla and was a reactionary in politics he was also, of course, attacked by leaders of the popular party. He was accused of prolonging an unnecessary war simply in order to enrich himself. Pompey who, above all things, wanted this command for himself, began to associate himself both with Lucullus's critics in the popular party and with those Roman financiers who conceived that their interests were being threatened by good government.

The senate, for a variety of reasons, wavered. Some senators were merely jealous of Lucullus's achievements ; others were deeply implicated with the financiers ; others feared that, if they continued to support an unpopular general, they would be forced in the end to give way to Pompey, whom they still could not forgive for his two triumphs and his consulship which had been awarded to him so unconventionally. They ended by doing what, from the point of view of their own interests, was the worst thing possible. They failed to back up the only first-rate commander in existence who could be counted upon to be always loyal to their own order, and they still further alienated Pompey from themselves. Other commanders, noted rather for their conservatism than for their military abilities, were sent out to replace Lucullus. There followed a mutiny among Lucullus's troops, just when they were at the height of their victories. This, too, was a sign of the times. For Lucullus, with every other quality that a general could wish to have, lacked that one quality which, in our days, is the most important of all. He was ignorant of human nature, was unable to draw upon its strength and scorned to play upon its weaknesses. He rightly asked much of his men, but gave them nothing in return—neither the assurance of comradeship which Marius and I have given to our troops nor the pleasures and excitements of that cynical kind of irresponsibility which Sulla used to display in his deliberate alternations between the strictest and the laxest discipline. Lucullus, in fact, relied on a kind of discipline which has become obsolete. In our days soldiers demand at least the illusion of being treated as human beings.

Had Lucullus received proper support from the senate and from his own friends, this mutiny would not have been serious. As it was he was abandoned by the government at home and was violently attacked in the army itself by his brother-in-law, young Clodius, who was at this time at the height of his great, if somewhat effeminate, beauty and was just beginning his career as a popular agitator. So for more than a month Lucullus could do nothing with his men and had the bitter experience of watching Mithridates, whose main armies had already been destroyed, winning back almost unopposed much of the ground which he had lost. Once again people began to speak in Rome of the danger from the east.

At the same time there was trouble even nearer home. The pirate fleets were now far more formidable than they had been at the time when I was captured on my way to Asia. They were better organised and more numerous ; and they had begun deliberately to attempt to strangle Rome by interrupting her supplies. They had destroyed a consular fleet in the harbour of Ostia; their raiding parties would intercept convoys not only on the seas but even on the roads of Italy where they ran anywhere near the coast. The prices of food were rising every day and there was also a scarcity of money, since the Roman business men were being deprived of the profits of their investments abroad. Both they and the poorer classes were united in demanding vigorous action.

It was a situation which seemed designed to suit the ambition of Pompey and Pompey made use of the situation cleverly. At the beginning of the year after my return from Spain, the tribune Gabinius, a personal friend of Pompey's, proposed a law providing that a supreme commander for the whole Mediterranean area should be appointed, that this commander should be given an enormous financial subsidy, a fleet of two hundred ships, an unlimited army and powers extending not only over the sea but over all the coasts for fifty miles inland. The name of Pompey was not originally mentioned; but it was clear to everyone that no one but he could hold the post.

This proposal of Gabinius was, as events were to show, an excellent one. It was enthusiastically supported both by the people and by all representatives of financial interests except Crassus who, though he stood to gain much from the suppression of piracy, would even rather have lost money than see Pompey given such extensive power. The senate was bitterly opposed to the bill. Leading statesmen such as Catulus and the great orator Hortensius went about declaring that it amounted to the setting up of a monarchy and the final destruction of liberty. They failed to observe that, though Pompey was being given adequate powers for setting up a monarchy, he had neither the inclination nor the ability to do so; and by " liberty " they meant little more than a perpetuation of the system by which limited commands were held in rotation by members of their own order. Marcus Cicero, who shared many interests with the financiers and who had already the highest reputation as an orator, might have been expected to support the bill. However, he remained silent. He intended to stand for the praetorship this year and wished to do nothing that might offend. So it happened that I was the only member of the senate who spoke in favour of Gabinius's proposal. For this action I was reproached by some members of the senate and described as a mere demagogue and a traitor to my class. In fact, though I certainly planned to secure the people's favour by supporting the bill, I saw rather farther ahead. I realised that the extraordinary command which was to be given to Pompey by a vote of the Roman people and against the wishes of the senate would create a useful precedent. As I pointed out to Crassus, who was particularly alarmed at the idea of what he called Pompey's dictatorship, the world extends beyond the coasts of the Mediterranean. There was Spain, for instance, there were the unsubdued and unexplored districts of Gaul and Germany; and there was the Kingdom of Egypt which might, by somewhat straining the terms of the will of a recent monarch, be annexed by Rome. This was a position of the very greatest strategic and economic importance. Any Roman statesman who could secure from the Roman people a commission to subdue and hold this area would be able to talk to Pompey on equal terms. Crassus was impressed by this argument, but even so his jealousy of Pompey was so great that he could not bring himself to say a word in favour of Gabinius's bill.

As I had expected, the bill became law in spite of every effort made by the senate to prevent this happening. Pompey set to work at once and I am inclined to think that this campaign of his against the pirates was the most brilliant one of his whole career. Within two or three months the whole sea was cleared of pirate ships and for the future freedom of navigation was secure. Though Pompey himself liked to consider his actions as uniformly spectacular, his real distinction was as an administrator, and it was as a result of the most careful and painstaking administration that this great victory was won. The result was certainly spectacular enough. Those who had supported the proposal of Gabinius could now point to an operation which had been more successful than anyone could have imagined possible. Those, on the other hand, who had claimed that such powers vested in one man would lead to a dictatorship could point to the fact that, at the conclusion of his rapid campaign, Pompey was showing no signs of being willing to lay down his command. Instead he was waiting in Asia to hear the results of the agitation being conducted during the winter in Rome by another agent of his, the tribune Manilius. At the beginning of January Manilius was to propose another law to the effect that Pompey should, while retaining his present command, be also entrusted with the supreme command in Asia against Mithridates. It was a proposal which would give Pompey at least twice as much power as he possessed already and would allow him to extend this power almost indefinitely. It was not surprising that in the senate old Catulus and others protested violently. This proposal, they said, meant the end of the republic and the domination of the world by one man. Events have shown that there was some truth in this view of theirs ; their only mistake lay in imagining that this one man would be Pompey ; for, if a man is unable or unwilling to use power except for limited ends, it does not matter how much power is put into his hands.

As in the previous year and for the same reasons I spoke in favour of the extension of Pompey's command. So, on this occasion, did Cicero, who had now been elected praetor and was anxious to increase his own popularity with the people and with the rich men outside the senate, most of whom were enthusiastic supporters of Pompey. Indeed, Cicero's speech was one of the cleverest he has ever made. In the course of it he succeeded in flattering almost everybody.

The result of the voting on the proposal of Manilius was a foregone conclusion. One year after Pompey had received his exceptional command against the pirates he was entrusted with another command which was even greater. Never in our history had such an extent of territory, such military and naval power been under the control of one man. Pompey received the news for which he had been waiting in Asia. Even his friends were somewhat disgusted by the way he took it. He is said, while reading the dispatches from Rome, to have sighed, to have wrinkled up his handsome brow, to have complained of the fate which drove him to greatness and to have declared that in fact all he wanted was to live quietly in the country with his wife. This story deceived nobody. And so far as his wife Mucia was concerned, I personally had the best of reasons for knowing that it was untrue. My relations with Mucia must have started at about this time. I was also intimate with the wife of Gabinius ; and from both these ladies I learned much which confirmed my own estimate of Pompey's character.

Indeed, Pompey revealed his character clearly enough himself soon after he took up his new command. This was on the occasion when a meeting had been arranged between him and Lucullus in Asia. It appears that at first these two great generals had attempted to be polite to each other. However, the facts of the situation, of character and of training were too much for them. Real power was in Pompey's hands, and it was not like Pompey to dissemble the fact. He refused to ratify any of Lucullus's wise arrangements for the administration of conquered territory and he succeeded in detaching from him the greater part of his army. Lucullus could only retort by means of words, and his words were bitter. Pompey, he said, was acting as he always had done. Like a vulture he was coming to pick the carcase of yet another war. So he had behaved in Spain, where the credit was due to Metellus and not to him. So he had behaved with regard to Spartacus. And so now he would claim the glory of conquering Mithridates, whose effective force had already been destroyed.

After a number of undignified scenes in which sufficient truth was spoken on both sides to enflame tempers to the uttermost, Lucullus returned to Rome for his well deserved triumph. He did not receive even this honour until several years later. It was scarcely surprising, therefore, that he withdrew himself more and more from politics, and indeed scarcely intervened in them at all except on those occasions when he was able to do harm to Pompey. He, too, was a sign of the times, and in the final ineffectiveness of Lucullus one may see, I think, the collapse of the whole system of ideas which was associated with Sulla. Lucullus was a better general and a more consistent politician than either

Sulla or Pompey. Why did he fail? One can only say that he was out of date. He devoted most of the rest of his life to landscape gardening, to the breeding of fish and thrushes for the table, and to the organisation of splendid, though tasteful, entertainments.

Meanwhile, in the east Pompey began almost immediately to reap the rewards of what Lucullus had already accomplished either by fighting or by diplomacy. There was little serious fighting; but in six months he had driven Mithridates to the Caucasus. News of his successes arrived every day in Rome. But at this time I myself was thinking of the next elections and of how, if elected, I could support the expenses of the curule aedileship.

CHAPTER III

A CONSPIRACY

THE NEXT six years were years of violence and of threatened revolution. In the course of them there was one occasion at least when my life was in danger and there were many occasions when I faced the possibility of complete political ruin. As it happened, my power and influence throughout this difficult period grew so remarkably that by the end of it I was able to negotiate with Pompey and Crassus on more or less equal terms.

Throughout most of this time I was very closely associated with Crassus. He helped me in my election expenses and, in the summer of the year when Pompey took up his command in the east, I was duly elected curule aedile. I was then thirty-six years old. Before the beginning of the next year, when I was to take up office, I borrowed still more money since I was determined to make my tenure of this post a memorable one. Crassus and Catulus were appointed censors for this year, and Crassus had promised that he would arrange for me to be given the responsibility of restoring and beautifying the Appian Way. This also would cost money; for though I should receive an allowance from the treasury, I intended to spend much more on this great road than the money which was likely to be allotted to me.

But before the time came for me to embark on any of these undertakings I became involved, at least to some extent, in a conspiracy. It was an absurd conspiracy and bore the stamp of Catiline's impetuosity rather than of Crassus's foresight; yet Crassus was implicated in it too.

Crassus himself, in all his ambitious and intelligent political planning, tended to act in a manner more characteristic of a financier than of a statesman. Something in his nature or training made him tend always to dissemble his aims and to work for them, so far as he could, through the agency of others. He took great pains to acquire the reputation of being a respectable and moderate character; he was often (as I have every reason to know) generous to those who owed him money; he was a good speaker and carried much weight in the senate where he made no secret of his dislike and fear of the great powers which had been given to Pompey. Yet all the time Crassus, much more deliberately than Pompey, was planning to undermine the authority of the senate and to gain for himself supreme power. In these plans of his he made use of agents who were neither respectable nor scrupulous and whom he often had to disown. His methods were devious and often appeared contradictory; but his final aim never changed. It was to secure for himself or for some other person on whom he could rely a great independent command either in Italy, in Spain or in Egypt, so that he would be in a position to confront Pompey on equal terms. It is ironical to reflect that when, in the end and through my agency, he did obtain his objective, it was to cost him his life.

Pompey had gained his great commands by means of direct appeals to the people. This still seemed to me the most likely way of attaining the ends which we had in view. But Crassus, again like a financier, wished to have many irons in the fire at once. In particular he wanted to have in office consuls who could be regarded as dependents of his. During these years he must have spent quite prodigious sums on the consular elections.

The plans were carefully laid even before the election at which I became curule aedile. If at this time the candidates supported by Crassus were elected to the consulship, it was proposed to bring in laws which would put in our control both Spain and Egypt. An ambitious, dissolute and, as it turned out, inefficient young man, Cnaeus Piso, was to be appointed to Spain. I myself was to have the commission of occupying Egypt. And, to make our position stronger still, Crassus himself, in his capacity of censor, was to bring forward a resolution for giving the franchise to the northern Italians beyond the Po. Had all these plans been carried out successfully, we should have had at our disposal a power which would have been as great as Pompey's own and which would have had the advantage of being based centrally on Rome.

One of the candidates for the consulship supported by Crassus this year was Catiline. It was only at about this time that I got to know him well and I should probably have avoided him entirely had he not seemed for a short period likely to be the man who would most capably advance our interests and, in particular, gain for me the commission to annex Egypt. As a matter of fact Catiline was not without good qualities. He was loyal to his friends and possessed very great courage, both physical and, if one can use such a word of him, moral. Like myself he came from an impoverished patrician family. From the beginning he had been determined to raise himself to greatness and from the beginning had acted with a complete lack of scruple. He had fought with distinction on the side of Sulla and during the terror had enriched himself at the expense of Sulla's victims. He had been lucky to retain his place in the senate when, during the consulship of Pompey and Crassus, so many of Sulla's partisans had been deprived of their seats by the censors. Probably even then Crassus had decided that Catiline might be useful to him in the future. So, with his debts constantly increasing, he had reached the position of praetor and, in the year of Pompey's campaign against the pirates, had held the governorship of Africa. Here he had extorted great sums of money from the provincials and, on his return to Rome, was threatened with legal proceedings. However, as an officially recognised candidate for the consulship, he hoped to have these proceedings postponed, and, once elected (as, with the support of Crassus, he felt sure he would be), he had little doubt that he would be safe for the future. Long before the names of candidates for the consulship had been announced he used to speak as though he were already consul, and his language was singularly indiscreet. He was indeed deeply committed to the policies designed by Crassus and myself and we should, at this stage, I think, have been able to control him had he in fact come into power. As it was, he liked to represent himself as a man of original ideas and he did much harm both to himself and to us by his violent and inconsistent pronouncements. He was to be the saviour of the poor, he used to say; he would relieve them of the crushing burden of their debts; and those who stood in his way would simply be liquidated. He suffered, in fact, from both vanity and enthusiasm, and had not grasped the obvious point that threats are quite useless unless one has the power to make them good in action. Catiline's threats never did him anything but harm. On this occasion the consul in charge of the elections refused to accept his name as a candidate, on the ground that he was a man waiting to stand his trial. As the accuser had not yet been appointed, this action of the consul, though, strictly speaking, legal, was both unusual and provocative. Catiline had no one to thank but himself for his disappointment.

Nevertheless, his disqualification need not have been fatal to our plans. There were other candidates for the consulship on whom we could rely. Crassus now began to spend his money and to use his influence on behalf of Publius Sulla and Lucius Autronius. With the aid of bribery on a very large scale, they were elected.

Sulla was a nephew of the Dictator and so related to me by marriage. He was a man of great wealth and considerable ability. Much later he held under me a responsible position in the battle that decided the fate of the republic. Autronius, the other candidate elected, had little to recommend him except that, being deeply indebted to Sulla and to Crassus, he could be relied upon to do as he was told. He was violent and reckless by nature. Recently he had secured his acquittal at a trial before the courts by letting loose a band of gladiators upon the jury.

With these two elected consuls, it seemed certain that we should be able to proceed successfully with our plans for the next year. Once again, however, Crassus was frustrated, and again the reason for his failure lay in his unfortunate choice of disreputable agents. Sulla might have been tolerable to the senate. Autronius was not. Nor did either of the consuls-elect command such support from the people that he could afford to neglect, as I did later on, any move that the senate might make against him.

In this case the senate moved quickly and successfully. Defeated candidates at the consular elections had been my Uncle Lucius, the youngest of the Cotta brothers, and Manlius Torquatus. These two brought a charge of bribery against the consuls-elect and, with the overwhelming support of the senate, won their case and were themselves declared consuls instead of Sulla and Autronius.

These events took place towards the end of November. It was, I think, early in December that Catiline, with Sulla, Autronius and some others, called late in the evening by appointment at the house of Crassus and began to outline to us (for I was there too) his extraordinary plan for seizing power. In the uncertain lamplight he seemed, I remember, an even bigger man than he was; he wore his toga well and made few gestures; those that he did make were rapid and spasmodic, like the movements of a hawk's foot and talons; when, in the course of speaking, he thrust his face forward into the lamplight, the long lines that marked it seemed to have been made not in flesh but on metal. The very lowness of his voice and precision of his language served to express his tremendous nervous energy and the desperate quality of his resolution. Indeed, what more evidence could be required of the strange fascination which he was able to exercise than the fact that he had already convinced his fellow conspirators, who included one or two sensible people such as Sulla, that his plan was practicable? He even came near to securing for it the support of Crassus himself.

His plan was characteristically daring and absurdly inadequate to meet the situation. Briefly, what he proposed was that on the first of January, when the new consuls were to take office, both should be murdered. They should be replaced by Sulla and Autronius who, once in office, would provide a legal cover for getting rid of any others who opposed the new régime. With the ground thus conveniently clear, all the plans that had been made by Crassus and myself were to be carried out quickly. Piso would be made governor of both the Spanish provinces and would raise armies in each. He was to be supported in Africa by an

adventurer named Sittius, who had commercial interests there
and considerable influence with the native tribes. I myself,
meanwhile, was to receive the commission of annexing Egypt.
Citizenship would be granted to the northern Italians and various
popular measures, including the reduction of interest on debts,
were to be passed in Rome. Many of the conspirators, including
Antonius Hybrida, the man whom I had once prosecuted, were
particularly attracted to the conspiracy by the thought of this
last proposal.

So, if all went well, we should be in control not only of
Rome and Italy but of all those areas from which Rome imports
the necessities of life, and of all the best recruiting grounds for
armies. To give cohesion to the régime and to make it still more
secure it was proposed that, at the appropriate moment, Crassus
should be declared Dictator and that I should be his Master of
the Horse. The part to be played by Catiline himself, other than
that of murdering the consuls, was left somewhat obscure, though
it was certainly assumed that for the time being he would be safe
from any judicial proceedings and that he would be elected to
the consulship for the following year.

The element of melodrama in this conspiracy offended me
greatly. Moreover, I have always been opposed to the use of
assassination as a political method. I had seen too much of it
in my boyhood. And in this particular instance it seemed to me
that Catiline was behaving with an extraordinary effrontery if he
imagined that I would acquiesce in the assassination of my own
uncle. I noticed, too, that his whole approach to the subject of
revolution in our time was a mistaken one. Certainly it would
be possible to organise rioting in Rome on a considerable scale
and even to seize power in the city ; but no revolt based solely
on the city could possibly be successful for long. For any permanent achievement it was necessary to have the support of
provinces and of legions. Provinces cannot be organised or
legions trained overnight. Meanwhile Pompey was in possession
of both and, if we were to inaugurate our régime by the kind of
butchery which both Marius and Sulla had made familiar and
hateful, Pompey would seize upon the opportunity to restore

order and, unless he was foolish enough to leave us three or four years to complete our preparations, he would be able to do so with the utmost ease.

These facts were obvious to me and some of them were quite adequately appreciated by Crassus. But, with his financier's mind trained to make something out of every possible contingency, Crassus was inclined to think that this conspiracy also could be used for his own profit. It was also true that Catiline's proposals had placed him in an awkward position. He needed Catiline for the future and had no wish to offend him now. Moreover, he liked to be prepared for every eventuality, including the very unlikely one of the conspiracy being successful. He therefore made it clear that he was, to say the least, interested, though he insisted that in public he must be free to deny having anything whatever to do with the conspiracy; in this way, he pointed out, he would be in a better position to help the conspirators, whether they succeeded or not. There is no doubt that Catiline left the meeting under the impression that Crassus was prepared to help and that I, who was so closely associated with Crassus, would also play my part.

For me the situation was a most awkward one. I was bound to Crassus not only by financial ties, but by friendship and by a community of interest. I was also bound, though less closely, to Catiline, many of whose supporters were friends and helpers of my own. On the other hand, I felt certain that the mere threat of this conspiracy would do more harm than good to the prospects of Crassus and myself. I was also, of course, concerned about the the danger which threatened my Uncle Cotta, and I should certainly, in some way or other, have arranged to have him warned of it, if Catiline himself had not made this precaution unnecessary. As it was, Catiline's inability to keep any kind of secret alarmed everyone. During the last days of December he went about Rome attended by bands of gladiators and armed slaves and, in whatever company he found himself, used the most unguarded language. It was quite clear that he was contemplating some violent action and the senate, acting on the basis of a number of rumours and much correct information, decreed that on the first of January the new consuls should, on taking office, be escorted by a formidable bodyguard of trained troops.

This was a most unusual measure and it had a profound effect not only on the conspirators, who immediately gave up their proposed attempt, but on public opinion generally. No one knew what to believe, and while some maintained that there had never been any danger at all, others were convinced that at any moment their houses would be burnt over their heads and that the massacres of the days of Marius and Sulla would be repeated. The consuls were as bewildered as anyone. My Uncle Cotta, who in those days was a very heavy drinker, drank more plentifully than ever and affected to believe that all talk about a conspiracy had been greatly exaggerated. I noticed, however, that he rather avoided my company. The other consul, Torquatus, openly declared that he did not believe a word of any rumour concerning a plot against his life. Partly in order to convince people of his sincerity, and partly as a kind of insurance for the future, he actually offered his services to Catiline as counsel for the defence in the trial that was now pending. Cicero did the same thing. He was proposing to stand for the consulship at the next elections and knew that, unless Catiline were condemned at the forth-coming trial, he would have him as a competitor. He wished, therefore, by making friends with Catiline, to secure his help at the elections and the help also of Crassus and myself. Catiline, however, while accepting the offer of Torquatus, whom he had proposed to murder, would have nothing to do with Cicero, whose ability he most foolishly underrated and whom he despised because of his humble origins.

In the senate there were a few who pressed for a thorough investigation into the alleged conspiracy; but the majority, either through timidity or from a reasonable desire to avoid stirring up still more trouble, were easily persuaded by Crassus and others to shut their eyes to the whole affair. For a short time it looked as though the judgment of Crassus had been more correct than my own and that we might really gain some solid advantages from Catiline's abortive plot. Its suspected existence had certainly made the senators nervous and they were anxious not to offend Crassus who, though he appeared to be acting respectably enough, was capable, it was thought, of throwing in his weight on the side of revolution. In these conditions Crassus succeeded, very early in the year, in having his nominee, Piso, appointed to the command of the Spanish provinces. This success, however, was short-lived. Piso, who in any case was an absurd choice for the position which he held, behaved with such arrogance towards the Spaniards whom it was his particular duty to conciliate that he was murdered by them within a month of taking up his command.

By this time the senate had recovered some confidence and, as I had expected would happen, showed that it was prepared to oppose any other measures that appeared either dangerous or unorthodox. The most important of our aims, and the one that was likely to affect me personally most closely, was the project for the annexation of Egypt. It was soon evident that this project would be violently opposed, and in the end when, through the agency of one of the tribunes, Crassus had the proposal put before the assembly of the people, it was defeated. This defeat was due partly to the energy of the more reactionary senators led by the old statesman Catulus ; but the really decisive factor was an extremely able speech made by Cicero. Crassus, like Catiline, had failed to recognise that Cicero, by his eloquence alone, was capable of being an important force in politics. He had consequently made no effort to conciliate him, though this should have been an easy thing to do, since Cicero has always been extremely vulnerable to flattery and at this time was eagerly looking for any support that he could find for his candidature for the consulship. Now, largely as a result of having been rebuffed both by Catiline and by Crassus, Cicero began to move away from our party and to look elsewhere for his friends and supporters. This was, from his own point of view, a clever enough move, since, in the course of this year a large section of the nobility became increasingly alarmed at the policies, real or imagined, of Catiline, Crassus and myself. They were thus willing to support a self-made man like Cicero, who enjoyed some favour with the people, simply in order to keep Catiline out of office.

So in this year none of our major objectives were attained. Even Crassus's proposal for giving the franchise to the northern Italians had been thwarted by his fellow censor, Catulus, who was susceptible neither to persuasion nor to bribery. Yet Crassus had widely advertised his proposal and he began to encourage numbers of able-bodied young Italians from the north to come to Rome and to put themselves under his protection. They might be useful, he thought, in certain emergencies. Here again, however, Crassus miscalculated. The senate had, at least for the time being, recovered its nerve and was not to be intimidated by this attempt of his to build up a private army in the heart of Rome. In the following year, when feelings regarding the elections were running particularly high, a decree was passed ordering the expulsion from the city of all Italians from beyond the Po.

It remains true, nevertheless, that, in spite of these political failures, most of which can be traced to errors in judgment on the part of Crassus, for me personally this year of my curule aedileship had been quite remarkably successful.

CHAPTER IV

SUCCESSES AND FAILURES

SINCE THEN I have, of course, done very much more to beautify Rome and to make a display of myself. Yet I can still look back with satisfaction to this year in my youth when for the first time I had the opportunity to leave a permanent mark upon the city and to bring myself, in an official capacity, before the eyes of the whole people.

In carrying out my duties I spent more money than had ever been spent previously by a holder of this office, and it was generally agreed that the money had been spent with taste, distinction and splendour. I borrowed very large sums from Crassus and I borrowed also from Bibulus who, rather unfortunately for himself, was my colleague as aedile and was later to be my colleague in the consulship. Bibulus remained until his death one of my most implacable enemies, and, so far as our relations during the time that we held the consulship were concerned, he had good reasons for his hatred. His frequent shows of bad temper towards the end of the year of our aedileship are less easily justified and did Bibulus himself no good.

His main ground of complaint was that I had used his money to gain for myself the entire credit for the splendid entertainments which marked the year. This was, in fact, what happened, but for this result Bibulus was himself to blame. I had pointed out to him that if he, who could well afford the expense, were to subscribe lavishly to the games and festivals which were to be offered to the people in our joint names, I myself, who had a particular talent for such things, would undertake the whole burden of their organisation. This was a convenient and honourable arrangement. Unfortunately Bibulus lacked the personality to profit from it. The curious blend in his character of naïvete and irascibility made it impossible for him to behave with grace and dignity on public occasions. Instead of sitting quietly in his place at the public spectacles and giving the impression that he himself was partially responsible for them, he would loudly express surprise at what he saw, admiration, and, in the end, indignation at what he considered to be my extravagance. The people were quick to notice his behaviour and were glad to be able to attribute to me, since I was already a favourite of theirs, all the credit for the performances. Yet I had fulfilled my part of the bargain and could not properly be blamed for the fact that Bibulus, because of his own insignificance, had failed to secure the reward for his expenditure.

There were also, of course, many undertakings of my own in which I received no help, financial or otherwise, from Bibulus. Apart from building permanent porticoes on the Capitol, where I exhibited my own collection of pictures and works of art, I spent much time and money on the decoration of temples and public buildings. Then, after receiving from Crassus, in his capacity of Censor, the appointment of Curator of the Appian Way, I spent on this great thoroughfare a large fortune in addition to the money allotted from the treasury.

The games which we held in spring in honour of the Great Mother were splendid enough and it was at these games that Bibulus first displayed his peculiar pettishness. But the Roman Games, held towards the end of our year of office, were more remarkable still. On this occasion I organised a show of gladiators in honour of my father. Not that my father had played a very important part in my life ; indeed he had died some twenty years previously and had so far not been commemorated in any way. Yet I could have wished him, if (as I do not believe to be the case) the dead retain any sense or understanding, to have known that, owing to my activities, our family was becoming, however, gradually, once more a force in the state. So I was determined to make this gladiatorial display the richest that had ever been seen. I engaged three hundred and twenty pairs of gladiators to fight in duels, and I should have engaged more still, if the senate had not hurriedly passed a decree limiting the numbers that could be employed by one man. These were most disturbed times and it is possible that some people may have thought that I was raising a private army for revolutionary purposes ; but the main purpose of the decree was to check, if possible, the prodigious growth of my popularity. As it happened the senate's action gave me an interesting idea. I spent the money which I had intended to spend on more gladiators in equipping the six hundred and forty I had already with weapons of solid silver. This produced a tremendous impression and made Bibulus, I think, more angry than anything else had done.

But what gained me the greatest popularity of all was the gesture I made, just before laying down office, in honour of my Uncle Marius. I arranged secretly for the making of a number of beautiful images of Marius himself and of Victory, carrying trophies in her hand. These images, all bright with gold and with appropriate inscriptions describing the great battles in which Rome had been saved from the barbarians, were carried through the streets of the city by night and set up in the Capitol. The effect was beyond my expectations. Next day the slopes of the Capitol and the whole forum were full of cheering crowds, jubilant at this reassertion of the glory of one who was still regarded as their leader and their comrade, and grateful, too, to me who had dared to give them this opportunity of rejoicing. I was almost intolerably moved when I heard together in the shouting that filled the city the name of "Marius" and the name of "Caesar."

As a result of this action I was vigorously attacked in the senate by old Catulus. "You are no longer undermining the state in secret," he shouted. "Now you have begun to plant your batteries against her in the open." There was some truth in this view, but I could afford to neglect the expression of it, and so, for the time being, I gave a courtous answer to the old statesman, who was always an enemy of mine.

As it happened, although some of the "batteries," as he called them, may have been visible, Crassus and I were still engaged in

operations that could be better described as "undermining."
During the year following my aedileship we made careful plans
not only for controlling the consular elections but for introducing, by means of our agents, some most far-reaching measures
of reform which would also have the effect of putting great power
into our own hands. Crassus worked all the more energetically
on this programme as he became more and more alarmed by the
news, which was constantly arriving, of Pompey's career of victory throughout the east. His armies had ranged from the Caspian
Sea to Syria and Arabia. The conquest was announced of peoples
whose very names were hitherto unknown and popular imagination was delighted at the thought of twelve kings at once paying
court to Pompey at his winter quarters. Crassus, however, was
far from delighted. He was convinced that in the end Pompey
would use his victorious armies to make himself dictator and he
was prepared to go to all lengths in order to prevent this happening. There were many in the senate (though I was not one
of them) who shared Crassus's apprehensions. On the other
hand, Crassus himself, who was constantly toying with revolutionary policies without ever declaring himself openly, was also
an object of suspicion. And once again his judgment of human
nature, particularly in the cases of Catiline and Cicero, was
seriously at fault.

Catiline was again eligible to stand for the consulship. His
trial, largely through the money and influence of Crassus, had
been so arranged that he had been acquitted against all the
evidence. By this time young Clodius had returned from the
east, where he had done much damage to his brother-in-law,
Lucullus, but not much good to himself, except in so far as he
had acquired a reputation for reckless and impassioned oratory
and for championing the interests of those who were supposed
to be oppressed. In private life he was as extravagant as I was
and more dissolute. He owed much money to Crassus and was,
on the whole, ready to do what Crassus or I proposed. It was
through the influence of Crassus that Clodius was appointed
prosecutor in the case against Catiline. He immediately came to
an understanding with the defence as to the selection of the jury

and then presented the evidence in such a way that even if the jury had been honest, they could scarcely have brought in a verdict of " guilty." The trial was certainly a scandal and since in the course of it Clodius could not resist the opportunity of violently attacking individual senators, both reactionary and moderate, the effect of it was to cause some unnecessary alarm.

However, Catiline was acquitted and it seemed likely that, with the financial support of Crassus, he and Antonius Hybrida, whom we also supported, would be elected consuls for the following year. The only other candidate who could be regarded as at all dangerous from our point of view was Cicero, whom Crassus continued to underrate. According to Crassus, Cicero, the son of a provincial squire who had never held office in the state, would, because of his birth, receive no support from the nobility. Nor was he likely to secure much from the people, since he had no policy of his own which could be called popular. He had attempted to secure favour from too many different sources at once : the senate, the people, the business men, Pompey, even Catiline had been flattered by him in his frantic efforts to raise himself to the consulship. In short, Crassus concluded, he was not a definite enough character to be taken seriously.

I have often noticed that people tend to attribute with particular vehemence their own faults to others. So, in these criticisms of Cicero, Crassus seemed unaware that his own chief failing as a politician was that, though certainly he had a definite policy, no one except his closest friends knew precisely where he stood with regard to it, so that he also gave the impression of being on opposite sides at the same moment. His estimate of Cicero was facile and incorrect. Cicero, in those days, was not only ambitious but extremely intelligent, though with the intelligence of a lawyer rather than of a statesman. So far as statesmanship is concerned, his ideas were, and still are, antiquated, sentimental or snobbish. He has always seen himself as a character intruded into a history book. Yet in certain moments of hysteria such a character as this can impose himself on others, especially if, like Cicero, he possesses really remarkable powers of grandiloquence. And in the particular situation in which Cicero was now to find himself, his very faults combined to be useful to his ambition. His high-flown phrases about "the unity and concord of class with class" was, strictly speaking, meaningless, since the interests of the various classes remained divergent and Cicero had no programme to offer which could possibly reconcile their antagonisms. Yet for a short time there was a majority of the middle classes which liked to believe that Cicero was talking sense, while the senatorial aristocracy found that in a difficult situation Cicero was much the most effective tool that could be used in their own interests. Not that Cicero was ever consciously their tool. He genuinely believed in his superior ability as a statesman and, such was his energy, his legal, literary and dramatic skill, that for a certain time he even looked like one.

Early in the year of his candidature for the consulship he showed his legal skill in a manner which was somewhat embarassing to me personally. I was anxious, after my aedileship, to continue to exploit the great success of my demonstration in honour of the memory of Marius; and so, when I received an appointment as judge in charge of the court dealing with cases of murder, I arranged to have brought before me some of those who had been most notorious in the massacres ordered by Sulla. I saw to it that two of these criminals were condemned. One of them had three murders proved against him; the other was the centurion who, at Sulla's orders, had stabbed his general, Ofella, in the forum. These cases were having the kind of effect that I had designed when Cicero intervened with a manœuvre which I ought to have anticipated. Through the agency of one of his friends he had Catiline summoned to appear before my court and charged with some of the murders which he, too, had undoubtedly committed during the period of Sulla's terror. Cicero of course must have known that since Crassus and I were supporting Catiline in his candidature for the consulship and were even bound to him by certain ties of friendship, I should certainly arrange to have the case postponed or abandoned. I would never make use of the law except against my enemies or political opponents. Yet even the mere threat to bring the case did some harm to Catiline, since it reminded the electors that both he (and, for that matter, Crassus also) had once been closely associated with the worst aspects of Sulla's tyranny ; and it placed me in a somewhat foolish position, since in order to be loyal to my friends I was forced to adopt a somewhat inconsistent attitude towards the strict interpretation of the law.

Meanwhile, though it still appeared probable to us that Catiline and Antonius would be elected to the consulship, Catiline himself continued to act with his usual arrogance and lack of feeling. He made scarcely any attempt to conceal his lavish expenditure on the buying up of votes. Even Crassus was worried by his behaviour and began to doubt whether in the end he would prove as amenable as he had hoped. He seemed, out of sheer bravado, to be deliberately antagonising all sorts of interests which in fact would benefit from the projects which Crassus and I had in view. In particular he did not bother to deny rumours that he intended to bring forward a measure for the cancellation of all debts. The result was panic among the business community and a great opportunity for Cicero. He made use of it cleverly and effectively.

Cicero has always believed that his conduct during this and the following year entitles him to a secure place in history as one of Rome's greatest statesmen. Such a claim is absurd. He has no conception of what is needed by the times and if he were to outlive me and engage again in active politics he would almost certainly be destroyed. Nevertheless, his case is extremely interesting and he will be, I should imagine, remembered not, as he would wish, as a statesman, but as an outstanding freak, an example of how, at certain times, supreme literary ability can be effective without any statesmanship at all. For his reputation as a literary man must be secure for all time. I, who have some pretensions as a literary man myself, have always admired this aspect of him. Even when I can see through every one of his arguments, I am delighted by the dexterity and fervour with which they are deployed. No wonder that, in these years when he appeared to be powerful, he was convinced by them himself.

Since then, of course, I have read a number of the books and poems in which Cicero has attempted to commemorate what he regards as his great achievements. I should not be surprised if these, alone of his works, fail to interest or even to reach posterity. Yet this would be a pity. For, though his vanity is childish, there is something pathetic and instructive about this kind of idealism. He harps continually on the theme of unity and order within the state. He is delighted to think that, under his leadership, there did once exist what he describes as "a union of all good men," a force co-operating towards the excellent aims of peace, justice and good government. And he is particularly pleased to think that he accomplished all this without the aid of an army. He even goes so far as to say: " Let arms give way to the toga," by which he means to suggest that the highest form of political life is that in which no armed force is involved.

It is possible that for some societies this may be true, but Cicero did not live in such a society. The unity which he imagined was quite illusory. His " good men " were not good men at all. They were the usual body of reactionaries who, for a short time, were supported by the majority of the middle classes who believed themselves threatened by revolution. Cicero himself did nothing to calm their fears but rather increased that atmosphere of hysteria in which alone he could hold power. Once the immediate danger, which he had so greatly exaggerated, had melted away, his party melted away ; his " good men " became what they always had been, bad ; and, with the arrival of Pompey from the east with his army, Cicero himself in his toga appeared almost negligible.

Yet, though finally not important, Cicero was for a time undeniably powerful. He, more than anyone else, disrupted the plans made by Crassus and myself and as a result of his activities I was myself in some personal danger.

In the days before the consular elections, when everyone, including Crassus, was becoming alarmed by the provocative behaviour of Catiline, Cicero made in the senate one of the best and most effective speeches I have ever heard from him. A motion had been introduced for increasing the legal penalties against bribery at elections and for banning most of the political clubs. The motion was, of course, aimed at Catiline but in itself it caused us no concern. It was easy to get one of the tribunes to veto the proposals before they could become law. There was nothing, however, to prevent the proposal being debated and in the course of the debate Cicero naturally took the opportunity to attack his rival candidates. He was dressed at the time in the white toga which is customarily worn by candidates for the consulship, and the speech was subsequently published under the title of " The Speech in the White Toga." Even at the time and before it was revised for publication, it was a remarkable performance and it transformed the entire electoral situation. I can still hear the vibrant modulations of his voice, the careful and often inspired transitions from a kind of frenzy to the deepest gravity ; the rapidity of certain sentences, the slow weight of others. He started, as he often did, nervously ; but this time he was almost immediately in his stride, and, harmful as I could see that he was being to Crassus and myself, I could not help hanging upon his words and admiring his brilliant use of them.

The invective was magnificent and ranged over the characters and careers of both Catiline and Antonius. Catiline, who was described conventionally enough as an adulterer and an assassin, was also accused of carrying on an intrigue with one of the Vestal Virgins. I personally thought this accusation not in the best of taste, since the Virgin in question was the sister of Cicero's own wife. However, from an oratorical point of view, the choice of words was admirable. By the very vigour of his language he contrived to give the impression of being a man of courage and resolution. In fact, Cicero is not a brave man, but he can, in a crisis and when assured of overwhelming support, act as though he were. On this occasion he had, just as he used to do in the law courts, accurately estimated the feelings of his audience. Many of these were bewildered and apprehensive. Pompey with his invincible army and unlimited power hung over their minds ; and nearer home was the threatening activity of Catiline, all the more terrifying because no one knew what was behind it. Cicero exploited the mood of impotence and turned it into a show of power. He spoke of Catiline with contempt, but he hinted that under cover of Catiline were working in secret forces far more dangerous and destructive. He never actually named either Crassus or myself, but he made it clear enough to whom he was referring. In a series of beautifully contrived emotional transitions he led his hearers on to contemplate the greatness of Rome, the dignity of the senate, the dangers with which both Rome and the senate were threatened, the glories of the past, and the certainty of glory and stability in the future, if only " the good " would unite. And what better leader, he suggested, could they find than himself, one who had reached his present position by the favour of the people and with the support of the moneyed classes, and yet who, with his sense of history and tradition, recognised and would assert the august and almost divine authority of the senate ? Let men of goodwill, in these desperate days, follow him as a leader from anarchy to greatness. His programme was a just and simple one : order, peace, prosperity at home ; dignity and efficiency abroad.

The senators, except for a few in our party, received this speech with tremendous enthusiasm. They united to support Cicero with all their influence at the election, being convinced, quite rightly, that he would best serve their interests. No one except Cicero himself took at all seriously his claim to be a " popular " leader. In fact, by this speech of his Cicero had finally cut himself off from the popular party, though he himself probably did not immediately realise this, since his vanity was so great that he was quite capable of believing that for the future all " good " citizens of whatever party would rally together under his leadership and remain, disciplined and contented, under his control. He seemed to be unaware that he had not the faintest idea of where he was to lead them, or any means, other than oratory, to control them. Instead of creating unity he had crystalised dissension.

However, for the time being his coalition, artificial as it was, certainly produced results. At the elections he was returned at the head of the poll. For the second place the voting was very nearly even, but Antonius, probably because both his father and his brother had held high office in the state, just succeeded in gaining the advantage over Catiline. For Catiline this was a very serious blow. He was not only disappointed in his ambition, but nearly ruined by debt. He immediately announced his intention of standing for election again in the following year, but he could no longer feel sure that Crassus would continue to support him. Indeed he was becoming a most doubtful asset.

CHAPTER V

CHIEF PONTIFF

THERE WAS much political activity during the autumn months which passed between the elections and the 1st of January, when Cicero and Antonius were to take office. We had imagined that Catiline would be in the position which Cicero now occupied and had planned to put before the people early in the year proposals of our own which would be backed by the authority of both the consuls. Now we had to revise our plans and were soon forced to recognise that, whatever the disadvantages of Catiline as a collaborator, he would have been of much more use to us than Antonius was likely to be. Catiline was at least a man of character, while Antonius was a natural subordinate, timorous, and interested above all in making money. Cicero, whose ambition and self-confidence had been greatly increased by his success at the polls and by the flattering attentions which were being paid to him by the great families, lost no time in eliminating his colleague as a political force. He did this by simple bribery, promising that after the year of their consulship was over he would forgo in favour of Antonius his own claim to the rich province of Macedonia. In return Antonius was, during their year of office, to support Cicero in every measure that he took and break off all relationships with revolutionary elements in the state—by which, of course, Cicero meant Crassus and myself. The arrangement suited Antonius admirably. He hated responsibility and he wanted money. He was lacking in those feelings of loyalty and gratitude which should still have attached him to Crassus, by whose help he had reached his present position. Antonius was, therefore, for the rest of the year a negligible factor.

Nevertheless, we were still determined to present our proposals to the people at the earliest possible moment. These proposals took the form of a new Land Law. In the drafting of it Crassus was chiefly motivated by his own fears and anxieties with regard to the return of Pompey. Personally I did not share this alarm of his and was more concerned to see to it that the law should appear popular and be useful. We proposed that ten commissioners should be appointed to buy up and redistribute public land throughout Italy and the empire. These commissioners were to be elected by the people and were to be present in Rome at the time of their election—a clause which would, of course, have the effect of disqualifying Pompey from holding one of these appointments. It was naturally assumed that Crassus and I would be among the commissioners and would, in fact, control the work of the commission, though the existence of eight other members would make our great powers look rather more democratic than they really were.

The effects of the law, if it were passed, would be important. Pompey, on his return, would need land to distribute among his veterans. For this land he would have to go to Crassus. It would also be possible without seriously misinterpreting some of the provisions of the law, to give one of the commissioners the opportunity of annexing Egypt. And finally, if the commissioners carried out their work with efficiency, they would deservedly win great popularity. The practical measures proposed were wise ones and would do much to relieve poverty in Rome, to strengthen the provinces and to encourage enterprise and initiative among those who, for a variety of reasons, had had no opportunity to develop these qualities. At various times in later years I have myself carried into effect many of the proposals which we then put forward through the agency of a tribune. On this occasion, however, we were once again thwarted by the intervention of Cicero.

Ever since the elections Cicero, months before he assumed office, had taken up the curious view that no political action could or should be planned without his knowledge and approval. He heard, naturally enough, that some sort of a Land Law was being drafted and he did everything he could to discover in advance what measures precisely were being proposed. Various agents of his were constantly approaching both Crassus and myself and suggesting that, if only Cicero were taken into our confidence, he would be glad to give us the advantage of his legal experience in the actual drafting of the bill. His motives in making these overtures were obvious. He had already made sure of his support in the senate, and now he wanted to ingratiate himself with the people by becoming, if he could, associated with a proposal which was evidently of a popular character. Naturally we refused to allow him to have anything to do with it. We knew that, if he got the chance, he would try to make alterations in the law which would deprive it of its effectiveness, since he would shrink from offending either Pompey or the great land-owners. Also it seemed important that Cicero, who had in fact aligned himself with the reactionaries, should be shown up in his true colours and not be permitted to represent himself as a reformer, which he certainly was not.

So Cicero knew nothing of the law until the 30th of December. On this day the new tribunes came into office and Rullus, the tribune with whom we had previously made our arrangements, introduced the proposals at a meeting of the people and posted up in the forum the text of the forty articles of which the law was to consist. Cicero had copies made immediately and, with no hesitation at all, decided to oppose the law as being a dangerous revolutionary measure.

As soon as he took office on the 1st of January he made a speech in the senate attacking the proposals of Rullus and, as usual, playing upon the fears, some justified, some entirely unjustified, of the reactionary classes. He then spoke at an assembly of the people in different, though still effective, language. To them he represented himself as a " popular " consul, who had nothing but their interests at heart. He also succeeded in con-fusing their minds and arousing their suspicions by various clever misinterpretations of the necessarily complicated provisions of the law. Finally he found a tribune to come forward with his veto, so that in the end the proposals of Rullus had to be dropped.

Crassus, chiefly because of his obsessional fear of Pompey, regarded this as a very serious defeat. I acknowledged the set-back, but took a less tragic view of the future than did Crassus. I was beginning to form, though still very indistinctly, a more or less correct estimate of how, in the next few years, the political pattern was to be determined. I saw that Cicero's majority in the senate was held together mainly by a dislike of change or, as they would have said, of revolution. Yet change, or revolution, was necessary. The measures proposed by Rullus had been good measures in themselves; they would have relieved poverty and increased economic stability; but in a very special sense some such measures were essential. Land would have to be found for Pompey's troops when they returned from the east; yet no large-scale distribution of land would be possible if landowners and financiers continued to co-operate in impeding the necessary legislation and administration. Pompey certainly, if he were to act as Crassus feared, had the armed power to force his will upon the senate. But I did not believe that Pompey had either the ability or the desire to become another Sulla. Yet if Pompey neither made himself dictator, nor received what he wanted from the senate, he could only satisfy his army and retain his own position by making a direct appeal to the people, as indeed he had done for the securing of his great commands against the pirates and against Mithridates. Should my own influence with the people continue to increase as it had been increasing in the last few years, I could easily imagine a situation in which Pompey would need my help and even, as had happened once before, the help of Crassus. For such a situation to arise it was essential, first, that Pompey should be alienated from the senate, and that, secondly, the popular opposition to the senate should remain firm and should know who its leaders were.

I myself, in this year of Cicero's consulship, was to stand for the praetorship and I could count confidently on being elected. I was also already considering a number of somewhat spectacular actions by which I could strengthen my own party and my own position with the people when, by the accident of the death of old Metellus Pius, the Chief Pontiff, I was presented with an opportunity of doing something much more spectacular than anything which I had previously had in mind. I determined, against all precedent and to the surprise of everyone, to stand for the vacant office myself.

I suppose that this was one of the most daring actions which I have ever undertaken. By it certainly I stood to gain much, but I also stood to lose everything. Though I could count to some extent on my personal popularity, I knew well that much expense would be involved in my candidature, and that, if I failed to be elected, I should not only appear ridiculous, but should be at the mercy of my creditors, who would in all probability turn on me at once. If they did so, I should be compelled to go into exile and to abandon my candidature for the praetorship. To abandon the praetorship would mean abandoning the prospect of a provincial governorship, a military command and, in due course, the consulship. All this I was risking for a title of honour and for a dazzling personal success. There was no prudence in the undertaking, since failure would be complete failure, and even success would still leave me far from the summits of power. I had, however, even then grasped the fact that what appears to be imprudence can be a valuable kind of tactic. Few things are more formidable than the unexpected or the incredible.

And certainly it seemed to most people incredible that I should venture to put my name forward for the highest position in the whole system of state religion. I had not yet reached the age of forty and had not yet even been elected praetor, whereas it had become an established rule that the Chief Pontiff should always be chosen from among the most distinguished elder statesmen who had already filled the highest offices. On this occasion my rival candidates were Catulus, the leader of the senate who had been consul at the time of the revolt of Lepidus, and Servilius Vatia, under whom, in the same year, I had served for a short time in Cilicia and who, after his victories over the Isaurians, had won a triumph and the title of "Isauricus." Against candidates such as these I should not have stood the remotest chance of being elected, had the election taken place in what had been, since the time of Sulla, the normal way. For

Sulla had passed a law depriving the people of their ancient right of electing the Supreme Pontiff and giving the power of election to the fifteen members of the College of Pontiffs. These would, without any question, have selected either Catulus or Isauricus, and when I, as a member of the College, put forward my own name as candidate, my action was regarded by my colleagues as a ridiculous and rather tasteless attempt at self-advertisement.

In fact, my gesture was of much greater importance than they realised. I was planning to pit my own personal popularity against the whole authority and prestige of the senate ; and in order to do this, I proposed to continue what had been my consistent and successful policy of gradually destroying every vestige of the Sullan constitution. My rivals had been friends of Sulla, and, under Sulla's law, one or other of them would certainly be elected. It was therefore necessary both in the interests of my own propaganda and my own electoral prospects to repeal the law of Sulla.

This was done through the agency of one of the tribunes, Titus Labienus, who for a long time was to work in the closest co-operation with me both politically and in the military field. I had first made his acquaintance when we were both very young men serving under Isauricus in Cilicia. Now Labienus, in his capacity as tribune, brought forward a bill to restore to the people their right of electing the Chief Pontiff. It was a measure which could scarcely be described even by Cicero as revolutionary, since the original revolution in the procedure had been made by Sulla. And even after the bill was passed, no great alarm was felt by my rivals, since it was generally expected that the people would conform to the ancient tradition and would never give their votes to a candidate who had filled no office higher than that of aedile.

However, my record in this office now stood me in good stead. I had not only won enormous popularity by the brilliance and splendour of my entertainments, but had also acquired a solid reputation for efficiency. If the position of Chief Pontiff was to be the reward of achievement, it could be maintained that in a short time I had achieved much, whereas the achievements

of Catulus and Isauricus were in the remote past. I could point
to the contrast between the restored Appian Way, the new
buildings and galleries with which I had beautified Rome, and
the sight of the still ruined temple of Jupiter which had been
destroyed by fire in the year of Sulla's return and which for the
last fifteen years it had been the responsibility of Catulus to
rebuild. Apart from a block of stone bearing the name of Catulus
himself as curator of the reconstruction, not much evidence of
the curator's efficiency was visible. I was also helped by the
reputation I had acquired by restoring the statues of Marius. It
was remembered that both Catulus and Isauricus had owed their
advancement to the fact that they had been friends of Sulla,
whereas I, in my early youth, had dared to disobey the Dictator.

All these considerations proved helpful, and it was not long
before my competitors became seriously alarmed. Catulus
actually attempted to buy me off, offering a large sum of money
if I would withdraw from the contest. This was a sign of weakness and I made full use of it. I widely publicised the offer of
Catulus and my own reply to it, which was that, poor as I might
be, I was prepared to borrow for my expenses even more money
than Catulus was prepared to offer. And indeed I did borrow
enormous sums, for, though the actual voting was only done by
seventeen of the thirty-five tribes into which, for this purpose,
the Roman people were divided, these seventeen tribes were
chosen by lot at the last moment. It was therefore necessary to
secure support in each of the thirty-five tribes.

On the day of the election, which took place in the middle of
March, I suffered from that strange feeling of apprehension
which I had known once before (at the time when I first paraded
the effigies of Marius through the streets and there was a moment's
silence before the applause), and which I was to know once again
on the day I led my army across the Rubicon into Italy. On all
these occasions events turned out for me much more favourably
than I could have anticipated ; but it seems that in the case of
some events, one is in awe of them until they have actually
taken place. Certainly at the time of this election I was not
joking when I left my house in the morning and told my mother,

as I was saying good-bye to her, that she would either welcome me on my return as Chief Pontiff, or else never see me again. I could not have borne the disgrace of failure, and I knew what I had to fear from my creditors. Nevertheless I rather fancied that I should be successful.

In fact I won the election easily. Among my supporters there were scenes of the greatest enthusiasm. On the other side I had made some irreconcilable enemies, but my position with regard to them was far stronger than it had been previously. I now held for life the most respectable office in the state. This fact alone would make it difficult for my opponents to describe me, as they had done in the past, as an irresponsible demagogue.

On the day after the election I moved with my mother and my wife from our old family home to the official residence provided by the state for the head of the state religion. I must own that I was delighted to think that, in one sphere at least, I now had no superior. I was impressed, too, by the ancient associations of my office. I reflected on how in the distant past the duties of the Chief Pontiff had been carried out by the Kings of Rome and it was with a certain awe that I found myself now established as it were at the heart or fountain of Roman history, close to the Temple of Vesta, close to the Regia, the ancient palace of the Kings where still most of my official functions were performed, and close to the forum. I thought of my own regal and divine ancestry and it seemed to me that I was in a place to which I was entitled.

CHAPTER VI

THE CASE OF RABIRIUS

I WAS now beginning to make enemies as well as friends. Chief of my enemies at this time were, I suppose, old Catulus and Cato. Both of them would claim that in attacking me they were performing a public duty, yet in fact their motives were less disinterested and the hatred which they felt for me was based largely on personal grounds. Catulus had never forgiven me for bringing back again into Roman politics the great name of Marius, who had killed his father. Cato disliked me because of my long and happy relationship with his half-sister Servilia, and he was jealous of the influence I had over Servilia's son, Marcus Brutus, who, even after everything which has happened since, remains my particular favourite. Probably Cato also objected to me because he was quite unable to fit me into any of the rather limited categories in which he was accustomed to think. I was, he considered, frivolous; therefore, according to his theories, I ought to be inconsiderable. He was incapable of modifying, in the light of experience, his own theoretical views of reality, and it must have been very annoying for him to find them so inaccurate when applied to my case. I myself, I must own, have always felt a certain antipathy towards Cato. I was irritated by his attempts to interfere between Servilia and me, and I disliked his affectation of rectitude and that deliberate rudeness which his friends called "freedom of speech." Not that he was insincere. He genuinely believed in himself as an example of ancient virtue. This made him all the more troublesome and unnecessary; he could not grasp the fact that he was not living in antiquity, and, in the name of ancient virtue, he obstructed every demand that was made upon him by modern times.

He, Catulus and others did their best during this year of Cicero's consulship to exploit that temporary feeling of panic and reaction which had carried Cicero himself to the highest position in the state. They evidently considered that now was the time to get rid, once and for all, of those elements which they would describe as " dangerous "; but they were neither strong enough nor resolute enough to do so. In the first place the senatorial majority was not quite certain who was dangerous and who was not. Most of them, certainly, would have agreed that Catiline, who was to stand again for the consulship this year, was dangerous. In the view of some, Crassus, who had so lavishly supported Catiline in the previous year, was an even greater menace to stability. Others, frightened by my rapidly increasing popularity, considered that the first person to be eliminated from politics was myself. Others again were chiefly concerned with their fears of Pompey, whose campaigns in the east were drawing to an end and who, when he returned to Italy, would have the power, if he wished to use it, to impose his will on everybody. In this complex situation it was not easy for the reactionary reformers to act consistently. In particular it was difficult for them to attack both Pompey and Crassus at the same time, and those senators, of whom Lucullus was the most important, who were chiefly moved by their fear and jealousy of Pompey, were determined not to forgo the advantages of having Crassus on their side.

I myself still saw much of Crassus and, before the year was over, events were to bring us even closer together in a common danger; but I was now pursuing a policy of my own, and Crassus was not always in agreement with me. His mind was entirely dominated by his fear and jealousy of Pompey and he was thus unable to see as clearly as I did that the real danger which threatened both him and me was that we might, owing to the clever oratory of Cicero and the weight of reaction which was behind him, lose our own influence and authority over the people. The alliance between the most conservative elements of the nobility and the wealthy classes outside the senate was, I rightly believed, a temporary phenomenon. But for the time being it was something to be feared. I could remember that in my childhood whenever this sort of alliance had, for a short period, come into existence, it had resulted in the death of one or more of those who, because of their influence with the people had been regarded as objectionable. It seemed to me, therefore, that in the interests not only of my future career but of my own safety two things were necessary: first, the people must be encouraged to realise their own strength and not be cowed into a lethargic submission; and secondly it must be made plain that Cicero's claim to be the leader of a general coalition of all classes must be exposed as the sham which it was.

I had these ends in view when I arranged to have some archaic and rather colourful proceedings instituted against an aged senator of the name of Rabirius who, nearly forty years previously, had been implicated in the murder of the tribune Saturninus. This event had taken place before I was born, yet I considered that I was affected by it, both because of the principle concerned and because my Uncle Marius had also been involved in the incident. I had often heard stories of it—of how Saturninus, once an ardent supporter of Marius, had alarmed senatorial opinion by putting directly before the people various proposals which seemed reasonable enough, and of how Marius, who was consul at the time, had (foolishly, as it seemed to me) allowed himself to be persuaded to crush Saturninus by armed force. The legal basis (if it can be called legal) for this use of force was in the passing by the senate of what is still known as " the last decree " in a form of words empowering the consuls to " see to it that the state comes to no harm." On this occasion Marius seems to have used his powers sensibly. With his customary efficiency he surrounded Saturninus and his followers on the Capitol, cut off their water supply and compelled them to surrender. It is certain that he had every intention of sparing their lives. However, he made the great mistake of withdrawing his troops too soon, and the enemies both of the people and of himself seized their opportunity. Armed bands of senators and of wealthy men (among whom was the young Rabirius) invaded the forum and slaughtered the prisoners without mercy or consideration. This brutal action had two effects : it discredited Marius for some time among his own real supporters, and it encouraged a belief that the passing of "the last decree" amounted to a state of martial law in which Roman citizens could be deprived of their right of trial.

In attacking Rabirius, who was now, of course, an old man, I planned to challenge this theory, and the methods I chose for delivering the attack were not only spectacular in themselves but were designed to show that the people's power over life and death is no modern innovation, but something that goes back to the beginnings of our history. There were some who laughed at my passion for a synthesis between the traditional and the revolutionary, and who regarded the whole of this case as a piece of stage management. Certainly it had its theatrical element and in my reversion to procedures that were so archaic I may have been partly influenced by the personal consideration of my own new office as Chief Pontiff, an office which linked me, in all my modern ingenuity and vitality, to the remotest past. Yet I am far from deploring this tendency of mine to draw strength and inspiration both from the past and the future. Neither a nation nor a man can be great without memory and anticipation. To-day, holding as I do monarchical power, I should like to see this situation regularised by an appropriate title, and to me the appropriate title is "King." Nor is it only because of my connections with the east that I prefer this word to others, such as "Emperor," which would certainly cause less offence in Rome. Unlike the majority of my fellow citizens, I really respect the past and am not a victim of prejudice. True that both Greece and Rome evolved from monarchy to systems of government which contained elements both of oligarchy and democracy. These systems have great achievements to their credit, but in the end have proved inadequate for orderly and efficient administration. No doubt the ancient Athenians resented the fact that Alexander was a King, just as my friend Brutus is indignant at the proposal that this title should be bestowed on me. Yet the fact is that the title not only corresponds to the needs of the times but also reflects the real desires of the majority of people, who, if they were not blinded by political pedantry, would recognise clearly that they are taking part in the final stages of one of those cyclical movements of history which leads them into the future by means of an apparent regression into the past. The monarch to-day requires very different techniques and abilities from those that were possessed by our early kings, who forged a state out of the conflicting interests and various skills of our remote and semi-barbarous ancestors, and, once they had achieved this elementary organisation, became unnecessary. But the need for a monarchy to-day is even greater than it was at the beginning of our history, and I sometimes think that the need will persist until the whole world is brought into one system of organisation.

I have reached these conclusions in later life and under the pressure of events. Yet even in those days when I was arranging for the prosecution of Rabirius and had just taken up my office of Chief Pontiff, I was aware, however dimly, of the trend in feeling and of the exigence of history which would once again bring the people into a direct relationship with the leader, thereby cutting out the whole complicated system of intermediaries, which, though valuable in its day, had now become merely obstructive. So, for the prosecution of Rabirius, I devised a method of trial which had been out of use for three hundred years. This was the Court of High Treason, which even in the time when Rome was ruled by Kings seems to have met on very few occasions. Indeed a considerable amount of antiquarian research was necessary in order to discover what, in those days, the Court was accustomed to do. I discovered that it used to consist of only two judges who were chosen by lot from a list prepared by the City Praetor. If the defendant were found guilty, he was to be condemned to a very unpleasant death. He was to be tied to a cross and then suspended from an "unlucky," that is to say a barren, tree. This procedure had no doubt been originally intended as some sort of a superstitious charm by which the city would be freed from the supposed pollution of a crime directed against herself. There was no appeal from the decision of the two judges except to the Assembly of the People.

Obviously, if my plans were to turn out as I wished, it would be necessary first to secure the active co-operation of the City Praetor. Without his permission the case could not be brought at all, and without his connivance one could not be sure that the two judges appointed to deal with it would give the required verdict. The praetor in office for this year was Metellus Celer, a rather stupid and choleric man and, like most of his family, unduly convinced of his own importance. However, I was able to make use of him and, later, of his brother, Metellus Nepos, more or less as I liked. This was very largely because the two Metelli were much influenced by women and the woman who had the strongest influence over them was their half-sister Mucia, Pompey's wife, with whom I had been for some time on very intimate terms. She had helped Metellus Nepos to secure a very lucrative appointment under Pompey in the east, and she now helped me to secure the co-operation of Celer in the case of Rabirius. Celer's wife, Clodia, was also helpful. If she can be said to have been fond of anything, she was fond of her brother Clodius and of her sister Clodia, who had just been divorced by Lucullus. This year Lucullus was to celebrate his belated and well-deserved triumph. He was once more taking an active part in politics and the main motive of his activities was to get even with those who had injured him. Though he regarded Pompey as his chief enemy, he had not forgotten how Clodius had instigated a mutiny among his troops and he was certain to do everything he could to impede the career of this very ambitious young man. Clodius, who aimed at acquiring the same influence and authority over the people as I possessed, was on the whole willing to support any measure that I initiated. And his sister, who was married to Metellus Celer, was able to do more or less what she liked both with her husband and with the majority of her innumerable lovers.

So, in spite of some opposition from the senate, the Court of High Treason was duly constituted. The two judges appointed by lot were, as previously arranged, myself and my cousin Lucius, a self-effacing man who could be relied upon to follow my lead. My old friend (I still like to think of him as a friend)

Labienus conducted the prosecution with ability and great fervour, and I, in my examination of the witnesses and of old Rabirius himself, took every opportunity of pointing out the importance of the case as a legal precedent. In it, I said, the whole rights of the people were at stake, since to acquit Rabirius would mean to recognise that the senate had the power at any time, whether in peace or war, to take violent action against Roman citizens and to deprive them of the opportunity of legal defence. Of course we found Rabirius guilty, and, with a certain amount of antique ceremony which pleased the crowd, we sentenced him to the form of death laid down by law.

Being a humane person, I had no wish to have the poor old man, who was now thoroughly frightened, put to death at all; besides, the carrying out of so brutal a sentence might, in the end, cause ill-feeling. But I was careful to give the impression that I was resolved to take matters seriously, since I wished the senate, and in particular Cicero, to commit themselves publicly in the support of an unpopular and reactionary cause. For Rabirius could only be saved either by a successful appeal to the Assembly of the People, or by the direct intervention of the senate. An appeal to the people would be unlikely to succeed, so that it seemed likely that the senate would be forced to place itself openly in opposition to the people's will.

This, in fact, was what happened. Once more Cicero came forward as spokesman for the reactionary elements through whose support he had been elected. On his motion the sentence passed by my cousin Lucius and myself was declared invalid, so that no question of an appeal against it could arise.

Cicero himself was proud of his action. He was already beginning to see in himself an idealised version of some great statesman from ancient history, curbing what was extreme, guiding what was good and loyal by the sheer force of integrity and of a deserved prestige. He had not yet begun to realise that he had neither a party nor a programme, that he was rapidly losing the goodwill of the people, and that the support now given to him by the nobility would melt away as soon as some new situation arose in which the real factors of our history were more clearly revealed than they were during the muddled and inconsequential period of his consulship.

Labienus and I decided that we would force him into a position where he would have to compromise himself still further. This time Rabirius was summoned to appear before the Assembly of the People on a number of quite different charges, many of which were invented for the occasion, and, at the last moment, to this list of offences was added an indictment for murder. By now the case had become one of prestige and Cicero himself appeared to speak for the defence. His speech, as might have been expected, was an extremely clever one. He attempted to suggest that the attack on Rabirius was really an attack on the great Marius, who had been consul at the time when the " last decree " was passed. This suggestion was totally unfair but had some effect in confusing the minds of listeners. Indeed I have often observed that statements which are the exact opposites of the truth are often more effective than reasoned arguments which respect the facts. However, with all his skill and eloquence, Cicero did not have a good hearing. He was defending a principle to which, thanks to our previous agitation, his audience was hostile, and, if a vote had been taken, it is likely that Rabirius would have been once again condemned.

However, I had decided that our interests would be best served by bringing the proceedings to a premature and somewhat theatrical conclusion. There was no point in continuing to persecute old Rabirius now that every object which I had had in mind had been attained. It had been demonstrated both that the people were opposed to the arbitrary use of the " last decree," and that Cicero, who had claimed to be a " popular " consul was, in fact, nothing of the kind. I had therefore arranged with the Praetor Metellus Celer that, before the voting could be taken, the Assembly should be dissolved by the simple, though unusual, method of lowering the red flag which, by long established custom, flew from the Janiculan Hill at all times when the people were officially in assembly. No doubt the original purpose of the lowering of this flag had been to call the citizens to arms in case of some sudden incursion of enemy troops, Samnites or

Etruscans, into what used to be the small territory of Rome. I was amused to find yet another of these curious survivals from the past fitting admirably into my own plans. For the lowering of the flag gave the Praetor an excuse for pronouncing that all business for the day was over. And so the crowds dispersed, pleased with themselves because they had enjoyed a good entertainment and had demonstrated their strength, but profoundly suspicious both of Cicero and of his senatorial majority. Most people also believed that it was Cicero who had been responsible for the lowering of the flag and for the suspension of business, and that he had taken this step because he realised how weak was the case which he had been putting forward.

Already as the summer approached so the tension was increasing between those two elements in the state which remained divided and whose division had been rather accentuated than healed by Cicero's splendid but dishonest oratory. It was becoming clearer and clearer that for Cicero " the good " were " the privileged." I myself, while waiting for the elections at which I was to stand for the praetorship, continued to make things as awkward for Cicero as possible. I spoke, for instance, in favour of a proposal put forward by one of the tribunes for the restoration of civil rights to the sons of those who had suffered in the proscriptions of Sulla. This excellent measure was one which, if Cicero had remembered his own early days, he should have supported himself. As it was, he spoke against it. His legalistic argument was that it was impossible to repeal one of Sulla's acts without repealing all of them and thus, in a time of threatened revolution, weakening the state. It was a thoroughly bad argument, but it proved successful, so many and so tenacious were the interests involved in perpetuating injustice. I myself, fourteen years after this time, have only recently been able to carry into law this admirable proposal—a sign, surely, of the extreme bitterness and intransigency of our age. Cicero's opposition to the proposal again provided evidence for the true nature of his consulship. Under the cover of the slogan "Unity of the Classes," the reactionaries had gained power and some of their opponents were being driven desperate.

CHAPTER VII

CATILINE LEAVES ROME

THE REVOLUTION which had been so often prophesied by Cicero did, in fact, break out before the end of the year, and to this day, I should imagine, Cicero believes that in dealing with this minor insurrection he saved Rome and the empire from extinction. In reality the conspiracy of Catiline, though interesting from a political point of view, was not a serious menace to the existing structure of affairs. Even the revolt of Lepidus had represented a greater danger. Yet Catiline's movement combined with Cicero's oratory certainly produced a remarkable condition of hysteria at the time.

I myself, unlike Cicero, realised immediately that the really important events of this summer and autumn were only remotely connected with Catiline. Overshadowing everything else was the news that Pompey had concluded his campaigns in the east and was shortly to return to Rome himself. When it was known in Rome that Mithridates had committed suicide and that his heirs had made submission to Pompey, a public thanksgiving to the gods, lasting for ten days on end, was decreed. Pompey's friends in the city did everything they could to magnify what had indeed been great achievements in themselves. They spoke of the fifteen hundred and thirty-eight cities which he had conquered (though how they arrived at this figure it is impossible to say), of the vast new revenue which he was bringing to the treasury, of new provinces constituted, of how the legions had penetrated as far as the Sea of Azov and the Red Sea. And, without actually using any threatening language, they pointed out that one who controlled such fleets and armies was in a position of absolutely irresistible power.

Yet Pompey's enemies in the senate were now stronger than ever before. They were jealous of his continual successes and of his exceptional commands. Now, though rather late in the day, they would refer, not without some justice, to Lucullus as the real conqueror of Mithridates, and, with no justification at all, would belittle Pompey's achievements. They were the better able to do this because of the splendid triumph which Lucullus celebrated this summer. An impressive feature had been the placards announcing not only Lucullus's victories but also the large sums of money which he had made available to Pompey both for his war against the pirates and for the Mithridatic war. Then there were sixteen thousand of Lucullus's veterans in Rome. These men had apparently forgotten how they had betrayed their general at the most critical moment of his campaign; they only remembered the victories, spectacular enough, which they had won under his leadership, and, to glorify themselves, they glorified Lucullus as well.

Crassus, of course, tended to side with the enemies of Pompey, but I was now pursuing a policy of my own. I lost no time in getting into touch with Pompey's chief agent, Metellus Nepos, who had been sent back to Rome by Pompey from the east in order to stand for election as tribune. Here again my friendship with Pompey's wife Mucia stood me in good stead, since Nepos, like Celer, was devoted to his sister. Mucia herself at this time was worried by the coldness of Pompey's letters to her which seemed to indicate some disapproval of her conduct in Rome during his absence. And indeed she had had many lovers apart from me. Nepos, however, insisted that she was misunderstanding her husband's attitude. Like all the Metelli, he was intensely proud of his own family and could not believe that anyone would not wish to be allied with it. This pride of his also caused him to underrate Cicero. He seemed to imagine that only the ancient families had a right to be vain, and he failed to observe that Cicero was also intelligent. So, too, in his relations with other members of the senate he showed an extraordinary lack of tact. He was genuinely devoted to the interests of

Pompey, but in his handling of affairs he acted rather more in my interests than in those of anyone else.

Not that it was at all easy at this time to act or plan consistently. Events seemed to be following no logical course and might well have led to different results. The only constant factor in the situation was its instability. There was a nervousness and restlessness both among the senate and the people. These were already marked enough by the time of the consular elections in the summer.

In these elections Catiline was again standing as a candidate, but this time with less good prospects than in the preceding year. He was now utterly desperate and was relying for his support almost exclusively on characters as desperate as himself. His aims went far beyond what was reasonable in the policies that up to now had been sponsored by Crassus and myself. Moreover, his declared aims were not only extravagant but vague. He talked of the cancellation of all debts and of great redistributions of land, but gave the impression that these measures could only be brought about as a result of a period of organised massacre and disorganised society. Naturally Crassus was alarmed. In the first place, as the greatest money-lender of the age, he had no wish to see his investments vanish overnight. He saw also that, if Catiline were to begin a civil war, one of the most likely results would be the recall of Pompey with his army to re-establish order. This would give Pompey just the legal position which he wanted and which Crassus most feared. On the other hand, it was not easy, at least before the elections, to dissociate oneself entirely from Catiline, partly because of old ties of loyalty, partly because the alternative would be to align oneself with those reactionary elements in the senate which we had for so long opposed. My own position was rather easier than that of Crassus. As I was myself standing for the praetorship, I was chiefly interested in my own election campaign, nor could anyone possibly expect to borrow money from me. As for Crassus, he acted, as so often, in an ambiguous manner. Without entirely withdrawing his support from Catiline, he ceased to finance him as he had done in the previous year, and he also went out of his way to show his favour to one of the rival candidates, Murena, an old officer of Lucullus, and therefore, so Crassus thought, one who would be opposed to Pompey. Murena could also depend upon the support of Lucullus's veterans who were now in Rome.

Another candidate for the consulship was a respectable character, Silanus, whose chief distinction was that he was the husband of my friend Servilia, and the step-father of young Marcus Brutus. Since he was supported by a number of powerful families, his chances of election seemed good. Even the fourth candidate, the famous lawyer, Servius Sulpicius, was not without some powerful backing. In fact it was clear that even before the day of the elections Catiline was already planning an armed uprising to take place in the event of his failure at the polls.

His plans were characteristically violent and ill thought out. The only real asset which he possessed was his popularity with the veteran soldiers of Sulla, particularly those in northern Etruria, who had been settled on the land and who, for one reason or another, had fallen into debt or difficulty. Among these Catiline's chief lieutenant was an old centurion of Sulla's, Manlius by name, who, before the elections, had brought to Rome large bands of these discontented soldiers who could be relied upon both to vote for Catiline and to terrorise his opponents. In Rome itself Catiline's following was smaller than he imagined, but it included a certain number of men of senatorial rank who were prepared to collaborate with him in any kind of reckless action. Among these was one ex-consul, Cornelius Lentulus. He had been expelled from the senate nearly ten years previously, but had gained readmittance by being elected praetor for the second time. His mind, never one of the strongest, seems to have been swayed by some prophecy to the effect that three Cornelii were destined to be Kings of Rome. There had already been Cornelius Sulla and Cornelius Cinna. Why should not the third be Cornelius Lentulus? This kind of desperate stupidity was characteristic of the conspiracy. Grandiose plans were made, but somehow the conspirators invariably failed to carry them out. Moreover, they were almost unbelievably indiscreet. One of them, for instance, Quintus Curius by name, had a mistress called Fulvia and, in order to impress this lady with the idea of his future prospects, was in the habit of boasting to her about what would happen when Catiline had seized Rome and describing to her exactly what had been said at each meeting of the leaders of the conspiracy. Fulvia rightly saw that much more solid advantages could be gained by her if she were to turn informer, and so, from the beginning, she kept Cicero acquainted with everything that was being said and done.

Anyone who reads the various accounts in verse and prose which Cicero wrote later of his consulship will be encouraged to believe that the consul was in complete command of the situation from start to finish. This is by no means true. Cicero's first attempts to get rid of Catiline as a political force were curiously ineffective. He began by passing a bill which greatly increased the penalties for bribery at elections. The bill was designed to operate against Catiline, but in fact did him no harm, since, not being fully supported this time by Crassus, he was spending much less money than usual. Indeed the only candidate who was really employing bribery on a great scale was Murena, who enjoyed the support of Lucullus and most of the senate and whom Cicero himself wanted to see elected.

The elections should have taken place towards the end of September, but at the last moment Cicero had them postponed and called an extraordinary meeting of the senate. At this meeting he openly accused Catiline of planning a rebellion and made it clear that in his view, if the elections were held at all, the presiding magistrates (himself and Antonius) should be provided with a bodyguard, just as had happened two years previously when Catiline had planned to assassinate my Uncle Cotta and Torquatus. However, Cicero was not in so strong a position as he imagined himself to be. He was unable to disclose that the source of his information was Fulvia, and his frequent repetition of the phrases " I have been informed " or " I have discovered " failed to impress his audience. Catiline himself treated both Cicero and his speech with an overbearing contempt and at the end of the meeting the general feeling was that Cicero had made a mistake in postponing the elections and had failed to show any sufficient reason why he should be provided with a bodyguard.

Cicero, however, for reasons both of self-advertisement and self-defence, had already organised his own bodyguard. On the day of the elections he appeared with a large following of enthusiastic citizens, mostly belonging to the business community—those people whom, in his speeches, he liked to describe as " men of goodwill." He himself wore very conspicuously beneath his toga a flashing breastplate, making it clear to everyone that he anticipated an attempt upon his life. These precautions were quite unnecessary since in any case the bands of Catiline were outnumbered by the supporters of Murena, who were mostly veteran legionaries and, if it came to fighting, would have been very much more effective than any body of men whom Catiline could have got together in Rome. Yet the demonstration was useful to Cicero himself and probably cost Catiline some votes. As it happened, there was no disorder of any kind at these elections. Catiline was again defeated. The consuls chosen for the next year were Murena, who had most notoriously broken Cicero's anti-bribery law, and Silanus, whose election gave great pleasure to his wife, Servilia.

Had Catiline been so dangerous a revolutionary as Cicero made him out to be, his plans would by now have been matured and would have been put into operation at once. As it was, more than a month passed before anything significant occurred. Yet, though Catiline's planning was certainly as inefficient as possible, there was no doubt at all that the planning was going on, and this was something which caused very acute embarassment both to Crassus and to me. A rebellion, we saw, was likely to break out and was certain to be suppressed. We ourselves were not implicated in it, but we had certainly been implicated with Catiline in the past, and it was evident that, once the rebellion had been crushed, our enemies would immediately accuse us of having been concerned in it. Things were made still more awkward for us by the behaviour of Catiline and his friends in Rome. They had failed to secure our support but they still wished to remain on good terms with us. Messages kept on arriving at our houses warning us to be away from Rome on the 28th of October, this being one of the days which from time to time were chosen by the conspirators to be the occasion of a general massacre. Some of these messages, no doubt, were meant kindly; others represented a clumsy attempt to incriminate us. It seemed clear to both of us that this must not be allowed to happen. Crassus in particular feared that in the end Pompey might be called in to restore order and he believed, without sufficient evidence, that Pompey would make use of any excuse to get rid of him. I had just been elected praetor. After my year of office in Rome I could look forward to a provincial governorship and then the consulship. It was one of the most critical periods of my career and I knew that there were many who would, if they could, try to prevent me from attaining the real substance of power which was now so close to me. It was therefore extremely important that I should be known to have dissociated myself from the conspirators. On the other hand, it was equally important that I should not associate myself with the reactionary policies of Cicero and his supporters. I had a party of my own and it was essential that this party should remain in being. Moreover, I was able to look a little way ahead. I realised that, at this juncture, Pompey's enemies and mine were the same. Pompey's agent, Metellus Nepos, with whom I remained in constant communication, had by now discovered how deep was the jealousy and prejudice felt against Pompey by numbers of the leading senators. Nepos himself, with the support of Pompey's faction in Rome, had been elected tribune. But Cato, with all the weight of senatorial influence behind him, had been elected tribune at the same time and had stood for the office expressly for the purpose of opposing what he declared were Nepos's schemes for the domination of the republic by one man. It seemed to me that my own interests would be best served by maintaining my position of independence and by making it clear to Nepos that I was prepared to use what influence I had against Pompey's enemies and my own.

In the meantime, however, I agreed with Crassus that for the safety of both of us it was necessary to have it put on record that we were not concerned in Catiline's conspiracy, though for my part I did not intend to pledge myself to support blindly any action which Cicero might take in dealing with it. I was more inclined to support Nepos in his demand that Pompey should be invited to restore order in Italy and I suggested to Crassus that he himself might again be associated with Pompey in this task. Crassus, however, would hear nothing of the idea. At this time I was perhaps more at variance with him in policy than at any other time in our lives. Probably we were only prevented from quarrelling by the thought that we were both in danger. For we remained in danger even after we had done our best to clear our reputations so far as the conspiracy was concerned. Crassus adopted a somewhat dramatic method of clearing his own name. On the night of the 20th of October he roused Cicero from his sleep and handed him a bundle of the letters, only one of which appeared to have been opened, containing warnings of the massacre planned for the 28th. I contented myself with giving Cicero some unimportant information about some of the more disreputable characters whom I believed to be involved in the conspiracy. In fact, Cicero, through Fulvia, was much better informed about the plot than I was ; but I was now in a position to say, if it were necessary, that I had helped Cicero rather than hindered him in the discharge of his duties.

The letters provided by Crassus were read aloud in the senate and produced a great effect, though of course Catiline disowned any responsibility for them and continued to treat Cicero in the most arrogant manner possible. But Cicero's position had been greatly strengthened. Now the senate passed "the last decree" empowering the consuls "to see to it that the state suffered no injury." Troops were raised to deal with the revolt that might at any moment break out in Etruria, where Catiline's lieutenant, Manlius, had already gone to organise his bands of Sulla's discontented veterans. In Rome the streets were full of companies of enthusiastic volunteers, mostly from the moneyed classes, who served no useful purpose except that of demonstrating the nervousness of the consul and the numbers of his followers. Slaves belonging to some of the suspects were put to the torture in the hope of extracting information from them. This cruel measure also served no purpose ; the slaves either knew nothing or would not reveal what they knew.

Catiline himself remained at Rome and Cicero, though armed with " the last decree," did not dare to touch him. The projected massacre of senators of which Crassus had given information had, of course, been postponed, like so many of Catiline's plans. Now that regular troops were being raised the very remote chances of success which he may once have had had entirely disappeared. His persistence in his constantly changing plans indicated desperation rather than any ability to manœuvre. He was still in Rome on 6th November, a week after news had arrived that Manlius, with an army of veterans, had already taken the field in Etruria. It was on this date, apparently, that he convened a meeting of the chief conspirators and made what were intended to be the final plans. Catiline himself was now to leave Rome and take over the command of the army in Etruria. When he got within striking distance of the city the other conspirators, who were to be left behind, were to do everything possible to disrupt normal life and public order. Fires were to be started in various districts ; looting was to be encouraged ; slaves were to be promised their freedom. Cicero, of course (this was an invariable item in any plan made by Catiline), was to be murdered almost immediately.

Fulvia's lover was no more reticent about this final meeting of the conspirators than he had been about others and Fulvia at once reported the revised programme to Cicero. I can still remember the speech which he made to the senate on the following day. It was a brilliant performance and, though it was not, perhaps, quite as effective as he could have wished, it did have the effect of isolating Catiline entirely from all who were not actually his fellow conspirators. There was much self-praise in the speech, but even Cicero's vanity ceased to be offensive through being expressed in such faultless Latin ; and the passages of invective were so powerful that even Catiline, who was bold enough to take his place in the senate as usual, scarcely ventured to interrupt and, before the speech was over, clearly revealed his discomfiture, as he observed that those senators who were sitting near him began to edge away from him, treating him already as an outcast. Cicero, in the most magnificent language, charged him with attempted incendiarism and murder and rebellion. He claimed that the " last decree " of the senate had given him, as consul, the power to arrest and execute him on the spot. Here he paused significantly, since what he hoped for was that there would be some kind of spontaneous outcry by the senate, or even another emergency decree, which would encourage him to take this course. I was gratified to observe that nothing of the kind took place. Instead there was an uneasy silence, a silence almost of shame, for many senators, had they dared, would have been glad to make use of this situation in order to get rid not only of Catiline, but of others including, quite possibly, myself. I could now see how effective had been the activities of Labienus and myself earlier in the year with regard to the case of Rabirius. We had made clear what the feelings of the people would be towards any magistrate who took the life of a Roman citizen without trial, and, though very few protests from the senators would have been heard if Cicero had decided to do so on his own responsibility, no one was willing to share the responsibility with him.

Cicero, being a singularly clever lawyer, at once sensed the feelings of his audience. He had failed to secure the kind of vote of confidence which he required, but he could still exploit what he knew about the future. In grave and almost humble tones he declared that, though Catiline's crimes cried out for vengeance, he was a merciful man and would never act in a manner contrary to the constitution. Then, raising his voice, he demanded that Catiline should declare himself openly. Let him leave the city and put himself at the head of his army of vagabonds, debtors, homosexuals and brigands. Then, perhaps, others beside the consul would recognise the situation for what it was.

Cicero of course knew that in any case Catiline was proposing to leave Rome on the following day. Indeed his position was becoming too desperate for him to do anything else. Before leaving he seems to have given his final instructions to Lentulus and the other conspirators in the city, who were desperate men themselves and, as events were to show, most singularly incompetent. He then, while people were still talking of Cicero's great speech, rode out of Rome with a few companions and proceeded to the camp of Manlius in Etruria. Here he appeared with the complete retinue of a consul—a somewhat pathetic gesture for one who had twice failed at the elections and who entirely lacked the resources to make his claim to the office good. Now indeed he had nothing left except his undeniable courage and that personal magnetism of his by which he was able to retain until the end the loyalty of his inconsiderable forces. Had he been subject to discipline he might, in better ordered times, have been a useful and distinguished person. As it was, he was a doomed man and had only existed as a symptom of disorder. After his flight from Rome he was declared a public enemy and he was soon confronted with a consular army commanded by, of all people, his old associate Antonius Hybrida. But before Catiline himself was finally disposed of his friends in Rome had acted in a way which cost them their lives and very nearly cost me mine.

CHAPTER VIII

THE DEBATE ON THE
CONSPIRACY

DURING THE last two months of Cicero's consulship events certainly seemed to play into his hands, though it must be admitted that, for the most part, he made good use of his opportunities. What he himself has always regarded as his great moment came in the early days of December.

On the third of this month a meeting of the senate was called in the Temple of Concord at the foot of the Capitol. Most of us who attended had already been informed that Cicero had ordered the arrest of Lentulus and four other leading senators. There was intense excitement throughout the city. Guards surrounded the Temple and, as Lentulus and the others were escorted through the streets, crowds gathered in great numbers. Every kind of rumour could be heard—that Catiline was at the gates of Rome, that the Gauls were invading Italy from the north, that one or both of the consuls had been murdered.

Once the meeting of the senate began it became evident that Cicero had at last got what he wanted, that is to say absolutely overwhelming evidence of the guilt of those conspirators whom he had arrested. Lentulus and his friends had acted with a stupidity which was scarcely credible and were left without any means whatever of defending themselves. They had planned, it seemed, to set fire to parts of the city and to organise riots, using both slaves and citizens for this purpose, on 17th December, the first day of the Saturnalia, when the slaves would be enjoying a holiday and could most easily be assembled and incited to violence. No doubt they hoped that by this time Catiline's army would be approaching Rome, though in fact there was not the slightest prospect of this. Probably this plan of theirs also, like so many of their previous plans, would have been abandoned in the end. However, they proceeded to make an irreparable mistake. Gallic ambassadors from the tribe of the Allobroges happened to be in Rome at the time. They had come to complain of the way their people had been treated by Murena, who had been their governor in the previous year and had undoubtedly been guilty of every kind of extortion. But Cicero would do nothing against Murena, who was to succeed him in the consulship, and the Gauls were evidently angry and discontented at the way their petitions had been received. It therefore occurred to Lentulus and the others that they might be able to secure for Catiline the assistance of large bodies of Gallic cavalry if they were to bring these Allobroges into the conspiracy. This they attempted to do and, showing no caution of any kind, revealed every detail of their various plots. The Gauls, however, were intelligent men. They accurately weighed up the chances of the conspiracy being successful and decided that their interests would be best served by selling their information to Cicero. By Cicero's directions they pretended to be ready to co-operate with the conspirators, but demanded that the promises which had been made to them should be written down, sealed and signed, so that they would have something to show to their fellow tribesmen on their return. Lentulus and the others fell into the trap and provided the required documents. The Gauls, as had been arranged, left Rome with the incriminating evidence and were arrested just outside the city gates.

Cicero told this story to the senate with his usual eloquence. He produced the evidence, overwhelming enough in itself, with great skill, and he arranged for a complete account of the investigation to be taken down on the spot and for copies of this account to be distributed throughout Italy. The conspirators could do nothing but admit their guilt. It was decided that for the time being they should be placed in the custody of various prominent senators. Both Crassus and I were among those who were appointed to act as gaolers. Cicero knew, no doubt, that his prisoners would be safe with us, since we should certainly be suspected of complicity if they escaped; and he also wished to give the impression to the public that the whole senate, without exception, was behind him. We were in no position to decline. I kept in my house a man whom I had never liked, called Statilius, and saw to it that he was closely guarded.

The effect of Cicero's revelations was enormous, both among the senators and among the people. On this day he must have received almost as much praise as even he could have wanted and a thanksgiving service was decreed in his honour. This, as Cicero was careful to point out immediately, was the first occasion in history when such a distinction had been conferred for civil services, and, in an address made to the people in the forum after the meeting of the senate was over, he did not hesitate to couple his own name with that of Pompey. Indeed he inclined to the placing of himself on an even higher level; for, if Pompey had carried Roman arms to the extremities of the earth, it was he, Cicero, who had saved the very heart of the empire from destruction. Such remarks as these were received with enthusiasm at the time, though they greatly angered the friends of Pompey and angered Pompey himself still more when they were reported to him.

In the hysterical atmosphere which prevailed for some weeks in Rome it seemed possible, however, to say anything and hope to be believed. Though Cicero kept on assuring the people that all danger was over, that, thanks to his own vigilance and firmness, all was and would be for ever well, he still continued to thrive in conditions where people were always wanting to hear him speak and could seldom resist an opportunity of harping upon such themes as incendiarism, pillage, a Gallic invasion and the cancellation of debts. Instead of disbanding the companies of young men who went about the city armed for its preservation, he encouraged all "the good" to enroll themselves as special constables. The "good," or rather the rich and moderately well-off, responded in a remarkable way, and among them, splendidly armed, was to be seen such an unwarlike and unpolitical figure as Cicero's friend, the rich banker, Atticus, who happened at this time to be in Rome on one of his brief visits from his estates in Greece.

It was an atmosphere most favourable to misunderstanding and to persecution and there is no doubt that there were some in the senate who saw the occasion as an opportunity for getting rid of their personal or political enemies. Crassus and I had, in the past, openly supported Catiline, and it was therefore easy now to suggest that we had supported him to the end in secret. Reactionaries such as old Catulus, the senior member of the senate, may even have believed this suggestion to be true. Cato also was quite capable of believing that those who did not share his views must of necessity be in some way criminal. Both Crassus and myself, therefore, found ourselves for the time being in a situation of some delicacy.

Indeed at the meeting of the senate on the day after the arrest of the conspirators, an informer was brought forward who openly charged Crassus with complicity in the plot. Crassus himself believed that this manœuvre was the work of Cicero, but it is equally likely that Catulus was responsible for it. The manœuvre was, in any case, a failure. There were too many senators who either owed money to Crassus or hoped to borrow from him, and there was an immediate outcry against the unfortunate informer, who was committed to prison until he should confess who had bribed or persuaded him to utter so evident a falsehood. Naturally enough, this confession was never made. Yet even this unsuccessful move was enough to make Crassus lose, for the time being, his nerve. He always felt himself threatened by Pompey; now he was threatened also by the anti-Pompeians—Cato, Catulus and the rest. He therefore began to make arrangements for retiring from Rome to the province of Macedonia, and at the meeting of the senate held on the following day in order to decide the fate of the conspirators he was not present.

This meeting, on 5th December, took place in a most unusual setting. The whole of the forum and the slopes of the Capitoline hill were filled with bands of Cicero's enthusiastic special constables, all armed and many anxious to use their arms. Some of my friends had advised me not to attend this meeting of the senate. They considered that both the senate house itself and the streets would be dangerous for me. But I am not inclined to show fear and so I neglected their advice. I soon realised that they had not been exaggerating matters. Though I was Chief Pontiff and praetor-elect, I was met, when I left my house, with angry shouts and actually encountered some obstruction. " The good," I could see, were unnaturally excited and, as often happens when people take up arms for no evident purpose, were eager to find a victim ; and the people as a whole, among whom my popularity was as great as ever, were for the moment cowed and over-awed by this demonstration of what appeared to them to be power.

However, I arrived safely and took my place in the senate. Here also I observed an atmosphere of extraordinary excitement. I had many personal friends among the senators and, before the meeting began, I took care to speak to them in as easy a manner as possible. But the behaviour of Catulus, Cato and some others was impossible to misinterpret. They looked at me with hatred and with a simulated contempt, as though I were a criminal.

After the customary religious ceremonies had taken place, Cicero, with an unusual brevity which was remarkably effective, introduced the business of the day—what was to be the fate of the conspirators ? In accordance with custom he asked the opinion of every senator in turn, beginning with the consuls chosen for next year. First to be asked was Servilia's husband, Silanus. He, no doubt as had been arranged beforehand, proposed that the five prisoners should be put to death. Murena, next to be asked for his opinion, agreed with the motion of Silanus, and so did all the ex-consuls, fourteen of whom were present. Many of them took the opportunity of making more or less lengthy speeches in which they dwelt upon the horrors which had been so narrowly escaped and upon the duty of those in authority to stamp out any vestiges of rebellion that might still remain.

After the consuls had expressed their unanimous opinion, Cicero turned to the praetors. I, as one of the praetors elected for next year, was the first to be asked to speak. I now had to choose my words with the utmost care, since indeed the situation was a most difficult one, as, no doubt, Cicero had intended it to be. I had no intention of supporting the opinion of the majority, since, if I did so, I would disappoint my own supporters, would lose the reputation of fearlessness upon which I prided myself, and would be instrumental, against my known views, in arming the senate with a most dangerous power which might, one day, be turned against me or my friends. On the other hand, if I were to express myself too openly or too defiantly, I would probably not get a hearing at all and would certainly be charged with being one of the conspirators myself. So that not only my reputation but also my life seemed to be at this moment in danger.

I therefore spoke with the greatest sobriety and moderation, using, to the best of my ability, my skill and experience in oratory, and attempting to gain the sympathy of my hearers not only by the matter but by the manner of my speech. I began by complimenting some of the previous speakers on their eloquence, and on their public spirit, professing myself in entire agreement with all that they had said concerning the guilt of the conspirators. Indeed, I pointed out, the facts could speak for themselves; they were grave and indisputable; and there might even be a certain danger in dwelling upon them too eloquently, if eloquence were employed to influence passion and to distort judgment. And in particular it was necessary for the Roman senate to act with dignity, deliberation and, above all, calm. In private life men could be allowed to act impulsively, or at least could be forgiven if they gave way, when injured, to such passions as revenge. But those who stood at the head of affairs must neither act out of resentment nor give the impression of having done so. Moreover, it must be considered that, while no punishment could be too severe in this case for the crime committed, most men would, in the future, tend to remember rather the severity of the punishment than the blackness of the crime.

By this time I was commanding a respectful hearing from the majority of my audience, even though it was becoming evident in what direction my arguments were turning. In order to keep their attention and to prepare the way for the statement of my main theme, I now delivered myself, with some solemnity, of some commonplaces on the subject of death and the death penalty. Death, I said, so far from being a torment, was a release from pain, suffering and indignity. To inflict the death penalty would not, therefore, be to increase the punishment which the criminals deserved to suffer ; it would be to free them for ever from all suffering. Moreover, there were some cogent arguments against the use of the death penalty in this case. In the first place it was unnecessary. Thanks to the vigilance and patriotism of the consul, the conspiracy was under control, and the forces of law and order everywhere supreme. In the second place it was unconstitutional, and, as had been already pointed out, no state of such extreme danger existed as could justify an unconstitutional act. Certainly, I hastened to add, no kind of illegal tyranny need be feared while the state was blessed with so excellent and upright a consul as Cicero. None the less it was necessary to consider the future. One must guard against creating a dangerous precedent. For there might be a time when an unscrupulous consul, in an unusual emergency, would attempt to arm himself with illegal powers in order to get rid of personal or political enemies. I therefore proposed that the goods of the prisoners should be confiscated and that they should be condemned, not to death, but to perpetual imprisonment in one or other of the Italian towns. Thus, I suggested, the gravity of their crime would be emphasised, their punishment would be the more severe, and the constitution would be left intact.

This speech of mine was remarkably effective. Old Catulus, certainly, that survivor of the age of Sulla, immediately protested against it and warned his fellow senators not to be taken in by mere rhetoric aimed only at weakening the authority of their order. Many other senators, however, now began to think again; for I had succeeded in making it clear to them that, whatever the state of opinion at the moment, there was a strong probability that in the future the people or the people's representatives would call to account those who voted in favour of putting to death Roman citizens without trial. To the general surprise, Quintus Cicero, the brother of the consul, who, like myself, had been elected to the praetorship for the following year, expressed himself in favour of my proposal. Others followed suit, and the debate was further confused by another proposal that the whole discussion should be adjourned until after the defeat of Catiline in the field.

Cicero, the consul, now intervened with a characteristically legalistic speech. He congratulated me on my patriotism, on the mercifulness of my disposition, and on my constant pursuit of the favour and interests of the people. Such compliments were, to say the least, double-edged. He then remarked that, in fact, my proposal was less merciful than the proposal of Silanus. For, as I myself had admitted, was not death preferable to perpetual imprisonment? As for the constitutional point, the conspirators, having been declared public enemies, had automatically lost their rights as citizens. And to be scrupulously considerate of such people might well be to show a lack of consideration, indeed real cruelty, to the state itself. He himself, the consul, was prepared to accept responsibility for any action which was supported by the authority of the senate.

This intervention of Cicero's was less effective than he had hoped. Many of the senators failed to grasp his insinuation that I was all the time promoting the interests of the people against the senate, and others were, in any case, averse to offending the people. Nor did his casual assumption that the death penalty was legal simply because the prisoners had been declared public enemies carry much weight. Everyone knew that, whatever Cicero might say, this was, in fact, a most disputable point. Moreover, in trying to give the impression of being judicial, Cicero had only succeeded in appearing not quite to have made up his mind.

As the debate proceeded, so the confusion grew. Silanus himself suddenly changed his mind and said that his original proposal had not been correctly understood. He had not really meant to propose the death penalty, but only the severest penalty that could legally be imposed. If this turned out to be imprisonment, he must have meant to say "imprisonment" rather than "death." He then still further confused matters by saying that on the whole he favoured the alternative proposal of adjourning the debate until Catiline and his army had been crushed.

It was at this point that Cato, as tribune-elect, made an impulsive, violent and characteristic speech which turned out to be decisive. Though still under thirty years of age, Cato had already acquired an important and indeed unique reputation. He had done this by his extreme pigheadedness, and by his affectation of what he imagined to have been the ancient virtues —an affectation so consistent and intense as almost to deserve the name of sincerity.

On this occasion he began by making a violent attack on Silanus for having changed his mind in the course of the debate. Silanus had indeed made something of a fool of himself, but had still spoken sincerely and thus did not merit the abuse hurled at him by Cato who was, after all, his brother-in-law. Cato's neglect of common politeness was known, however, to his followers as "plain speaking," just as his conviction that those who disagreed with him were scoundrels went by the name of "integrity."

From Silanus he passed on to me and accused me, with some reason, of having deliberately confused the councils of the state. He then went on to attack my entire political record, which he described as that of a disloyal and disreputable demagogue. If, he said, the state was now trembling on the brink of ruin, the fault was as much mine as Catiline's. Moreover, I was, in all probability, implicated in the plot myself. I ought to be thankful that I was not at the moment in the same danger as that from which I was attempting to rescue the conspirators, those monsters of iniquity who were, no doubt, my friends. Now or never, he concluded, was the time for the state to take firm action. He himself, since Silanus had weakly retracted his proposal, would now propose the punishment of death.

The fury and vigour of this outbreak changed the temper of the whole meeting. Cato was applauded on all sides and before long not only was his proposal generally acclaimed, but in addition to this it was proposed that the property of the guilty men should be confiscated, as had been originally suggested by me as an alternative to the death penalty. This was, of course, a move designed to make it appear that I was to some extent associated with what was now evidently the determination of the majority. Feelings were, by this time, running high, but I neither wished nor could afford to keep silent. I protested strongly against retaining what was most severe in my own proposal, namely the confiscation of the prisoners' property, while rejecting what was merciful in it, namely the saving of Roman citizens from an ignominious death. And I replied with vigour to the aspersions made upon my own character by Cato. While I was speaking, warmly enough but now to an audience that had become hostile, I was approached by a messenger who handed me a note. Cato immediately jumped to his feet and, in his usual unbalanced way, demanded that the contents of the note should be made public. In all probability, he declared, it was a communication from one of the conspirators and it was characteristic of my known effrontery to receive such communications in the sacred atmosphere of the senate itself. So hysterical, by this time, had become the feelings of the senators that there was a general outcry in favour of Cato's hot-headed and, as it turned out, ludicrous intervention. By this time I had glanced at the note and had discovered it to be a message from Servilia, Cato's half-sister and Silanus's wife. Servilia had been most anxious for my personal safety at this meeting of the senate and she had not been able to restrain herself from writing to me in the warmest possible terms. So, after protesting that my own private affairs could have little interest for so stern a moralist as Cato, I passed the note to him, and invited him to read it aloud. It was a somewhat awkward moment for Cato who, finding that he had in his hands a love-letter addressed to me by his sister, and at the same time that he was the object of the most anxious attention of those senators who believed that he was now about to produce something remarkable, scarcely knew how to proceed. In the end he acted with characteristic stupidity and indelicacy, flinging the letter back at me with the words, "Take it, you drunkard!" The indelicacy was in the action, the stupidity in the words; for, while Cato himself was a notoriously heavy drinker and would often sit up all night with his wine, discussing, so far as his fuddled wits were capable of it, the principles of morality, drunkenness is one of the few vices with which I have never, even by my enemies, been charged.

The incident of the note, however, scarcely interrupted the fervour of the debate. I continued to oppose the motion for the confiscation of the prisoners' property and appealed to the tribunes of the people to support me with their veto. The tribunes, however, were afraid of the majority opinion, and gave me no support. Finally Cicero, rather to expedite matters than for any other reason, withdrew the motion for confiscation and simply put before the house Cato's proposal of the death penalty. This was passed by a large majority and among scenes of great and savage enthusiasm. Those few of us who abstained from voting found ourselves the centre of hostile attention. I myself, while leaving the senate, was surrounded by a band of Cicero's armed guards, who approached me with drawn swords which they seemed ready enough to use. Some of my friends gathered round me and protected me with their togas, but there were others who, under the influence of the emotions roused by Cato, called out to the guards to do their duty and make an end of a traitor. The guards, however, waited for the authority of the consul, Cicero, and Cicero, though he is said later to have repented of his action, raised his hand to forbid them from proceeding further. I was therefore able to reach my house in safety, while Cicero himself, attended by the majority of the senators and by crowds of armed supporters from the moneyed classes, went slowly through the forum to the prison and place of execution. Here the prisoners were soon brought and, after having been lowered through a hole into the underground dungeon, were soon strangled. Cicero, after supervising the execution, pronounced in a loud voice to the expectant crowds, "They have lived," and was then escorted to his own house by a large, distinguished and hysterical following, who, greatly to his delight, saluted him as the second founder of Rome, the saviour and father of his country.

I myself did not witness this indecent spectacle ; nor for the rest of the year did I attend meetings of the senate. This was not because I feared that my life was in danger, but rather because I wished it to appear that this was so. I knew that the unnatural "union of the classes," so dear to Cicero, could not last and I was already, with the aid of Metellus Nepos, the friend of Pompey, taking steps to hasten the inevitable process of its dissolution.

BOOK FOUR

CHAPTER I

DISORDERS

THOUGH I was not frightened of personal violence at this time, I had every reason to be apprehensive of other forms of attack. I could remember how in my childhood my uncle, Caius Cotta, had been tried by a summary court and forced to go into exile for no better reason than that he had been the friend of a reforming statesman and it seemed to me certain that my enemies would, in their present mood of confidence, take some such action against me. It was from fear, not only of Pompey, but also of this kind of persecution that Crassus had now retired from Rome to his estates in Macedonia. Crassus could afford to do this; he was already a man of consular rank and his immense riches would always preserve him in the end. I, on the other hand, was so burdened with debts that I could not hope to survive, let alone to advance my fortunes, unless, at the end of my year's term of office as praetor, I received a provincial governorship. I felt that, if I were now to relax for a moment, I would certainly lose everything, and so I determined to attack before I was myself attacked.

The new tribunes, amongst whom were Metellus Nepos and Cato, came into office less than a week after the execution of the conspirators. They thus had some weeks of activity before the first of January, when the higher magistrates took up their duties. In these weeks Cato and Nepos revealed, emphasised and extended the division of opinion that had never ceased to exist. Their bitter quarrels were mostly concerned with the political future of Pompey, but this question involved many others, including the whole conduct of Cicero with regard to the conspiracy.

Cicero, to do him justice, saw more clearly than did the majority of his supporters. He realised that if his cherished " union of the classes " was to survive, some sort of an alliance with Pompey was necessary ; but in his attempts to organise such an alliance he showed himself singularly inept. He failed altogether to control Cato and other fanatics in his own party who, either from principle or because of jealousy, were determined that Pompey should become a private citizen like anyone else, and in his own communications with Pompey he made the ridiculous error of addressing him as though he were his equal, if not his superior. He was deeply hurt by the fact that Pompey had made no public announcement from the east congratulating him on having saved Rome and the empire from revolution, and he lacked the imagination to see that Pompey was in fact extremely annoyed with him. For Pompey, who never liked laying down a command, had planned to be recalled to Rome at the head of his army in order to crush the rebellion himself. This obvious reflection never seemed to occur to Cicero, whose vanity was such that he could not understand why Pompey's letters to him were so cool in tone.

His vanity was still more wounded by the attacks made on him at meetings of the people by Metellus Nepos. Cato, certainly, organised rival meetings and at one of these gratified Cicero enormously by saluting him, amid general applause, as " the father of the fatherland." Gratifying, however, as these empty titles were, Cicero became seriously alarmed when Nepos, in one of his speeches, declared that a person who had put to death Roman citizens without trial ought himself to be refused the right of speaking. It was the kind of remark which gets repeated and was widely interpreted to mean that Nepos was prepared to use his right of veto when, on the last day of December, Cicero, in laying down his office, would make the customary speech to the people. The prospect of being deprived of this unique opportunity for self-glorification was, to Cicero, a terrifying one. He immediately got into touch with the two women whom he rightly considered to have influence with Metellus Nepos, though he was wrong in believing that they would use their influence in his behalf. One of these women was Mucia, Nepos's half-sister and wife of Pompey; the other was Clodia, wife of Nepos's brother, Metellus Celer, who was at this moment operating in the north against Catiline. Both Clodia and the two Metelli despised Cicero as a self-made man, though Clodia was interested in him to the extent in which she was always interested in anyone who had made a name for himself and was rich; she was particularly impressed at this time by the fact that Cicero had begun to negotiate with Crassus with a view to purchasing, at an enormous price, one of the most splendid private houses in Rome. Moreover, she enjoyed having Cicero at her dinner parties. On general subjects he was a brilliant talker; on politics he was singularly indiscreet; on the subject of himself and his great actions he was always ridiculous, and his boasting both amused the guests at the time and could be used as amusing anecdotes on subsequent occasions. Clodia was also pleased with the fact that Cicero's wife deeply resented his going to her house, since she was convinced, quite without reason, that Clodia had designs on him. She therefore encouraged Cicero to believe that she would do what she could to restrain the violence of Metellus Nepos, though she had no intention of doing anything of the kind.

Nor was Mucia of any more help to him. She was, if not precisely faithful to Pompey, at least devoted to his interests and she had been extremely offended by Cicero's supporter Cato, who was constantly warning the people of what he conceived to be Pompey's plans to make himself an absolute ruler.

Thus Cicero's diplomacy had no effect other than to promote quarrels between himself and his wife. On the last day of the old year Metellus Nepos carried out his threat and, on the grounds that Cicero had not allowed other Roman citizens to speak in their own defence, forbade him to address the people and told him to confine himself to the usual oath that he had carried out his duties to the best of his ability during his year of office. Cicero, profoundly wounded though he was, behaved on this occasion with dignity. He advanced to take the oath and then, in his ringing, well-trained voice, shouted out, " I swear that this city and this empire have been saved from ruin, and saved by me alone." Though both arrogant and untrue, this claim was received with tremendous cheering, and Cicero was escorted back to his house by large numbers of those whom he liked to consider as " the good."

This was, however, almost the last occasion on which " the good " appeared on the streets of Rome in any large numbers ; and what was significant about this occasion was not the applause which Cicero had received, but the fact that Nepos had been able to exercise his right of veto at all.

Next day I took up my own office as praetor. I lost no time in openly attacking the most powerful of those whom I knew to be my enemies. Instead of attending the ceremonies on the Capitol which were taking place at the inauguration of the new consuls, I went with my lictors to the forum and mounted the platform from which, during this year, I was to preside over legal cases. I had arranged that large numbers of my supporters should be present and so I had a considerable audience to address. I announced that I proposed to bring to justice the old and respected statesman, Catulus, and was glad to notice that my words had a powerful effect. My own party was delighted to see me acting again in a bold and unusual manner. They had believed me to be, as in fact I was, in danger, and this display of confidence now made them think that I had some secret source of strength, though, in reality, the strength of my position came entirely from the confidence which they were beginning again to have in me. Others were simply astounded that anyone could venture to attack one who was, as it were, the father of the senate and who liked to imagine himself as above and beyond controversy.

But I had not forgotten that Catulus with Cato had openly charged me with complicity in the designs of Catiline. I now accused him of inefficiency in his work as superintendent of the reconstruction of the temple of Capitoline Jupiter and demanded that an inquiry should be held into his use of public money. I also accused him of having exceeded his powers by having put up an inscription under his own name on the still unfinished temple. I proposed that this inscription should be deleted, that Catulus should be censured for his incompetence or worse, and that both the work of completing the temple and the honour (to be recorded in a new inscription) should be taken away from him and given to Pompey. I added that I was entirely in agreement with the views of Metellus Nepos, who was rightly suggesting that Pompey should be recalled to Italy to establish once more the rule of law and order.

The reaction of Catulus and his party was immediate. As soon as Catulus himself was informed of what was taking place in the forum, he tore himself away from the official ceremony on the Capitol, though it was the kind of formal occasion in which he delighted, and, accompanied by a number of his friends, came down to the forum and demanded a hearing. It would have been normal for a praetor, dealing with an old statesman of such distinction, to have invited him to mount the platform and to address the people from there. But I knew from experience that Catulus was an irreconcilable enemy and I had determined to humiliate him in every possible way. I therefore directed him to speak, if he had anything to say, from the level of the street, like an ordinary person. This deliberate insult to the senior statesman of the republic had the effect which I had anticipated. It greatly encouraged the members of my own party and aroused the utmost fury among " the good," who were still in sufficient force to be dangerous. Catulus himself was rendered almost speechless, but before long a crowd of his supporters had assembled in such numbers that I judged it wise to adjourn business in my court for the day ; nor did I proceed any further with what would have been a most complicated and difficult prosecution. The gesture which I had made and which was most widely spoken of at the time was sufficient for my purpose. I had made it clear to Catulus and others that, if attacked, I was prepared to defend myself ; and I had accentuated the differences which already existed between Pompey and the senate.

Next day Metellus Nepos proposed in the senate that Pompey be recalled in order to crush Catiline and to re-establish order in Rome. As it was well known that Catiline's small army was already surrounded by government forces, and had little chance of survival, Nepos was unable to pretend that Catiline was any longer dangerous. He therefore devoted most of his speech to an attack on Cicero, who, furious as he was with Nepos for having prevented him a few days previously from displaying his oratory in public, now produced some fine passages of invective and some wearisome reiterations of his conviction that Rome owed her continued existence to his own efforts. His speech was warmly applauded by the majority of the senate and Cicero himself, in his pleasure at receiving such applause, failed to notice that the effect of his oratory was not at all that which he would have desired. Not only Nepos, but others such as Cato, would interpret it as an attack on Pompey, with whom Cicero was, in fact, most anxious to be on good terms. Cato indeed took the opportunity of saying that, while he was alive, Pompey should never lead his troops into Rome. This remark also was greeted with applause and Nepos, seeing that there was no hope of securing support for his proposal in the senate, now threatened that he would pass his bill whether the senate liked it or not by putting it directly before the Assembly of the People.

I had pledged myself to support Metellus Nepos in taking this step, which, in the circumstances of the time, was a bold one. In the days when Gabinius and Manilius had, in opposition to the senate, passed their laws which gave to Pompey his exceptional powers against the pirates and against Mithridates, the state had been in real danger, and, in particular, the moneyed classes had been anxious about their investments and so had thrown in their weight against the senate. Now, however, these classes were, for the time being, firmly allied with the most reactionary elements in the senate. Many people, both in the senate and outside it, genuinely believed that Pompey was planning a dictatorship. Many others were simply jealous of him. We were sure, therefore, to be confronted with the hostility of the most powerful sections of society and for our support could only rely on my personal popularity (which had been somewhat shaken by the events connected with Catiline) and on the large numbers of common people who would still respond to the emotional significance of Pompey's name, "the Great."

Personally I never believed that our agitation in this instance would be successful in the sense that we would get a decree passed to recall Pompey, though here Nepos disagreed with me. What I aimed at was once again to emphasise the existence of the people's power, to show how false had been Cicero's rhetorical statements that he had been the leader of a united Italy, and to put Cicero himself into an impossible position politically. As it was, Cicero was one of the few in the senate who was intelligent enough to see the advantages in treating Pompey with the respect and consideration that were due to him. He was now forced to take the side of Pompey's enemies—Lucullus, Cato and the rest—since he could certainly not associate himself with a proposal which amounted to a vote of censure on his own conduct as consul.

The riots which resulted from the action of Nepos and myself were the worst that had taken place in Rome for many years. The day was the third of January, and, while it was still dark, Nepos had occupied the forum with considerable numbers of armed men. Soon after dawn he and I, with our personal supporters, also entered the forum, taking our places on a platform in front of the temple of Castor. We immediately prepared to have the bill read out to the people. We had counted on opposition from Cato and from one of the other tribunes, a man called Thermus, but at first the opposition failed to appear in sufficient strength. Cato, who had been indulging in one of his drinking bouts, arrived late upon the scene and had to send out hurriedly in all directions for bands of men capable of resisting our own supporters. Senators, including the consul Murena, and large numbers of the moneyed classes began hastily to assemble. But for some time they were in a minority, and at the very beginning of the proceedings Cato and Thermus were almost the only members of their party present. It must be admitted that they acted with courage and resolution. Since they were tribunes, the guards made way for them and, amid angry shouts, they climbed on to the platform. Cato ostentatiously took his place between Nepos and myself, shouting out as he did so, "I am sitting here to prevent them planning another conspiracy together." Then, as the clerk produced a copy of the bill and began to read it aloud, he rose to his feet and interposed his veto as a tribune, forbidding him to read another word. There was already some fighting in the crowd and soon it broke out on the platform. Nepos, disregarding Cato's veto, now began to read the bill himself. Cato snatched it from his hand and trampled it to the ground. Nepos, holding Cato off with one hand, began to recite the bill from memory; but now the other tribune, Thermus, intervened and clapped his hand over Nepos's mouth. This was the signal for the fighting to become general. Stones and sticks flew in all directions. Our party, who were at this stage the more numerous and had also the support of Nepos's armed guards, began, slowly at first, then in a general rout to drive our opponents from the forum. Still, with blows raining down on him, Cato stood firm and continued to shout out sentences which were, in the din, unintelligible, but in which the words "tyranny" and "liberty" were frequently employed. Finally he was rescued by the consul Murena, who threw his own toga over him and escorted him to safety inside the temple of Castor. Then he, too, with the rest of the senatorial party, took to flight.

It cannot be denied that the forum presented an indecorous spectacle. Everywhere were to be seen bleeding heads and noses, discarded arms and garments, stones torn from the pavement and other evidence of riot. It was in order to make the proceedings appear somewhat more respectable that Nepos now dismissed his armed guards and, after what seemed a decent interval, began once more to read aloud his bill. However, during this interval, Cato and his friends had been active. They had reorganised their own followers and, once they discovered that the way was clear for them, they rushed back into the forum in full force and began to stone the supporters of Nepos who had remained behind. It became necessary to retreat. I myself, who had not far to go to my own house, retired in a dignified manner, closely escorted by members of my own party. Nepos was forced to retreat more hurriedly.

I was far from admitting defeat on this occasion. In fact I

felt much more secure than previously, though for the next few days appearances seemed to contradict my confidence. As I expected, my enemies made further attempts to eliminate me from political life, but I was now able to confront them with better prospects of success. The Roman people had, as it were, come to life again and they were determined to protect me. They had begun to realise that after the oratory and excitement of Cicero's consulship, things were exactly the same as before. Indeed, during the whole of his year of office Cicero had only passed one measure which was even remotely connected with efficiency in government and administration. This was his law about bribery at elections, and it had been most notoriously broken by the present consul, Murena, who had been supported throughout by Cicero himself.

Now the senate attempted, without success, to recreate the atmosphere of hysteria which had prevailed at the time of the execution of the conspirators. At a meeting held on the same day as that of the riots they all put on mourning clothes, as though for some national calamity, and proceeded to act as if Rome were in the hands of revolutionaries. Again the " last decree " was passed, empowering the consuls to take what action seemed best to them for the preservation of the state. And this was followed by another decree, wholly illegal, by which Metellus Nepos and I were forbidden to exercise our functions as magistrates.

Remembering what use had been made of " the last decree " in the case of the Catilinarian conspirators, we recognised our danger. Nepos called a meeting of the people in the forum, bitterly complained of the way in which he, the emissary of Rome's greatest general, had been treated, and announced that, in order to save his life, he was forced to flee from Rome and to seek protection with Pompey. He asked me to come with him, but I had different plans and let him go alone. I did not wish to approach Pompey as a refugee. I had a party of my own and, whatever the risk, I intended to keep it in being. So, for some days, I merely ignored the decree passed against me by the senate. While taking care to see that I was properly guarded, I went down as usual to the forum and continued to deal with the business that came before the court over which I had been elected by the votes of the people to preside. The people were delighted at this act of defiance ; my enemies in the senate were outraged. In fact it soon began to appear that the extremists among them, such as Catulus and Cato, might get their own way and have me placed under arrest. They would then, in all probability, produce some informer or other to declare that I had been in league with Catiline. This was certainly a danger to be guarded against, and so, after declaring publicly that the Chief Pontiff could no longer go safely about the streets of Rome, I retired to my official residence and for some days took no part in public business. During these days I was extremely busy in organising what was made to appear a spontaneous demonstration in my favour.

On the day which I had chosen for this demonstration some thousands of people, many of them armed, gathered together outside my house. They were addressed by various speakers who attacked violently those who had proposed in the senate that duly elected magistrates of the Roman people should be deprived of their offices. Sitting inside my house, I could hear the swelling cries of " Caesar ! Caesar ! " as they called for me with the intention of escorting me through the streets and forcing the senate to reinstate me. Meanwhile I had been informed that the senate had met hurriedly and in a panic, anticipating more violence and perhaps a revolution. They were still in session and were being informed constantly of what was happening outside my house. Many of those who brought them information were, in fact, agents of my own. I was particularly careful to see that the speech which I now proceeded to make was quickly and accurately reported to the senators.

The crowd, when I made my appearance, was even more excited than I had anticipated and at first I was almost swept off my feet by their enthusiasm to march with me directly to the place where the senate was in session. However, I managed to obtain a hearing and I spoke with a calm and a moderation which soon had the desired effect. After thanking them for their solicitude for me personally and for the constitution, I begged them to return to their homes in a quiet and orderly manner. I admitted that there were people in the senate who were enemies both of myself and of the established principles of law and order; but there were others, I said, who would soon realise that in my case they had acted illegally and they would of their own accord attempt to repair the injustice that had been done.

In this way I calmed the agitation of the crowd and forced the hand of the senate. As soon as my speech and its effect had been reported, those senators who were my friends turned at once on those who had been accusing me of incitement to revolution. They were supported by the great majority who feared above all things another day of rioting. Before the morning was over a deputation from the senate arrived at my house. They had been instructed to thank me for my loyal and public-spirited action and to invite me to return with them to the senate, where I was to be reinstated in my proper position as praetor.

CHAPTER II

SCANDALS

It was fortunate for me that I had acted so promptly and vigorously at the very beginning of the year. Soon after the demonstrations Catiline's small army was brought to battle and annihilated. Antonius Hybrida, complaining of an attack of gout, had taken no part in the fighting, but his troops had been led resolutely by his subordinate, Petreius. Catiline himself had died fighting bravely in a cause which for a long time had been hopeless.

Now, as I had expected, a number of prosecutions were brought for reasons of personal malice against people who at any time in the past had been associated with Catiline. I was an obvious target, but I had now greatly strengthened my position and, when my enemies made another attempt to ruin me, I was able to act with assurance and severity. First they produced an informer, Vettius by name, who denounced me before the court of the quaestor, Novius Niger. In his preliminary statement Vettius claimed that he could produce a letter addressed to Catiline in my handwriting. As I had frequently corresponded with Catiline in the past, it is quite possible that he may have been able to do so. At the same time a more damaging attack was made on me in the senate by the traitor, Quintus Curius who, having at first been a conspirator himself, had in the end joined his mistress, Fulvia, in the more profitable role of informer and had already received a reward from the senate for his activities. Like most informers, he did not know when to stop and he was no doubt hoping for another reward if he succeeded in incriminating me.

But I was now angry and felt myself to be powerful. In the senate I at once appealed to Cicero and demanded that he should state publicly that, in the early days of the conspiracy, I had acted patriotically by giving him information which I might have withheld. Here I had to take a certain risk. Curius had certainly been very useful to Cicero and, for all I knew, Cicero might have been among those who were now inciting him against me. On the other hand, I knew that Cicero's loss of favour among the people had greatly alarmed him and I doubted whether he would risk increasing his unpopularity by joining in with my enemies. I knew, too, that in the purchase of his new and splendid house he had put himself under great obligations to Crassus and, even though Crassus had at the moment retired from politics, he would resent an attack on me which might well be followed by one on himself. So, as I had anticipated, Cicero decided to clear my name and openly congratulated me on the public spirit which I had shown, not only recently, but at the time of the conspiracy.

I was now able to deal with my accusers as they deserved. Curius was convicted of having proposed to bring a false charge against a fellow senator. He was deprived of his original reward and disgraced. As for Vettius, I allowed some of my supporters to wreck his house and pillage his property. He was then dragged into the forum and nearly torn to pieces by the mob. In the end I saved his life by having him committed to prison. I also imprisoned the quaestor, Niger, for having exceeded his powers by allowing a magistrate of senior rank to be accused in his court. So for the time being my enemies left me alone.

Their attacks, however, had made a difference in me. They had aroused feelings of bitterness and anger which I had seldom known before. I became impatient and intolerant of opposition and no doubt many of my actions could be described rightly as high-handed and dictatorial. Partly, I suppose, this change, if change it was, in my character was the natural reaction of one who feels himself hunted and has to fight for his existence. I was also shocked, as I had been in the case of the pirates, by stupidity, conceit and inefficiency. Morally, too, I was offended by the contrast between my own willingness to make friends and to forgive with the implacable and irreconcilable enmity which, among a few, I undoubtedly aroused. Previously I had been content to laugh off and to forget those manifestations of ill-will which I had encountered. Now I began to guard and to assert my dignity, sometimes, perhaps, too vigorously.

There was, for example, the affair of the young Numidian prince, Masintha, who had greatly charmed me by his appearance and manners. I undertook to defend him in the senate when Juba, the son of the King of Numidia, came to Rome in order to secure support for his father, who claimed that this attractive young man owed him tribute. Juba's only contacts in Rome seem to have been with my enemies and, in speaking before the senate, he conducted himself most improperly. This bearded African addressed me in a contemptuous manner, hinting that I was both a revolutionary and a bankrupt and that I was only undertaking the defence of Masintha because of the vicious propensities which I shared with the young man. He even ventured, no doubt put up to this by Cato or one of Cato's imitators, to reproach me with effeminacy because of the fringed sleeves which I wore on my tunic and which, through my influence, were becoming fashionable in Rome. I could not bear to be insulted in this way, and so I crossed the floor of the senate, took Juba by the beard, and, after pulling him violently forwards, backwards and sideways, threw him to the ground. I then returned to my place and told the Numidian to continue his speech but, in the rest of it, to show proper respect for the elected magistrates of the Roman people. This action of mine had a disconcerting effect both on Juba himself and on those Romans who had encouraged him to make light of me. They were again disconcerted when, after it had been decided that Masintha must pay his debts and should be kept in custody until he had done so, I took the young man under my protection and declared that I would detain him at my own home. There were some protests, but I had my way. In fact, Masintha was with me for more than a year. At the end of this time, when I left Rome for my province in Spain, I smuggled him out of the city with me and finally set him free to return to his own country.

Apart from political and personal quarrels, I suffered from some domestic vexation in this year of my praetorship. The main scandal, which concerned Clodius and my wife, did not take place until the end of the year; but before this time I was deeply concerned to find that Pompey, by all accounts, seemed to be determined to divorce his wife, Mucia. Though I myself had been no more deeply implicated in her infidelity than had several others, I was sorry for her personally, since she enjoyed the position of being the wife of Rome's greatest citizen. Certainly I had no notion at all that the next wife that Pompey would choose was to be my own daughter. In fact, during this summer it appeared that all the calculations which I had made at the time when I was working in collaboration with Metellus Nepos had been entirely mistaken. Pompey's vanity had been gratified, as I intended it should be, by some of the things which Nepos and I had said about him. But he had been alarmed by the extent of the opposition which we had encountered and he was now following exactly the opposite policy to that which I had anticipated. He was actually proposing to make a marriage alliance with Cato's family and, even before he definitely divorced Mucia, his agents had approached Cato on this subject.

Very fortunately for my own future, Cato was foolish enough to turn down their suggestions. He had already committed himself to the view, for which no evidence existed, that Pompey aimed at setting up as King, and he could not resist the opportinity of once more advertising that mulish element in his character which he described as his integrity. He went about boasting of how he had rejected Pompey's offer and of how he, alone among the Romans, would always refuse to be bribed to give up any one of his convictions.

I see now that, though I had never had a high opinion of Pompey as a politician, I had in fact credited him with more intelligence than he possessed. He had failed to conciliate Cato and now, being too proud to go back on his decision to divorce Mucia, he alienated the Metelli and her other powerful friends. Nepos, who had reported to Pompey all the events which had led to his flight from Rome, had been angry enough when he found that Pompey had no intention of intervening with armed force and on the slender excuse that he was defending the rights of the tribunes ; he became more angry still when Pompey proposed to divorce his sister and to ally himself with the very man who had driven him out of the forum. The other brother, Metellus Celer, was even more incensed by the treatment which Mucia was receiving. Celer was now governor of Cisalpine Gaul and had a good prospect of becoming consul in two years' time. He was fond of Mucia, but he was even fonder of the idea of the importance of his family. An insult to a Metellus seemed to him something much more dreadful than treason. He became Pompey's implacable enemy and, in so doing, served, as things turned out, my own interests most admirably.

Metellus Celer himself held no strong views on the duties of wives to husbands. Indeed, since he was married to Clodia, he was in no position to do so. This year, while he was away in the north, Clodia continued to behave as she always had done, yet, so far as humanity is concerned, this year must have been the only valuable year of her existence. From her husband's province and probably with an introduction from him, the young Veronese poet Catullus arrived in Rome. He was a most learned and agreeable, if rather hot-tempered, youth. Personally I have always liked him and always taken an interest in his work. Indeed I was greatly upset when, some years later, he employed his great talents for vituperation against some of my officers and against me myself. His poetry is always good, though some of it suffers from excessive scholarship. I should guess, however, that the poems which he addressed, both in love and anger, to Clodia will still be read when his more ambitious efforts are forgotten. As soon as he appeared in Rome, he, like so many others, fell in love with Celer's wife, and, like so many others, was, for a short time, accepted as her lover. For Clodia, who was ten years senior to the young man, this love affair probably had little remarkable about it, but to Catullus and to the world in general it was an event of the greatest importance. For Catullus celebrated his joy, his passion and, finally, his despair in poetry which immediately and justly became famous. His first poem to

"Lesbia" (the poetical name which he gave to Clodia) was a brilliant imitation of Sappho. His later poems showed little trace of Greek influence and were altogether remarkable for their simplicity and strength. It is possible to laugh at the young man's extraordinary infatuation for Clodia, whom at first he evidently regarded not only as a kind of goddess but as a woman of pure and disinterested feelings. No one was surprised when, after a short time, he was replaced in her affections by another young man, Caelius Rufus, a friend of Cicero's and, later, a rather unreliable partisan of my own. But no one with any taste could find the poetry itself ridiculous and even in the very misguidedness of the poet's affections there seemed to be something grand. I myself, who would have been incapable of Catullus's aberrations in judgment, was profoundly moved not only by the verbal dexterity of these verses but also by a sincerity, depth and simplicity of feeling which were altogether admirable.

It was poetry of a new kind in our language and as soon as it appeared it made the work of other poets seem more like the clever exercises of schoolboys than the real effusion of genius. Up to this time Cicero, I suppose, had the highest reputation as a poet, though he was now lowering this reputation by the great numbers of verses which he was always turning out on the theme of his own consulship. My own poetry, too, is not bad. It is simple and direct, like the prose which I write on military matters. But I should be very vain if I imagined that it had the real fire of genius which I recognise in Catullus. I wish that he had lived longer. We need poets for the new world that is being born, and, as this new world takes shape, I should not be surprised to see a great poet prepared to devote himself to some great political or national idea rather than to the customary themes of love and idleness. I wish I had time to attempt this task myself. As it is, my only poetical works are, apart from a few tragedies, love poems and epigrams. Young Octavius actually suggested that, since I am worshipped with divine honours, I should suppress this early work of mine. But it is not, I think, without merit, and it will be good for posterity to remember that some generals are also literary men. I am not such a good poet as Sophocles, but I am probably a better general than he was. I greatly excel Sulla in both capacities.

As it was, few people at the time realised the importance of Clodia's new love affair. Much more gossip was provoked by the scandal in which her brother Clodius and my wife were concerned. This was a foolish enough affair in itself, but it caused me some embarrassment and, because towards the end of the year no one would talk of anything else, must have been very annoying to Pompey. For Pompey had, after a year of processions and parades, laid down his command. No doubt he would have been pleased if he could have found some pretext for keeping his army in existence, but no such pretext existed. So he disbanded his army and, with only a small escort of friends, rode northwards from Brundisium to Rome. He had presented enormous gratuities to his officers and men, and had promised to provide land for his men in the near future. He had destroyed the pirates and Mithridates ; he had settled the affairs of the whole east ; and finally he had behaved strictly in accordance with the constitution, thus showing how baseless had been the agitation conducted against him by Cato on the one side and by Crassus on the other. Naturally he expected to be received with honour and with gratitude. He was used to being regarded as the greatest man in the world.

However, in Rome he found that there was already in the senate a strong party aligned against him. Cato was not apt to admit that he had been ever wrong, and still insisted that Pompey was aiming at absolute power. Lucullus had already given notice that he would oppose the terms of the settlement of the east. Cicero was sulking, and aggrieved because Pompey had not yet congratulated him warmly or publicly enough on his handling of the conspiracy of Catiline. And, possibly most aggravating of all, the general subject of conversation at Rome was not the conquest of the east, but the affair of Clodius and my wife.

This affair had taken place in December. The occasion was the Festival of the Good Goddess which this year was being held at my house under the supervision of my mother and wife. It is an interesting festival and, though the women who take part in it are forbidden to reveal or to discuss with men anything in connection with its sacred rites, I have, of course, made myself at least partially acquainted with what goes on. The proceedings, it seems, are often of a somewhat orgiastic character and the ceremonies concerned with the display of various holy objects seem to indicate an eastern origin for the cult. The women take it very seriously, so much so that by no means all of them are willing to gratify one's curiosity on the subject. Since no men are allowed even to be present in the house when the ceremonies are taking place, I myself had gone away early in the evening, intending to return after dawn. Soon after midnight, however, I received an urgent summons from my mother. By the time I reached the house most of the women had already left, but those who were still there showed every sign of agitation and excitement. My wife Pompeia was shut in the bedroom, clearly in a state of hysteria. All she could do was to beg me not to believe anything that my mother might tell me and to assure me that my mother had always hated her. I was sorry for her under the circumstances, since I did not dislike her ; but I knew that my mother's word was a great deal more dependable than hers.

I soon received from my mother a true account of what had happened. Young Clodius, whose natural tendency was always to perform actions which, if known, would be shocking, had made his way into the solemn ceremony disguised as a girl and had been discovered. He had been actuated not by any interest in religion but by his passion for my wife, and certainly it would have seemed to him a most attractive idea to enjoy an assignation with a woman in circumstances which would have seemed to everyone quite impossible. There seems no doubt that Pompeia, though she always denied the fact, had entered into the spirit of this escapade and had concerted plans with Clodius beforehand. Unfortunately for both of them their plans were not made efficiently. Clodius had apparently taken such pains with his toilette that in any case, from the very richness of his clothes, he would have been likely to attract attention. Since he flattered himself on his powers of impersonating the opposite sex, instead of immediately going to find Pompeia he had mingled with the other women and began to gratify his curiosity with regard to the sacred objects which were being unveiled and the sacrifices which were about to take place. It appears that then one of my mother's women, attracted by the appearance of Clodius, began to make certain advances to him and that Clodius, in rejecting these advances, so far forgot himself as to speak loudly in a male voice. There was an instant alarm, in the course of which Clodius managed to escape and to hide himself in the room of one of Pompeia's maidservants. However, my mother then took matters in hand. She ordered that all the ceremonies should be stopped and that the sacred objects should be covered up. The house was then searched and before long Clodius was discovered and recognised. The women had been outraged at his impudence and had driven him out of doors in the most ignominious fashion. They had then returned to their homes very much earlier than they had been expected by their husbands.

Naturally next day and for some time afterwards all Rome was talking about Clodius. The affair was taken up with particular violence by the reactionary nobility who saw in it an opportunity both for ruining Clodius, whose influence with the people they rightly suspected, and for discrediting me, in whose house and for the sake of whose wife the sacrilege seemed to have taken place. I had some hopes that the affair might merely provoke gossip for some days. Most people expected me to divorce my wife immediately, but I had no wish to make myself ridiculous in the role of an outraged husband, and so I did what I could to pretend that the whole story had been greatly exaggerated. At a meeting of the College of Pontiffs over which I presided no mention was made of the guilt of any particular person. We merely declared that an act of sacrilege had taken place and that the sacrifices must be performed again. I had no personal animosity against Clodius and indeed was anxious to protect him. Most of his enemies were mine as well. He was an able speaker, a great favourite of the people and could be, I fancied, useful to me.

However, a small element in the senate continued to agitate for a public inquiry. Catulus, Lucullus and Cato were the leaders of this party and Cicero foolishly allowed himself to become associated with them. In the end it was decided that Clodius should be brought to trial, and it was only after this decision that I divorced my wife. She had ceased to be useful or attractive to me and, whether in this instance she was guilty or not, I could not afford to be suspected of conniving at her guilt. In getting rid of Pompeia I also pleased both my mother and my daughter.

The whole business of the trial of Clodius dragged on for several months into the new year and was extremely vexatious to me since, apart from everything else, it delayed my departure for Further Spain, which had been allotted to me for my province. The trial itself was more of a scandal than had been the original sacrilege. When proceedings were first instituted against Clodius, Cato had spoken of vindicating the claims of morality and Cicero had demanded a return to what he still regarded as the purity of public life which had marked his own consulship and which had so remarkably rapidly disappeared. Again he considered that " the good " should unite. But it was soon evident that the trial would only emphasise the existence of disunity and the power of corruption. Clodius was of course supported by his two sisters and by the many men whom they were able to influence. The sisters became all the more active when it appeared that Lucullus was prepared to give evidence of the incestuous relations that had existed between them and their brother. Even more powerful support came to Clodius from Crassus who, greatly surprised to find that he had nothing to fear from Pompey, had now returned to Rome and wished to assert himself against those who, like Cato and Catulus, had shown themselves to be his enemies. Clodius himself was also active. He had collected and bribed numbers of witnesses who were to declare that, at the time of the sacrilege, he was ninety miles away from Rome, and he had engaged bands of armed men who were to intimidate those few members of the jury who had not already accepted bribes from Crassus.

Even so it was only narrowly that Clodius escaped. The evidence against him was so overwhelming that it may be said that it required some courage to vote against it. His alibi was effectively demolished by the testimony of Cicero, who revealed the fact that Clodius had called upon him personally in Rome some hours before the women's festival was due to begin. In giving this testimony Cicero made, as later events were to show, a most dangerous enemy, and indeed I believe that shortly before the trial he had wished to withdraw from it all together. However, he had been subjected to persistent hen-pecking from his formidable wife, Terentia, who had convinced herself that any lukewarmness shown by her husband in the case could only be explained by some secret understanding between him and Clodia.

I myself was called as a witness and contented myself with denying all knowledge of the events alleged to have taken place at my house. Why, I was then asked, had I divorced my wife? I replied that my experience had shown me that it was necessary not only to be guiltless but also to be free of the suspicion of guilt. This reply of mine has, curiously enough, been remembered and is often quoted to-day as an example of the strictness of my morality, which has indeed, with the years, become rather stricter than it was then. At the time, however, I was merely referring to the fact that I myself had, not so long ago, been unjustly attacked on the suspicion of having been allied with Catiline.

My testimony was probably of some use to Clodius and he remained grateful to me. The verdict, in spite of the bribery, was a close one. Twenty-five of the jury voted against Clodius and thirty-one voted for his acquittal.

CHAPTER III

GOVERNOR IN SPAIN

I WAS eager to leave Rome at once, since in Spain I had much to do. Now, for the first time in my life, I was to command a regular army. Two legions were waiting for me in Spain and I had determined to raise another one when I arrived there. I was over forty and, though not completely ignorant of military affairs, was certainly inexperienced in them. Naturally I chose my staff with care. In particular I was glad to have the services of my friend Balbus, who is not only one of the most efficient administrators and engineers whom I have ever met, but is also a most lovable man and an admirable diplomatist. Since he began life as a citizen of Gades and had spent his early years in Spain, I had also the advantage of his expert knowledge of the country and of local conditions. Long before we left Rome we had planned roughly the lines on which our operations were to proceed. Time was short. In the following year I intended to stand for the consulship. I needed military prestige and, above all, I needed money.

As it was, I found it hard enough to get away from my creditors in Rome. Unpleasant threats were made to the effect that my baggage would be seized and I myself arrested if I attempted to leave the city without paying back at least something of the sums I owed. This I was in no position to do. I should have needed an enormous fortune in order to be worth nothing. So, even after the trial of Clodius, there were tiresome and dangerous delays. Once again I was saved by Crassus, who advanced to me a great sum of money, in fact a quarter of the total amount for which I was in debt. In this way I was able to satisfy the most pressing of my creditors. The rest, including Crassus, had to be content with speculating on my future success. I am glad that their investment has turned out for them so profitably.

Now that I was myself freed from the fear of arrest, I had to secure the safety of Prince Masintha, whom I could not honourably leave behind. I took him with me in my own litter until we were clear of the city boundaries and later arranged for him to take ship for Africa. Then, with Balbus and a few other friends, I went as rapidly as possible through northern Italy, through the Alpine villages and, after the rich land of the Province, across the Pyrenees into the different and gigantic landscapes of Spain.

It was already summer and, in a year from this time, I intended to be back in Rome as a candidate for the consulship. It was therefore necessary to begin operations immediately. I got to know the officers and men of my army while actually on the march and, as has always happened to me in every campaign, I not only got to know them but, in a strange way, came to love them. Indeed, my feeling for the soldiers and centurions under my command has been, I think, in some ways deeper than any other feeling that I have known. Only one or two great and intimate friendships can compare with it. And at this stage of my life both the feeling itself and the activities in which it was expressed were new to me and infinitely exciting. I revelled in the long marches beneath the summer sun and, whether riding or on foot, would go bareheaded, making no effort to conceal my increasing baldness. Indeed in every one of the physical aspects of warfare, except the mere shedding of blood, I took a delight which was very surprising to some of my friends and to most of my enemies. I was known already as a force in politics and I had also the reputation of a man of fashion, a connoisseur of the arts, an innovator in certain features of dress, a pursuer of women and one most careful of his personal appearance. Now, and almost immediately, I began to get a reputation of a very different kind. Stories were told of my incredible feats of horsemanship, of the rivers which I had swum across, of my endurance of heat and cold and hunger, of the care I took of my men, of their zeal for the undertaking of impossibilities, of the reckless- ness with which I myself would, at critical moments, expose myself to danger. Many of these stories were, of course, exaggerated. It is true, for instance, that I possessed a very remarkable horse, an animal of great size and strength, which no one except myself was able to ride. But it was not true, though the story is still repeated, that my horse's hoofs were split into five toes like that of the human foot.

Apart from the delight I discovered in physical exertion and in the sharing of danger, hardship and exultation, I also found this new way of life satisfying and enchanting from an intellectual and spiritual point of view. I had already exercised my faculties in the difficult and devious processes of Roman politics ; but in this military command it seemed to me that will, initiative, intellect and resolution could operate more honourably and with greater precision. This is not, I think, because the problems of a military commander are simpler than those of a statesman, or that he is more free from external control. It is rather a question of urgency ; for, whether his problems are simple or not, they must be dealt with immediately and continuously ; and, however free he may be from the supervision of others, he is directly and again continuously controlled by the necessity for keeping him- self and his men alive, strong and ready for action. Though, ideally speaking, we fight wars for the sake of peace, there is a sense in which war has more reality than peace can ever have. Life, death and honour, when pressing constantly upon one, have a different meaning from that in which these words are used in speeches before the people or the senate. In warfare the whole personality is engaged at every moment. Survival will depend on instantaneous decisions and on the real dexterity and perseverance both of body and mind. Even unworthy char- acters can be great in war ; they can become, as it were, better than they should be and can genuinely and generously share in the determination, the disappointments and the triumphs of others who are more courageous and intelligent than themselves.

So also the commander can love his men for their weakness as well as for their strength. But in peace time these common human weaknesses immediately appear reprehensible and inconvenient; and in peace time a man must be exceptionally gifted if he is able to exercise his own vitality to the full or recognise without envy the distinction of others.

How used I have become now to every aspect of warfare! Yet still I cannot resist its appeal and even now, when there is so much to detain me in Rome, when I am safe from every danger except possibly that of assassination, I must still pursue what seems to be my destiny and is certainly my pleasure. A soothsayer has told me to beware of to-morrow which is the Ides of March. I do not attach much importance to soothsayers, and the day after to-morrow, if all goes well, I shall again be on my way to join my army and to add in the east another province to the empire. My zest for the performance is as great as it was in those old days in Spain when for the first time I heard the voices of Roman soldiers saluting me as " Imperator."

My first campaign there was against the mountain tribes of Lusitania south of the river Tagus. These people were virtually independent and had become used to living, at least for some part of every year, on the profits made from plundering the more settled tribes who were under Roman protection. When I invaded the area I knew that my enemies in Rome would accuse me of deliberately provoking a war to suit my own interest. This indeed was precisely what I was doing; but, as has so often happened, my interest coincided with the welfare of those whom it was my duty to govern and protect. Cato, far away in Rome, would describe these savage mountaineers as the " innocent " and " harmless " victims of an " unprovoked " attack. The merchants of Gades and the peasantry in the plains knew better.

Before the beginning of winter I had cleared the mountains, defeated the enemy in a number of minor engagements, taken many prisoners and driven the still unsubdued tribesmen first to the Atlantic coast and then to an island off the coast. For the latter part of these operations we had been in country hitherto

unknown to the Romans and scarcely known even to my Spanish
troops. This Atlantic ocean, into which Sertorius had wished to
sail, was the end of the known world. I immediately decided to
explore it further, though for the time, with winter coming on,
all I could do was to make an unsuccessful attempt at forcing
a landing on the island where the rebellious tribes had taken
refuge. We had no landing craft more efficient than a few
unwieldy rafts and bad weather made the use of these extremely
difficult. Indeed the attempt, which resulted in some loss, should
never have been made, though its failure had no effect either on
the ultimate issue of the war or on the morale of the soldiers who,
apart from this one episode, had enjoyed continuous success and
retired to winter quarters considerably enriched and elated with
their achievements.

I spent the winter at Corduba, at Gades and at other towns
in the province and was continuously busy with various administrative tasks. In a short time I was able to do much to improve
the economic position both of the province and myself. I found
that many of the towns were still economically distressed by
having to pay indemnities that went back to the Sertorian war.
By either cancelling or reducing these contributions I increased
the prosperity of the towns and led them to abandon what had
hitherto been their hostile attitude to Rome. I dealt, too, with
the very acute problems of private indebtedness. As a debtor
myself and one who had recently escaped from the threat of
financial and political ruin, I felt strongly on this subject. I fixed
a limit of the percentage of a man's income which could be
claimed by his creditors. It was a measure which restored confidence to many who had been in despair and had a most salutory
effect on Spanish economy.

Then there were innumerable treaties and commercial agree-
ments which I went through and revised where necessary. There
were building projects, particularly in the town of Gades. Here,
too, partly as a matter of interest and partly for the sake of
efficiency, I thoroughly investigated the whole organisation of
religious worship. In this town an immense variety of cults had
been practised and I was able to bring about, with the consent

of the inhabitants, some notable reforms, including the abolition of human sacrifice. This barbarous custom must have dated from the time of the Carthaginian occupation and had still not entirely died out.

Throughout all this time I was in constant touch with Rome. My friends in the city kept me informed of every change in the political situation which continued to develop much as I had expected. During the autumn the chief news was of Pompey's triumph—the greatest that had ever been seen. Yet by the winter it became evident to me that Pompey had won nothing more than wealth, glory and what was to him no doubt the gratifying distinction of being allowed always to wear in the senate the purple toga of an imperator. I could well imagine him sitting in the senate and staring down with satisfaction on this coloured garment; but I could not imagine him making an effective speech or creating a party of his own strong enough to stand up to his political opponents. So far his only political success had been to secure the consulship for the following year for his own nominee, Afranius. His choice here had been a very bad one. Afranius was an excellent soldier, but was so lacking in culture and in political experience that he was apt to make himself a laughing stock whenever he opened his mouth. He owed his election entirely to the enormous sums which Pompey had spent in bribing the electors. No one had ventured to invoke Cicero's anti-bribery law against so great a figure as Pompey, but Cato had gone about self-righteously congratulating himself on having refused to be connected by marriage with one who could so notoriously transgress the laws. Moreover, the other consul elected was Metellus Celer, an even more stubborn character than Afranius and very much better connected and more influential. He was a bitter enemy to Pompey and would be supported in the senate both by that party which, since the recent death of old Catulus, was led by the even more reactionary Cato and also by Lucullus and his friends. People had imagined that Lucullus had retired from politics in disgust and was only interested in the breeding of great bearded mullets that would feed out of his hand, in planning pleasure gardens and in organising the most extravagant entertainments. But he had not forgotten how he had been treated by Pompey in Asia and he now began to act with his old energy. It seemed to me obvious that Pompey, who could only count on Afranius and one of the tribunes, was likely to experience great and perhaps insuperable difficulties in attaining the two ends upon which he had set his heart—ratification of his settlement of the east and land for his veterans.

Another piece of news from Rome concerned my friend Crassus and I saw immediately how important it was. Crassus had sponsored in the senate an appeal made by a powerful corporation of business men for a reconsideration of their contract for collecting taxes in Asia. Even Cicero, it seemed, regarded this claim as unjustified, but he was wise enough to see that, if there was to remain any reality at all in that " union of the classes " on which, in his view, the safety of the state depended, some consideration ought to be given to the interests of these powerful financiers. He had therefore, though rather reluctantly, spoken in their favour. Cato, however, acting on those strict moral principles of his which almost invariably did harm to his own party, had attacked both Crassus and the financiers in the most savage terms and had succeeded in blocking all attempts to debate their supposed grievances. The bitterest ill-feeling had been aroused and, so I was informed, Cicero himself had been heard to remark that the " union of the classes " had become a thing of the past.

I now conceived in a more vivid form an idea which for some time, I think, had been dormant at the back of my mind. Up to now I had been closely associated with Crassus in politics and I had also gone out of my way to show friendship towards Pompey. Yet Pompey and Crassus themselves appeared to be irreconcilable enemies. If, in my candidature for the consulship next year, I were to approach one of them for his support, I should automatically alienate the other. But now they were both involved in difficulties with those who were my own enemies. It seemed to me that I was on the verge of what might be the opportunity of a lifetime. A political alliance between myself, Pompey and Crassus would be regarded by almost everyone as an impossibility. Yet, if it did take place, it would be, in the present disposition of forces, absolutely overwhelming.

This powerful idea was constantly presented to me during the winter work of administration and during the renewed warfare in the spring. I began military operations very early in the year, since I wished to accomplish quickly what I had planned and then to return to Rome. During the winter Balbus had seen to the building of a fleet in Gades and by January all our plans were completed for a combined military and naval expedition up the Atlantic coast.

By the early summer the whole campaign was over. I had set out at least a month earlier than expert advisers had regarded as possible. Here I had certainly taken a risk, but, in view of my further plans, the risk seemed justified and, as it happened, everything went well. The sudden appearance of both fleet and army entirely demoralised the defenders of the island from which we had been repulsed in the previous autumn. We had no difficulty in making a landing and took considerable numbers of prisoners. I then sailed still farther north and received the submission of a number of tribes which had never yet been incorporated into the Roman province. Had it been possible for me to have spent more time on these conquests, I should have proceeded farther still, since everything I saw was unknown and for that reason fascinating. But I had already done everything that I had set out to do. I had been saluted by my troops as "Imperator," and, on the strength of their acclamation and our achievements, would be able to claim a triumph when I returned to Rome. I felt some reluctance when I ordered the fleet to turn again southwards, since no such fleet had ever been seen before in these waters and in front of us lay so much that was unexplored and unsubdued. In fact, however, I was on the threshold of events which were to prove for me and for the world decisive. I could still only dimly discern their pattern, but what I could see was enough to fill me with a mounting excitement. Every report I received from Rome indicated that the opportunity for which I had been waiting was at hand. In order to grasp this opportunity it was essential that I myself should be there in person.

CHAPTER IV

THE CONSULAR ELECTION

SINCE TIME was of such importance I disregarded the law which forbids a provincial governor to leave his province until his successor has arrived to replace him. I planned to arrive outside the gates of Rome in June, to claim the triumph which I had earned, and then to stand for the consulship. As the elections were to be held in August I should have little time for canvassing and most of this canvassing would, in any case, have to be done for me by my friends and agents, since I myself was debarred by law and tradition from entering the city until the celebration of my triumph. Officially, too, candidates for the consulship have to hand in their names in person to the appropriate magistrate in the city on a fixed day about a month before the elections. I fancied, however, that I should be allowed to do this by proxy if I had still not celebrated the triumph by this time.

My popularity was, I considered, sufficiently great for me to count with certainty on being elected ; and as a result of the sale of prisoners in Spain and the many gifts which I had received from the provincials I was in a fairly sound position financially, though it was still necessary to borrow money both for my election expenses and for the organisation of the triumph. It was the last time in my life that I did so.

I was kept busy enough with the election campaign and with the preparations for the triumph which, of course, I wanted to be as splendid a spectacle as possible. But far the most important of my activities were concerned with the secret negotiations into which I was entering with Pompey and Crassus. I found Pompey in a predicament which, for him, was ignominious and to me appeared pathetic. He was used to giving orders and to deploying immense forces towards some definite end. Now, in the unfamiliar world of politics, he found his will disregarded, thwarted or derided, and he had no instrument by means of which to make it effective. He was like some splendid though not very resourceful animal caught in a net from which he lacked the ability to extricate himself, and surrounded on all sides by enemies much inferior to him in force and determined, in their malice, to take the fullest advantage of this moment of his distress. His first and most humiliating failure was in connection with a Land Law that had been introduced early in the year by the tribune Flavius, who was acting as his agent. The chief purpose of the law was to provide land for Pompey's veterans, but it also contained provisions for redistributing land among impoverished citizens who had not served in the army. Altogether the proposals seemed to me to have been sensible enough, though not so thorough or far-reaching as those which had been designed by Crassus and myself and had been rejected during Cicero's consulship. But these proposals of Pompey were even more bitterly resisted than ours had been. In the senate the consul, Metellus Celer, had shown so violent and uncompromising an attitude that the tribune Flavius, no doubt with the consent of Pompey, had actually arrested him and kept him in prison for a short time by setting down his tribune's bench against the prison doors. Had the other consul, Pompey's friend Afranius, been a man of any political ability, or had Pompey himself any notion of how to organise public opinion, this gesture might have been effective. As it was, it had been a complete failure. No spontaneous rising of the people occurred—and indeed the people very rarely do rise spontaneously. Nearly everyone was shocked at the episode and it was soon found necessary not only to release Metellus but to obey him. The proposals of Flavius were dropped and the whole question of land legislation indefinitely postponed. So Pompey, in spite of a prestige greater than that of any Roman in history, had found himself incapable of keeping his promises to his own troops. Nor was he any more successful in securing the ratification by the senate of his settlement of the east. On this subject he found himself opposed by the violent moral fervour of Cato and by the intelligent informed criticism of Lucullus. Even Crassus, who had his own reasons for hating Cato's party, supported them on this issue simply because of his personal antagonism to Pompey.

As soon as I arrived outside the city, I began to enter into the negotiations which were, as things turned out, to be the most important ones in which I have ever engaged. In these negotiations a great part was taken by Balbus, a friend both of Pompey and of myself and one who had genuinely at heart the interests of the two of us. Balbus was able to recall to Pompey the many services which I had already rendered him—the fact that I alone in the senate had supported the motion for Pompey's command against the pirates, my collaboration with Pompey's agent, Metellus Nepos, and much else, indeed a record quite sufficient to outweigh any feelings against me which Pompey may have entertained on account of the scandal which connected my name with that of Mucia. More important still were the promises which I could give for the future. Here it was true to say that I and I alone could, if I were elected consul, guarantee to carry out, whether the senate liked it or not, the measures which Pompey desired to have passed. Disappointed and bewildered as Pompey was, he was at first inclined to doubt my powers; but after I had met him personally in secret, he came to see that these promises could be made good; for Pompey was not stupid, only inexperienced and ill-suited for politics. In dealing with him, it was necessary to employ great tact, for his feelings were easily wounded and had already been wounded not only by his enemies but by the blundering attentions of his friends and in particular by Cicero, who was continually giving the impression that he regarded the suppression of Catiline as a more considerable achievement than the conquest of the whole east. I did not make any such mistake. I scarcely mentioned my own recent campaign but took the keenest interest in Pompey's accounts of the destruction of the pirates, the capture of Jerusalem, the equipment and training of native troops and much else. My interest in such matters was genuine and professional. From these conversations

I learned much and was rewarded by receiving from Pompey one or two complimentary remarks to the effect that I myself seemed to possess an unexpected and not inconsiderable aptitude for military science. Gradually a confidence that was akin to friendship began to spring up between the two of us and, being now certain of Pompey's support in my candidature, I was able to pass on to the second and more difficult stage of the negotiations, that is to say to attempt to bring about a reconciliation of Pompey with Crassus and Crassus with Pompey.

Here again it was necessary to use the greatest tact, for ever since their joint consulship ten years previously the two had been open enemies, each jealous and mistrustful of the other, and even though it was easy enough to convince each that, by forgetting the past, enormous advantages for the present and future could be secured, neither of them showed the least willingness to perform this act of forgetfulness. For my own interests, the support of Pompey was more important than that of Crassus ; but I was bound to Crassus by heavy financial obligations and I was extremely anxious to secure by means of Crassus the powerful support of the business community. This I could obtain simply by promising to revise the contracts made by the collectors of taxes in Asia, a manœuvre which would immediately disrupt the so-called " union of the classes " and would leave the irreconcilable element in the senate isolated and powerless. The certainty of this event appealed both to the military mind of Pompey and to Crassus's own financial sense. Each of them, moreover, had been in different ways offended by the intransigence of Cato and his supporters. Indeed it is probable that Cato's puritanical and egotistic statesmanship played as large a part as my own tact and diplomacy in finally bringing about an uneasy but none the less effective understanding between Crassus and Pompey.

These negotiations were carried on throughout the summer and in secret. There was no secret, however, about my candidature for the consulship, and the mere fact that I was standing for this office at all aroused the bitterest feelings among my enemies. These feelings would have been more bitter still had the real situation been known ; for though I was ready and anxious to act with moderation, I was not to be humiliated and so had, before the election took place, equipped myself with what, if I were forced to use it, would prove an overwhelming power. I knew that I could count on the support of the Assembly of the People and, if the senate were to prove recalcitrant, I was prepared, as other reformers had done in the past, to legislate by means of the Assembly and over the head of the senate. Nor had I any need to fear for myself, as these earlier reformers had had every reason to fear. I would enjoy, at least for the time being, the support not only of the people but of the moneyed class outside the senate. Most important of all, there was no military power from outside which could intervene in the interests of my enemies. The only military power that existed was that of Pompey and with Pompey I was in close alliance. The mere threat to recall Pompey's veterans to their standards in order to enforce the just claims made for them by their leader would be enough to indicate that all opposition to my decisions would be hopeless.

Before the election my enemies, and Cato in particular, attacked me spitefully and ineffectively. In July, at the time when it was necessary to give in one's name in Rome as a candidate for the consulship, I was still outside the city, having already made the most splendid preparations for my triumph. I had asked permission of the senate to have my name handed in by proxy and my request was debated on the day before nominations for consular candidates were due to be made. There were several precedents for the granting of such a request as this, and in fact the majority of the senate were disposed to grant it on this occasion. Cato, however, to the great delight of a small circle of his partisans, succeeded in depriving me of the honour which I had earned. His simple expedient was to remain on his feet interminably uttering moral platitudes or untruths until it was past the hour when it was legally possible to take a vote on the subject of my request. So I was compelled either to forgo the triumph or the consulship. Of course I did not hesitate between the alternatives, nor could anyone have supposed me likely to have done so. I abandoned my claim to a triumph and entered the city on the following day to hand in my name as candidate for the consulship. I was attended by very large crowds of my supporters inside Rome who, together with my old soldiers, had been infuriated by Cato's mean and petty piece of obstructionism. Indeed the anger of those picked troops of mine whom I had brought from Spain to Italy far surpassed my own annoyance at having lost, for the moment, the honour of a triumph and at having already wasted so much money on preparing for it. For the troops had entered into the preparations with the utmost enthusiasm. The greatest pains had been taken with their equipment and, though they were trained in the first place as fighting men, they had, for the occasion, learned and practised a precision of movement on parade which, they were convinced, would eclipse anything that had ever been seen before. They had composed verses in honour of their general and they had already rehearsed the singing of them. The verses were not always respectful, but were invariably affectionate. One of them had the refrain :

> *A bald-headed lecher we bring into town*
> *Look out for your wives, boys, he'll knock 'em all down.*

This verse and others with reference to my friendship with the King of Bithynia became very popular in the army, but were not sung in a triumph for many years to come. At this time the angry feelings of the soldiers, disappointed of the honour they felt due to their general and to themselves, reinforced the already embittered feelings of the majority of Roman citizens who, in my absence, had lacked a leader and were now enthusiastic at my return. Indeed this popular demonstration in my favour must in itself have made it evident that my election was a certainty, and those who most feared me now gave up all hope of preventing it. Instead they concentrated their efforts on hampering me while in office and on depriving me of the honour that would be properly due to me when my year of office was over.

A competitor at the elections who could be relied upon to do his best, if elected, to hamper me was Bibulus, my old colleague in the aedileship. Ever since we had held this office together he had disliked me both personally and politically, yet now he had once again approached me with a view to securing my influence with the people on his behalf in return for more of that financial support which he had afforded during our aedile-ship. Soon, however, he changed his tactics. He was now Cato's son-in-law and he began to feel that his prospects for election would be improved and his sense of his own importance best satisfied if he were to come forward definitely as my opponent. In so doing he would gain the support of all Cato's party and no doubt fancied that just as Metellus Celer had so successfully dealt with Afranius, so he, with the same backers, would be able to deal with me. A fund was started to buy votes for Bibulus and Cato himself subscribed to this fund. " The general good," he was reported as saying, " must make me sacrifice even my own notion of right and wrong "—a sophistry which came very badly from this arch-moralist who had so often proclaimed that no consideration of any kind could induce him ever to forsake the strict rule of right and who had boasted that, so far as he was concerned, the whole world could collapse in ruin so long as what he conceived to be " justice " was done. As for Bibulus, he was greatly heartened by the notice which was being taken of him. He pledged himself to act consistently in opposition to me, if he and I were elected consuls together. Neither he nor those who were spending such large sums of money to purchase his election realised that I had already secured for myself a position of such strength that it could make no difference to me whatever whether Bibulus were elected or not.

A final and most provocative move against me was made on the eve of the elections, when it was customary to decide in advance what provinces would be allotted to the new consuls when their year of office was over. After my successes in Spain it was naturally supposed that, if I were elected consul, I would wish afterwards to exercise another military command. I myself was already thinking in terms of Gaul. My enemies, however, rightly judging that my election was certain, now did what they could to ruin my future and to deprive Rome of my services. They succeeded in passing a decree in the senate providing that the two new consuls should, against all precedent, not be allotted provinces at all. Instead they were to be entrusted with a vague commission described as "forests and cattle-runs," a purely civilian appointment which could be handled competently by any intelligent clerk.

I myself was still prepared, if at all possible, to act with moderation ; but when I saw how determined my enemies were in their attacks on my honour and my future safety, I, too, became prepared for hostility and was gratified to reflect that I could confront them with a determination at least as great as their own and with forces much more powerful than any which they could muster.

In August I was elected consul, with Bibulus as my colleague. I devoted the remaining months of the year to preparing the legislation which I proposed to bring forward as soon as I took office on the first of January. Though much of my planning was still secret, I attempted, in a general way, to secure support from all quarters except those of the extreme reactionaries. I even, through the agency of my friend Balbus, made an effort to win Cicero over to my side. On this occasion Balbus, who is an admirable negotiator, very nearly succeeded in his aim. Cicero had already become alienated from those extremists by whose help he himself had gained power and he was, it seems, greatly impressed when Balbus suggested to him that I wished to have the inestimable advantage of being guided by his advice. Indeed it would have been wise of him if at this time he had accepted the offer of my friendship. As it was he acted with irresolution. He was afraid of offending those who had been his powerful supporters in the past, even though he knew them to be politically unreliable or worse. Nor could he imagine any coalition of which he was not himself the head. He was still, so Balbus told me, incapable of seeing beyond the period of his own consulship, and he had insisted on reading to him long extracts from the Latin poem which he had composed on the subject. In Balbus's view, which has turned out to be correct, Cicero was not likely to be in the future either very helpful or very dangerous to me.

It was from Pompey, of course, that I had hoped most and

I became more closely associated with Pompey than I had imagined possible. It is, as experience will show, not at all uncommon for middle-aged men to fall passionately in love, and Pompey now fell in love with my daughter Julia. Nothing, of course, could suit my own interests better than to have Pompey as my son-in-law; moreover, I was beginning to like him and could see that he would almost certainly make my daughter happy; Julia, too, was attracted both by him personally and, not unreasonably, by the prospect of becoming the wife of one who was still known as the greatest man in the world. It was arranged that the marriage should take place early in the year of my consulship. Before then I had the somewhat embarrassing task of persuading my old friend Servilia that it was necessary to break off what had amounted to an engagement between Julia and her own son, young Brutus. Here, as so often, Servilia showed herself extremely sensible. It was about this time, I think, that I bought for her a pearl for which I paid more money than had ever been paid before in Rome for a single piece of jewellery.

So the time approached for me to take up the chief office in the state. Towards the end of the year there took place a sudden and most devastating storm and inundation of the Tiber. Much valuable property was destroyed, a whole theatre of wood was washed away, and ships in the harbour of Ostia were thrown up on to the land. There were high winds, heavy rains, thunder and lightning. In later years people have often spoken of this storm—"the storm in the consulship of Metellus," they call it—and profess to have regarded it as an omen threatening the break-up of the state and the beginning of the civil war. It is true that from this moment the balance of power was altered, but it was altered in the direction of efficiency. As for the civil war, my enemies and my friend Pompey brought that upon themselves.

CHAPTER V

CONSUL

I used to be told in my childhood by my tutors that the greatest day in the life of a Roman noble was that day on which, accompanied by his friends and followers, he went to the Temple of Capitoline Jupiter to sacrifice the traditional bulls and to enter upon his year of office as consul of the Roman people. Even old Marius would speak with veneration of this ceremony and of the dignity of the office and of the occasion, though he himself had gained his first consulship not by any political ability but solely because of his military record and his vulgar, though popular, attacks on the very concept of aristocracy. I, on the other hand, so far as warfare was concerned, was almost unknown. Leaving aside Pompey and Lucullus, there must have been at least twenty men in the senate who had greater claims than myself to any military distinction. I had risen to the consulship by my skill in political manœuvre, by my reckless extravagance, by my ability to make friends and by hard work. I had shown, too, a certain consistency and fearlessness which commanded respect. For this year at least I should be able to shape affairs as I wished to shape them. I knew that it was in this year that I must secure the future, and as on the first of January I ascended the slopes of the Capitol to take my part in the sacrifices of bulls, I gazed on those images of Marius which I had caused to be re-erected and my thoughts turned to my early days in which I had learned the lesson that, in the final analysis, power depends on force of arms. I thought of the many men whom I had known who had perished violently in the convulsions of our times. I wondered, as I still wonder, whether I was likely to prove an exception and could avoid either slaughtering or being slaughtered by my fellow citizens. Now, certainly, it was too late for me to go back. I had, up to a certain point, forced events to follow my guidance, but I also was in the forcible grip of events. Even to be secure I had still to increase my power. I had reached an eminence which might satisfy others and which could be regarded as the end of a long and laborious passage of my life. Beyond it, however, lay further heights and an unknown country towards which I was impelled both by ambition and by necessity. Even if the future had been revealed to me I could not have acted differently. Even to-day, when no power in the world exists that is comparable to mine and when the only danger I have to face is that of assassination, I must still advance, still conquer and still increase the realm of order. Yet in this necessity I find my freedom. I am not, as Marius was, a prisoner of passion. I know what I am doing and it was I myself who chose to become an instrument of necessity.

I have never, except sometimes in my dealings with native tribes, chosen violence where conciliation was possible. So, at the beginning of this first consulship of mine, I did everything I could to allay the suspicions of my colleague Bibulus and to win the good opinion of moderate elements in the senate. If only Cicero had listened to Balbus and openly given me his support, I might have been successful, for I was concealing the powers of compulsion which in fact I possessed and would not have employed them if I could have got my way without their use.

I began immediately by bringing before the senate a Land Law which was designed both to alleviate poverty and to satisfy the claims of Pompey's soldiers. It was unprecedented for a consul in person to introduce a Land Law. Such legislation had always been promoted by tribunes and was always, however wise it might be, regarded as revolutionary. I had hoped, by personally sponsoring the law, to give it an appearance of respectability. And indeed the law which I proposed for the redistribution of state land was singularly moderate. I was careful to point out that there were to be no compulsory expropriations, and that the rich land of the Campagna, the chief source of income of the great land-owners, was specifically excluded from the provisions of the bill. I made it clear that I myself would not serve on the commission for redistributing the land and I expressed myself ready to agree to any modifications or alterations of any clause in the bill that were approved by the senate. I pointed out how admirable a thing it would be for a united senate to pass, after due deliberation, a popular and just measure, and I carefully refrained from any threats as to what my conduct might be if the senate refused to be persuaded.

This may well have been the last time in our history when the senate had the opportunity of acting as a wise, independent and constructive governing body. They threw the opportunity away. My reasonable attitude and the politeness of my manner had made it hard for them to oppose openly a measure which was in itself so moderate and necessary. But Cato, Lucullus and their party were not going to agree to any measure which would do Pompey good and increase my own popularity. For weeks they avoided, by various tricks of debating, all serious discussion of the bill, and for weeks I remained patient. It only needed, I thought, the intervention on the side of reason of some such respected senator as Cicero for the law to be passed quickly and without disorder. But Cicero had, as it were, gone into hiding. It was a moment when he might have been of real service to the state. As it was, his inaction and irresolution helped to produce the very violence which, in all his speeches, he claims he has done his best to avoid. The year started under the name of " the consulship of Caesar and Bibulus " ; before it was over it became known as " the consulship of Julius and Caesar." This was not by my choice.

I am, I think, more patient than most people. Certainly none of my friends would complain that I am easily angered. Yet I have been, on some very few occasions, quite overcome by ungovernable rage. Cato, more than any other man, used to be capable of exciting this feeling in me. He did so at one meeting of the senate when, after I had again attempted to induce a reasonable discussion of the Land Law, he rose from his seat and, speaking with deliberate insolence, said, " People in general ought to be very happy with the constitution which we have. I regard any kind of innovation as unnecessary." Suddenly I found the man intolerable. I ordered my lictors to seize him and to put him into prison for a time. There, I thought, he could reflect at leisure on the merits of a constitution which, from the time of my boyhood, had never worked in the interests of efficiency, but had been most apt to frustrate genius and, at the cost of continual bloodshed, to delay what was necessary and to crush what was desirable. At the same time I wished to show his party that I was not prepared to put up for ever with their calculated insincerities and their ignorance of real facts.

However, my action was a mistake. Instead of raising the disturbance which I had expected, Cato behaved with dignity. In complete silence he allowed himself to be led away, and this silence of his was more effective than any words could have been. Some of the senate rose to follow him on his way to prison and refused to listen to me when I asked them to resume their seats. I saw then that the moment which I had expected, but had endeavoured to postpone, had come. I cancelled my orders to the lictors and allowed Cato with the other senators to take their places again. For some seconds they may have imagined that they had won a victory, but they became alarmed when I began to speak.

I told them that I had put the Land Law before them so as to give them the fullest opportunity of amending it and correcting it. Instead of carrying out their duty, they had merely obstructed matters and had not even got so far as a preliminary discussion. Now, I said, the law would go directly before the people and the people alone should decide upon it.

My words were intended as a declaration of war and were received as such. Many of the senators, knowing how great was my personal influence with the people, were overawed. They, too, would have to appeal to the people at subsequent elections and their careers depended on the votes which they would receive. Many others, however, still followed the guidance of Cato and Lucullus. They now began to hold private meetings at the house of Bibulus and to concert measures for frustrating my intention. They were undoubtedly prepared to use force, but, being so far ignorant of the understanding that had been reached between Pompey, Crassus and myself, were not aware that, if it came to force, all the force was on my side.

I held several preliminary meetings in the forum which were attended by large numbers of people. When Bibulus appeared at one of them, I treated him with the greatest courtesy, begging him to listen to what the people themselves said, to withdraw his opposition to the law and to avoid an unnecessay cleavage of opinion between people and senate. I urged him to speak to the people himself to reassure them. Bibulus, however, had by this time acquired a very exaggerated idea of his own importance. He merely stepped forward and said, " If every one of you want this law, you will not get it—not while I am consul." Though extremely stupid, he was a brave man, and stood up well to the hissing and cat-calling that followed his words.

It was now time, I considered, to reveal plainly our strength which was, in fact, overwhelming, though it might still be resisted. At the next meeting of the people which I organised I was, to everyone's surprise, accompanied by both Pompey and Crassus, who gave every impression of being on excellent terms with each other. I called upon both of them to speak and each admirably supported the other. Pompey in particular produced a great impression. He went through every clause of the law in detail, complained of the ingratitude with which he personally had been treated by his enemies and congratulated both Crassus and myself on supporting the just claims of his soldiers and the real interests of the people. I then turned to him and shouted out, " Pompey the Great, I the consul and the people appeal to you. If this law is attacked by violence, what will you do to uphold it ? "

There was an expectant hush and Pompey, who, though not a speaker of much ability, always was capable of rising to an occasion, replied, " I hold no office. I am a private citizen. But I am honoured by being asked for help by the consul and by the Roman people. I say that, if your enemies produce swords, I can produce legions."

His words were followed by tremendous applause and were

soon repeated everywhere in the city. It must now have been evident to everyone that our combination of power and influence was irresistible, and in fact the majority of the senate did recognise this fact immediately. Cato, Bibulus and their friends suddenly found themselves isolated, but only gradually came to realise how inconsiderable, from the first, were the forces which they claimed to represent. First Bibulus, in an absurdly legalistic way, attempted to prevent the holding of a legislative assembly of the people. He announced that every day for the rest of the year he would take the auspices and that thus on no day would it be legal for an assembly to be held. I took no notice whatever of this intervention and went on with my arrangements.

This time there were no mistakes such as those which occurred at the assembly organised by Metellus Nepos during my praetorship. We had in any case the almost unanimous support of the people and, to prevent any interference with the proceedings, I had distributed throughout the forum reliable detachments of men, some of them armed, using for this purpose both Pompey's veterans and some of my own troops from Spain who were still in Rome. I came into the forum myself at dawn and prepared to speak from a position at the top of the steps of the temple of the Dioscuri.

The expected interruption soon occurred. Bibulus, accompanied by Cato and by the ex-consuls Lucullus and Metellus Celer, began to make their way through the crowd. They were flanked by guards of their own and were allowed to reach the foot of the steps of the temple where I stood. Bibulus was certainly acting with courage. Indeed, had I not given express orders that his life must be spared, he would probably have lost it. As soon as he attempted to mount the steps, the crowd fell upon him. He was rolled on to the ground where someone threw a basket of dung over his head. The rods were torn from the hands of his lictors and broken ; his guards were swept aside and driven out of the forum. He himself somehow managed to get to his feet. Wiping the filth from his eyes, he bared his chest and shouted out, " Make an end of me ! Kill your consul ! And let that be remembered as one of Caesar's acts ! " But I had no intention

of allowing Bibulus to become a martyr. Both my own supporters and his friends hustled him out of the way to the safety
of an adjoining temple.

Cato now attempted to follow the example of Bibulus and
rushed up the steps. He was even more severely handled, but,
though he was beaten with sticks and cut about with stones and
chased through the crowd with blows raining on him from all
directions, he managed to slip round to the back of the temple
and then, appearing through a side door, had the courage to make
a second attempt at interruption. This time he was beaten more
severely than before. He left the forum cursing and groaning,
scarcely able to stand upon his feet. Lucullus and the others had
already disappeared.

I then proceeded to the passing of the bill and added to it a
clause that all members of the senate and all candidates for office
must swear on oath to abide by the law and not seek in any way
to alter it. Next day I called a meeting of the senate and informed
them of the necessity under which they lay. I found the senators
more amenable than I had expected. No one dared to blame me
personally for the violence that had been shown to Bibulus and
Cato. Most had already grasped the fact that opposition was
useless, and Bibulus, deeply offended by the timorousness of his
party, which he had believed to be larger than it was, announced
his intention of remaining in his house during the rest of his
term of office. This was another legalistic expedient of his,
designed to give an excuse for maintaining that any laws which
I might pass in his absence could be considered invalid.

A few senators, however, still asserted that they would refuse
to take the oath. I was in no mood now to consider their dignity.
At another assembly of the people I passed a law which imposed
the penalty of death on those who still refused to obey the people's
will. I would have been most reluctant to have had to act in
accordance with this law, and fortunately it was unnecessary to
do so. After some hesitation, even Cato consented to swear the
oath. He was persuaded by Cicero that Rome could not do
without him.

I had now fulfilled the first of my promises to Pompey. It

was easy to fulfil the second. I informed Lucullus that, unless he withdrew all opposition to the ratifying of Pompey's settlement in the east, I should arrange for an official inquiry into his own conduct in Asia and into the ways by which he had acquired his enormous fortune. Lucullus was terrified. He was one of the greatest generals whom we have had ; yet, he could not bear the thought of losing his fishponds and his artificial gardens. He was never active in politics again. It would now, I knew, be easy to have Pompey's arrangements for the east established as he wished them to be. Finally, when the commissioners for the distribution of land had been appointed, I passed an additional law which made it possible to buy up land from the great estates of the Campagna. Pompey was delighted. He intended to superintend personally the work of the commission in this area, and he was now in a position to fulfil all the promises which he had ever made. Within three months that political coalition of his enemies and mine which had seemed to him so powerful had been rendered, at least for the time being, entirely innocuous.

Before leaving Rome to take up his appointment in the Campagna, Pompey had become my son-in-law. This marriage more than anything else disturbed our enemies. Opinions were divided as to whether I was making use of Pompey or whether Pompey was making use of me for the furtherance of some plot for seizing absolute power. No such plot, of course, existed either then or later, though naturally we advanced each other's interests and would, I think, have continued to do so to the end, if only Julia had lived. Pompey's love for her and her love both for Pompey and for myself were, though our enemies could not see this, most important factors making for peace and security. I had every reason to be glad when I saw how passionately devoted Pompey was to my daughter, and I despised those who mocked at him for what they described as an old man's dotage for a girl. Pompey was very far from senile. If one could criticise him at all, it would be for not having grown old enough. He still retained the vanity of his youth and the desire not so much to be, as to appear, the greatest ; and he remained ignorant and even frightened of politics.

At about the time of his marriage to Julia, I also married again and I also was fortunate in my choice. Calpurnia has seen little enough of me in the years since her marriage, since nearly all of them have been spent in warfare. But she has been a good and affectionate wife. She is also extremely sensible, and it is strange to find her, as she has been this evening, nervous and distraught. She has some kind of superstitious fear about my leaving the house to-morrow. Knowing her normal good sense, I am half inclined to pay attention to her. Yet now, when I can so easily afford to offend the senate, I am rather reluctant to do so unless for some good reason. They will be meeting to-morrow in Pompey's theatre and will expect me to be there. And once again, when the meeting is over, I shall be leaving Calpurnia behind.

When I first married her I certainly calculated the advantages of the match. Her father, Piso, was a respectable character politically, a moderate and just one of those whom I wished to win over to my side. He was to stand for the consulship this year and Pompey, Crassus and I had planned to support both him and Pompey's old friend and lieutenant, Gabinius. It was necessary that we should have our own men in office for the following year in order to prevent the kind of agitation which Bibulus and his friends would certainly try to organise if they could.

In particular I was anxious that there should be no attempts to disturb the arrangements for my provincial command. Here I made use of the tribune Vatinius, one of the ugliest men I have ever met, with the most unfortunate swellings all over his face and neck. But Vatinius is a good fellow, excellent company, quite fearless in front of a crowd. I have even found him a competent commander of troops. It was through his agency that I was now freed from the humiliating restrictions which the senate had attempted to impose on me by allotting to me, after my consulship, a province which consisted of cattle runs. Again we proceeded directly to the assembly of the people. Vatinius proposed a law cancelling the senate's previous decree and providing that I should receive as pro-consul the governorship of Cisalpine Gaul and Illyricum for the exceptionally long period of five years. I was to have a force of three legions and the authority to choose my own officers. The law was passed without difficulty. Some protests, in particular from Cato, were made in the senate ; but, after their recent humiliation over the land law, most of the senators were wise enough to accept with as good a grace as possible what the people had decided. The province offered to me was, from the point of view of the ambitious military operations which I intended to carry out, the best available. I would have preferred Gaul beyond the Alps, since we were already receiving news of dangerous movements among the tribes in that area, and I had even conceived the idea that those vast territories in the west which were hitherto almost unknown might be subdued and brought over to Rome. However, what was at this time the small Roman province beyond the Alps had been allotted to Metellus Celer. I was therefore making plans for an expedition eastward from Illyricum towards the Danube and the Black Sea when I received an opportunity greater than any I had expected.

Metellus Celer, after a short illness, died before taking up his command. Some say that he had been poisoned by his wife Clodia, who by this time, I think, had left Catullus and was engaged in a love affair with young Caelius Rufus. But it would have been unlike her to murder a husband for the sake of a lover, and Rufus, whom I knew well, though he came to hate her in the end, never suggested that she had committed this sort of a crime for his sake. At the moment of Celer's death reports from the north were particularly alarming. This was the area in which my Uncle Marius had won his greatest victories and again, it seemed, Rome might be threatened by a Gallic or Germanic invasion. I at once approached Pompey and my father-in-law, Piso. Through them both the people and the senate were urged to add Transalpine Gaul with an additional legion to the command to which I had been appointed already. Even the senate submitted quietly. Probably my enemies believed that by passing this decree they might be getting rid of me for ever. They could scarcely imagine me in the role of a Pompey or a Lucullus and they both hoped and expected that my career as a soldier would end in defeat, disgrace, and, quite possibly, death. But to me it seemed that I had acquired more than I had ever hoped for. I was inexpressibly delighted and, when some senators hinted that I was unfit for a command of such extent, I was angry enough to tell them that from this moment I should be able, if I wished, to trample on them as a cock tramples on hens. One of them, trying to wound me by an allusion to the persistent story about my relations with King Nicomedes, replied, " That is scarcely the position for a woman to take up," but by this time I had regained my good temper. I told him to remember that there had once been a great queen in Syria by the name of Semiramis, and that the Amazons, all women, had in the past overran the whole of Asia.

So in a few months I had reached and surpassed every one of my main objectives. It remained to counter the opposition that was now beginning to grow and to secure the future.

CHAPTER VI

BEFORE THE DEPARTURE

THE OPPOSITION was, of course, centred round Bibulus and Cato. It derived its main strength from a group of young nobles who were either jealous of our power, as Bibulus was, or were influenced by the doctrinaire political theorising of Cato. Among the latter was young Brutus. I should imagine that even to-day, when I have done so much for him, he still hankers for that impossible thing of the past, the republic of our ancestors. In spite of his efficiency and his many good and agreeable qualities, he has in him a streak of sentimentality and might even now, if he were not an honourable man with a true sense of gratitude, be induced to join some conspiracy against my life. It seems that he and others came near to doing so in the year of my first consulship. But these young men were not dangerous in themselves. In subsequent years I won nearly all of them over by paying their election expenses or by other means. More dangerous was the praetor, Domitius, who went about saying that at the end of the year he would bring in a bill to declare all the acts of my consulship illegal. He was always an enemy of mine and indeed his hostility was so great that, though he was both unscrupulous and a coward, I could never keep him quiet either by bribery or by threats. However, at this time he carried very little weight in the senate and hardly any with the people. I considered that the person who could, if he wished, do us most harm was Cicero, and, before taking steps to have him eliminated from political life, I did everything I could to conciliate him. Unfortunately Cicero would not act either in his own interests or mine. I did not mind his witticisms at the expense of Crassus, Pompey and myself. They were, though ill-natured, usually funny and much less vulgar than the stream of published material which was issued every day from the house of Bibulus and described by him as his consular edicts. In these so-called edicts, which were posted up in the streets and widely read, Bibulus gave what were supposed to be detailed descriptions of my behaviour so long ago with the King of Bithynia and described the present state of affairs as a " Kingdom " in which Pompey was the King and I the Queen. Others of the nobility joined in this diverting game of vilification, and Cicero, who rightly prided himself on his wit, was among them. Personally I did not take these lampoons seriously. Pompey, however, found them very hard to bear, as also did the tribune Vatinius who, because of his personal appearance, was a very obvious target for abuse. In fact I had to restrain him from leading a crowd of my supporters to the house of Bibulus and burning it down. Crassus, I think, was secretly pleased that Pompey and I came in for more abuse than he did.

It was a more serious matter when Cicero began to show signs of attacking us on real political grounds and from the great resources not of his wit but of his measured eloquence. He did this on the occasion of the trial of his old colleague in the consulship, Antonius Hybrida, who, on his return from his province, was very rightly accused of corruption, extortion and cowardice in the face of the enemy. Cicero, probably because Antonius still owed him money, had consented to defend him and in the course of his speech he had some very damaging things to say about the present organisation of affairs. In part, I think, he was genuinely shocked at the concentration of power which had taken place and which seemed to conflict with his own ideal image of what a constitution should be and indeed had been once—during the period of his own consulship. In part he was merely vexed that he himself was not at the head of affairs. It did not occur to him to think that, if he had accepted my offer and had given us from the beginning the support of his authority, the violence of the first three months of the year might have been avoided and he himself might have occupied a safer, a stronger and a more responsible position than he did now. As it was, I could see, as soon as I received a report of his speech, that he was again toying with the idea of some coalition of " the good " with himself as their leader. He had not observed that the greater part of " the good " was already lost to him. The whole business community had been delighted when, as I had promised Crassus that I would do, I had secured for them the concessions which they had demanded and which had been rejected in the previous year. Many of the more foresighted financiers were already beginning to speculate on the results of my governorship of Gaul. Very few at this stage of affairs could have been brought to align themselves with Cicero or with Cato. So, though by nature not a reactionary, Cicero, if he was to exert any important influence on politics, would have had to fall back once again on those reactionary circles who had given him his consulship and who remained hostile both to Pompey and to myself. I did not wish to see my enemies strengthened, and on the same day as that on which Cicero made his speech in defence of Antonius Hybrida, I took steps to ensure that Cicero would himself be, at least for some time, powerless. With the support of Pompey I arranged to have Clodius, Cicero's bitterest enemy, adopted into a plebeian family so that he would be eligible to stand for the tribuneship at the elections in the summer.

There was much that was cruel, depraved and affected in the character of Clodius. He was also warm-hearted, charming and, up to a point, reliable. Already he had great influence with the people and, in a curious way, he felt a devotion for the lower classes which was both deep and sincere. It was thought, for instance, a ridiculous affectation on the part of his sisters and himself to spell their names as though they were endeavouring to disguise the fact that they belonged to the Claudian family, which is perhaps the greatest of all the patrician families in Rome. Yet, so far as Clodius himself was concerned, there was more than affectation in the gesture. He felt at home with the city mob, much as I felt at home with my soldiers. He took a genuine personal interest in the affairs of his followers and, had he been less violent in his affections and animosities, he might even have been a considerable statesman. As it was, he had no policy except the general one of giving larger and larger grants of free food to the poor and of attacking all those members of the aristocracy who were not personal friends of himself or of his sisters. Ever since the time of his trial, when I had refused to give evidence against him, he had regarded me as his friend ; but his feelings of gratitude towards me were less strong than the hatred which he had conceived against Cicero, whose evidence at the trial would certainly have led to his conviction had there been more than a handful of honest men among the jury. Now that he could stand for the tribuneship (and he was certain to be elected), he announced his intention of bringing to justice anyone who had in the past put a Roman citizen to death without trial. The threat, clearly, was aimed at Cicero and Cicero, as I had intended, became alarmed. I myself had no wish whatever to injure him. In fact I have always wanted to have him on my side, partly because I admire him as a literary genius and partly because of the value of his prestige. And he, too, would have been happier if he had not chosen to align himself with my enemies. He is not by nature a reactionary and he respects good government. He has always, for example, expressed the greatest admiration for the law I passed in this first consulship of mine which was designed to protect the provinces from the greed of Roman governors. Yet, like many others who have risen from humble origins, he has an exaggerated reverence for traditions which have outlived their usefulness. He seems fated to find himself always uneasily upon the losing side.

On this occasion both Pompey and I did what we could to save him from the violence of Clodius. We did not wish to ruin him. We only wanted to be certain that he would keep quiet. First we offered him an interesting and lucrative appointment in Egypt where, in return for a very large sum of money, we had recognised the existing régime. I then attempted to persuade him to come with me to Gaul, pointing out that there he would be safe from prosecution and that, as soon as the agitation had died down, he could return to Rome at his leisure. I left this offer open until the last possible moment. Only when I was on the point of setting out for Gaul did I allow Clodius to proceed with the plan that ended in Cicero's exile. At about the same time we got rid of Cato, again through the agency of Clodius, who proposed and carried a law by which Cyprus was to be annexed and Cato given the commission to occupy the island and reorganise its government. So, shortly after the end of my year of office as consul, the only two figures who commanded enough respect to be able to head an effective opposition had been removed, at least temporarily, from the scene.

That these measures were necessary had been proved by events that took place during the summer and autumn. It was clear that after the initial shock of the first three months of my consulship, my enemies were beginning to rally and to contemplate more serious steps than the writing of lampoons. There were one or two hostile demonstrations against Pompey and myself in the theatre, not important in themselves, but very upsetting to Pompey. There was even, it seems, some sort of a plot to assassinate either Pompey or myself or both of us, though to this day I am not certain how serious this plot was or how reliable was the information we received about it. Certainly the information came from as untrustworthy a source as possible. Once again it was the informer Vettius who attempted to gain either money or notoriety for himself, as he had done when he tried to implicate me in Catiline's conspiracy. On this occasion he was arrested in the forum with a dagger in his hand and announced that he had been employed by a certain group of people to assassinate Pompey. When asked to name his employers he stated that they were a party of the younger members of the nobility led by young Curio and by Brutus. It is just possible that there was some truth in what he said. Brutus was then and, I suppose, still is something of a fanatic and may, from quite honourable motives, have believed that by getting rid of a most eminent and efficient commander he was somehow acting in accordance with the highest principles. I much doubt, however, whether he would have sunk to the method of assassination or that he would have had any serious relations with so disreputable a character as Vettius. In any case, because of my affection both for Brutus himself and for his mother, I was anxious to see him cleared of all suspicion. On the day after the arrest I had Vettius brought before a meeting of the people and examined by the tribune Vatinius and by myself. Probably Vettius was aware of my interest in Brutus and thought that he might make more money if he was to give the kind of evidence which he imagined I would like to hear. He now declared that the real instigators of the plot had been Lucullus, Cicero and the praetor Domitius. Again it is just possible that there may have been a little truth in what he said, though Cicero, certainly, would not have been implicated in such an affair. Domitius, however, may well have been. He also, as praetor, had access to the prison where, at dawn on the following day, Vettius was found strangled. Domitius was both an impulsive and a cowardly man. I have always assumed that he was responsible for this murder, which was not even necessary, since Vettius had already so far contradicted himself that his evidence could obviously not be taken seriously.

The affair of Vettius, however, was useful to me in so far as it resulted in a much firmer attitude being taken up by Pompey. He had been happy in his marriage and happy in the popularity that he had won by his excellent work on the Land Commission. It seemed to him intolerable that there should be any suspicion that he could be unpopular in Rome itself and, during the last months of the year, he energetically supported me in all the measures which I was taking for my security and for his.

On the last day of the consulship my colleague Bibulus again put in an appearance, prepared to justify himself and to attack me in the speech that he proposed to make before laying down office. Clodius, who was now tribune, treated him as Metellus Nepos had treated Cicero, though Clodius acted more violently. Instead of merely announcing his tribunician veto, he clapped his hand over Bibulus's mouth and kept it there until Bibulus had signified that he would not attempt to say a word.

So ended my consulship in a gesture that may be rightly described as both brutal and sordid. Has anyone, I wonder, ever attained power by means which were entirely honourable and dignified ? Now, however, I had an army and a great command. I had still to remain in Rome for more than two months, busying myself with more political intrigue until I had become certain that no effective move could be made against me in my absence ; but during this time I was conscious of the fact that one period of my life had ended and that another was beginning. The period that was past had been one of continual danger and difficulty. I had been hampered from the beginning by lack of money and by the complete ruin of the party of Marius and Cinna to whom I had looked for opportunities for advancement. Now, at the age of forty-three, I had only a fraction of the military experience which had been possessed at this time of life by Lucullus or Pompey or even Crassus. I believed myself, however, to have no less ability than they and I knew that, in these years during which I had struggled upwards from the status of a youth hunted by Sulla's executioners to that of a consul of the Roman people, I had acquired a rather exceptional knowledge of politics and of human nature. In these fields I should not make the mistakes that had been made by my Uncle Marius. I hoped and indeed (though I do not believe that the gods intervene in human affairs) I almost prayed that I might prove not unworthy of him in what had always seemed to me the richer, brighter and more honest field of warfare. I did not know that in the course of the next ten years I was to take by storm more than eight hundred cities, to subdue three hundred nations and to fight at various times pitched battles with three million men. Nor did I know that these achievements were only to be the prelude to a still more desperate struggle. All I knew was the strong invitation of a greater future. I was eager to join my army at the earliest possible moment. Meanwhile I sent Titus Labienus on ahead to Gaul.

THE END

GAUL

THE ALPS

CISALPINE

TRANSALPINE GAUL

GAUL

R. Po • VERONA

THE PYRENEES

I T A L Y

R. Tiber

ROME
OSTIA

SPAIN

S

GADES

NUMIDIA

AFRICA

THE
ROMAN EMPIRE
in 100 B.C.

  THE ROMAN EMPIRE
and its BOUNDARIES

············ PROVINCIAL
BOUNDARIES

—·—·—·— OTHER BOUNDARIES

MILES

100   0   100   200   300